For Chris:
Partner and fellow carbon-cyclist.
Definitely a keeper.

Contents of

THE CARBON CYCLE

FOREWORD
by Jonathon Porritt

'It's like pedalling a bike. Values are the downstroke, actions are
the upstroke. And it's the downstroke that moves things along.'
Kim Stanley Robinson, *Pacific Edge* [1]

Even at the best of times, America is a pretty baffling country for most
Europeans. And these really aren't the best of times. A $4 trillion bill
for the two wars in Iraq and Afghanistan, a continuing refusal on the
part of the US to show any kind of leadership in addressing climate
change, and an unnerving amalgam of religious fundamentalism and
bizarre Tea Party politics, all make for an instinctive 'out of kilter'
feeling with our allies across the pond.

So when my good friend Kate Rawles declared her intention
back in 2006 of undertaking a cycle ride of some 4,500 miles from
El Paso in the South to Anchorage in Alaska, some of us wondered
if she'd gone just a little bit bonkers! She is, after all, the UK's first
and best-known 'outdoor philosopher', and prone therefore to bouts
of excessive enthusiasm at the prospect of being out there in the wild.
But there's out there and there's 'out there'!

Kate's not like most philosophers I know. For one thing I can
understand what she's talking about, and her work-a-day belief that
the principal purpose of philosophy is 'to question the assumptions
of our age' keeps even her most abstract reflections grounded in an
admirable way.

Not that there's any problem here about staying grounded. Grinding out the daily miles does that in spades! I'm an enthusiastic cyclist,
with nearly forty years experience of survival cycling in London, but
this kind of cycling adventure is so far beyond my imagination as to
leave me literally awe-struck at the doing of it.

Like most cyclists, I'm familiar with headwinds that never, ever,
turn into tailwinds – but not for 10 hours a day, sometimes in
temperatures in excess of 100°F – so hot that even the cacti give up

---

[1] Kim Stanley Robinson (1995) *Pacific Edge* Collins

and die! I'm familiar with punctures, troublesome gears and the endless running repairs – but not day after day with a frequency that would induce despair even in a cycling angel. And I'm familiar with heavy legs and inescapable fatigue – but not the spirit-crushing fatigue that Kate so eloquently describes.

We are truly into 'agony and ecstasy' territory here. The agony resides primarily with Kate herself 'doing battle with her head'. The ecstasy comes with her immersion in the natural world, as much in the stark, unforgiving landscapes she is riding through, as in staggeringly beautiful scenery. As much in the daily contact with the mundane (including the mosquitoes!) as in moments of startling intimacy with bald eagles, wolves, beavers, and even a lynx appearing out of nowhere on the final run into Anchorage.

So much for the adventure – and the weather. Then there's the equally serious business of the climate.

In the spirit of inclusive, open-ended enquiry, Kate asks everyone she meets what they think about climate change (or 'global warming', as she finds herself having to call it), and what causes it. The whole gamut of responses is revealed, from involvement in full-on climate activism (underpinned by a touching belief that the US could still become a leader in addressing climate change), to equally full-on denial. With much more of the latter than the former.

Unfortunately, there are still so many reasons for Americans to remain sceptical, not least the ubiquitous and malign influence of Fox News – a 'highly effective, right-wing echo chamber', as Kate describes it.

It's an extraordinarily revealing portrait, or rather a revealing series of vignettes. And who knows the degree to which they are representative of where America stands today. I took away a powerful sense of a nation no longer at ease with itself, in which 'the American Dream' has for so many turned into a nightmarish rat race, with more and more people working more and living less.

Long gone are those simple, heady days where it was seen as 'America's manifest destiny' to get out there and conquer the wild. And then conquer the world. Redefining the remnants of this 'manifest destiny' is what makes the climate change story so emblematic of contemporary America, obstinately hanging on to what once made them great (as George Bush Snr once put it, 'The American way of life is not up for negotiation') whilst sensing that their future may look very different.

For some, the first response is to turn to technology to dig them out of the hole, to innovate like crazy to provide the energy they need from renewables rather than from coal, oil and gas. And there is indeed great hope to be had here. The latest technology assessments are boldly claiming that technologies such as solar power (generated from photovoltaic cells) will soon be providing energy at the same price as coal, gas or nuclear.

Philosophically, that sits a little uneasily with Kate. Techno-fixing may be necessary, but it certainly isn't sufficient. The words of Aldo Leopold are a constant reminder to Kate and Chris (her heroic partner and companion for the second half of the journey) that 'to see things properly' we have to dig down a bit deeper than swapping out one technology for another:

> 'We abuse the land because we regard it as a commodity belonging to us. When we see land as a community to which we belong, we may begin to use it with love and respect.'[2]

In this regard, the contrast between the town of Aspen ('a monument to consumerism') and their encounters with various First Nations people, both in the US and in Canada, brings it all right back to a question of values. Values embodied in new stories, in a re-dreaming of what it is that makes America so special, in the extraordinary 'kindness of strangers' that they encounter all the way along the route, in the deep connectedness of people and communities to the natural world that still sustains them.

All of which provides a wonderfully rich and insightful narrative. We should all be very grateful that Kate managed to overcome her own carbon-sensitive scruples in order to put herself and her beloved Rocky on a plane to El Paso – first to do the 4,500 miles, and then, eventually, to overcome the even greater barrier of getting it all down on paper!

Jonathon Porritt is Founder Director of Forum for the Future
www.forumforthefuture.org.uk

---

[2] Aldo Leopold (1949) *A Sand County Almanac* Oxford University Press

ACKNOWLEDGEMENTS

Thanks are due to many people in many ways.

To all those who read and commented on drafts, or parts of drafts or, in some heroic cases, multiple drafts – your comments and feedback were much appreciated. Particular thanks here to Jeanni Barlow, Liz Campbell, Alison Crumbie, Ian Jones, Chris Loynes, Antje and Janos Peters, Jonathon Porritt, John Rawles, Kaye Richards, Shields Russell, Carole Ward and Rebecca Willis.

Charlie Kronick, Jonathon Porritt, Sir Crispin Tickell and Vandana Shiva all agreed to give interviews before the trip. These have not in the end been included in the main text of the book, but were immeasurably useful in helping me think through the issues. Material from these interviews are available on The Carbon Cycle website.

Various people and organisations supported the cycling side of things. Rocky would not exist without Charlie Ralph, and we probably wouldn't have got all that far without support, expertise and kit from Gill Cycles, Ulverston – a huge thanks due there to all the staff, and Dave and Claire especially. Thanks also to Reynolds Tubing and Lyon Equipment and all the mechanics in all the shops who helped en route.

Friends – or in some cases, friends of friends or even strangers – who gave generous hospitality on the road include Jonathan and Mela, Tom and Rosalind, Susan, Kevin, Chenoa, Liam and Lhasa, Bill and Steph, Julian and Saundy, Colin and family, Wayne and Nina at the Round Lake Resort, the wonderful folks at Spring Creek Farm, Pete and Alys and Paul, who not only looked after us royally in Anchorage, but ensured we caught the ferry home (which departed some considerable distance from Anchorage along a road which included an extended tunnel forbidden to cyclists).

I'm grateful to all those who gave up their time for talks and interviews, including Mayor Martin Chavez, Larry Gamble, Bryan at New Belgium Brewery, Jim Halfpenny and his neighbour Sandy, Nathan Glasgow, Michael Deme, Colin Funk, Annie and all the other people along the way who were willing share their views with a random stranger on a bicycle. And to Nick at the Verizon phone store for ensuring that communication across the pond remained possible.

Martin of 'Design Jack' designed the original, striking and still much-used 'Carbon Cycle' logo – much appreciated.

The Winston Churchill Memorial Trust Travelling Fellowship transformed the financial feasibility of taking a chunk of unpaid leave. They were always gracious and helpful.

To my Outdoor Studies colleagues and mates, a huge thanks for tolerating repeated 'book weeks' and for (literally) years of support and encouragement.

Thanks to Jacqui for the life-saving fourteen songs; to Jacqui and Emma, Mitch, Kaye and Dr Lia for being the best imaginable mates; and to Antje for saying yes to the Andes all those years ago. To Bella for inimitable spaniel exuberance and hours of hill-walking that always put writing back into perspective – and to her other humans, Hannah, Wendy and Vicky for friendship and good wine, as well as generous dog-sharing arrangements!

Above all, perhaps, thanks are due to the following: to Jonathon, for enduring friendship and inspiration, as well as for writing the Foreword (and reading the manuscript first). To Sharon and David at Two Ravens Press for agreeing, against all our expectations but in line with our wildest hopes, to take this on; and to Sharon for critical feedback that was always, always constructive, and for patiently taking a complete greenhorn through the publishing process. To my remarkable dad, John Rawles, still cycling (or tricycling to be precise) and still full of *joie de vivre* despite a truly horrendous car/bicycle encounter that changed us all. Thanks for a lifetime of love and support. And of course to Chris, unfailingly loving, patient, tolerant and calm ... who has supported the book, the Carbon Cycle, and me in so very many ways.

Needless to say, there are bound to be omissions – for which I apologise. Please don't take it personally! Any and all of the other shortcomings are, of course, my own.

Introduction
Ordinary Adventures

The body, stronger. The mind, sharper.
The air, cleaner. The grass, greener.
The pretzels, crisper. The beer, colder.
The weekday, shorter. The weekend, longer.
The sun, brighter. The sky, bluer.
LIFE IS BETTER WHEN YOU
RIDE BIKES!

Gary Fisher

Adventures. I grew up fantasizing about having them, and reading a great many books by Wilfred Thesiger. Adventur*ers*, though, always seemed like other beings: strong, tough, talented, somehow free of normal life and not at all like me. I was a weedy child, a bit of a swot, rubbish at school sports – though I loved being outdoors – and what's more, I was a girl. Later I discovered the Crane cousins, who cycled up Kilimanjaro before mountain bikes had even been invented and ran the length of the Himalaya in running shoes, carrying little more than a sawn-off toothbrush and overtaking fully kitted-out international expeditions on the way. These guys, with their low-tech high-humour approach – very different from the more conventional adventuring type – were inspirational to me. But they still felt utterly out of my league. The Cranes – and even Thesiger – never, I'm sure, set out to present 'adventurers' as a different order from the rest of us. But the sheer fact of what they'd achieved made them seem like another species. If I ever became adventurous myself, I thought, I'd want to try to inspire other 'ordinary' people to think they could do the same.

I started cycling as a way of getting to a gap-year job at a riding stable. Horses were my passion at that point, not bikes. The bike was just a means to an end. I spent months struggling to master the prescribed British Horse Society riding style, the finer details of therapeutic horse-shoeing, and how to make a decent bran mash. It wasn't until I failed my BHS final exam, gave up thoughts of being a riding instructor, and went off to Sweden to work as a lowly groom instead that my wanderlust was re-ignited. Southern Sweden was so close and yet so different. The immense flat landscapes, vivid with primary colour. Blue sky, green grass, red poppies, yellow fields of rape seed. The language. The price of alcohol. The names of things on the shop shelves. The taste of their chocolate. Close and yet different; the ordinary world no longer taken for granted in the background but suddenly full of intrigue and sharply in focus simply for being 'foreign'.

Back in Scotland as a student I joined the university riding club, but the horse thing – or at least, that kind of horse thing – was on the wane for me. I wanted to get out of the city and explore. And that's when I began to realise that a bike could offer a whole lot more than a cheap way of commuting. Not only could an athletically challenged person like myself quite quickly develop the ability to cycle for ten, twenty, thirty, forty miles with minimal training – and not that much pain – but, in the process, familiar landscapes were brought back to life. On a bike, you are really *in* the landscape. You can smell it and hear it. Hills you don't even notice in a car are suddenly all too real. You feel more alive. And people respond to you differently. Turn up in a small town outside Aberdeen or Glasgow in a car and nothing much happens. Turn up on a bike – especially by yourself on a bike – and, more often than not, all sorts of people stroll over and chat. 'Where have you come from? How far have you been? Don't you own a car?' The bike is a magician, transforming the ordinary world into something of endless interest. Making adventures possible for normal, non-adventurers, like me.

Over the years I got bolder. I meandered around the outskirts of town in all directions and gradually rode further away. I cycled to youth hostels and stayed a night or two. Then a boyfriend talked me into cycling across Scotland, east to west. We took two (badly) home-made panniers between us and bungied our sleeping bags and tent direct to the bikes, stuffed into bin-liners. He was not keen on spending money and suggested we do the trip while living entirely off road-kill. For me the mileage was challenge enough; I put my foot down and insisted on pub lunches. I was not very fit and I struggled with the distances, with riding every day, with the Scottish weather, with midges and above all with wet sleeping bags when the bin-liners disintegrated. But there was something absolutely magical about putting everything we needed on the back of our bikes and simply cycling away. I was hooked.

Venturing on to the far shores of France, a friend and I followed the Rhone from its mouth near Marseille to its source in the Alps. Taking a leaf out of the Cranes' book we used the Rhone ride to raise money for charity. Primarily, though, that trip was about the sheer joy of being on the road with mountains all around and a growing love of physical challenge that initially took me by surprise. I found I was tougher than I knew; that even when I thought I was totally done in I usually had another twenty or thirty miles in my legs; that I actually enjoyed the harder rides and totally relished the feeling of getting stronger and fitter as the trip progressed. I was not fast but I did seem to have an endurance mentality. Forget that I was only in the athletics B team because my school was too small to have a C team: that formerly weedy child could now ride a bike a long way. It made me feel *good*. Cycling in consistent warm sunshine was a revelation. And there was the point about being ordinary. 'If I can do a trip like this,' I said after writing an exultant 'Made It!' on a postcard of the Rhone Glacier, 'then pretty much anyone else could, too.' We'd inched onto the glacier in slippery cycling shoes after climbing the spectacular hairpins of the Furka Pass – as in the fabulous car chase in the James Bond movie 'Goldfinger' – and then swooped gleefully down the other side into Switzerland and a celebratory double-fondue. It was biking at its best.

And so cycling in mountains – hot, sunny mountains for preference – became my thing. In my free time and between jobs I cycled in the Picos de Europa in Northern Spain; I cycled in the Rockies; I cycled in Israel and Jordan and eventually, many years after bin-liner man and I had gone our separate ways, a girlfriend and I cycled for 2000 miles in the Northern Andes, from Venezuela through Colombia and on into Ecuador. Our families thought we were crazy. Our friends thought we were crazy. Even Venezuelans thought we were crazy, warning of various dire outcomes should we venture across the border into Colombia and advising us in the strongest possible terms to transfer from Venezuela directly to Ecuador by plane.

The only time our proposed route hadn't received the 'you're insane and will surely die' response was at the Royal Geographical Society. Entering that travellers' Mecca for the first time, I was simultaneously awestruck and liberated. There, amongst the preserved wooden kayaks and portraits of real adventurers, our trip was rendered utterly unexceptional. No longer a life-threatening deed of sheer madness but an enjoyable amble, barely of note. 'Colombia gets awfully bad press in the west,' the founder of a well-known travel guide told me. 'Most people, most places are friendly and helpful. Keep your wits about you but start from a position of trust. You'll have a fantastic time.' I was deeply grateful for this sole piece of encouragement amongst the dire warnings. And what's more, she was right. Cycling across Colombia, overwhelmingly friendly and spectacularly beautiful, was the highlight of the whole journey. On the one occasion we did come upon minor drug barons – readily identifiable by their extremely large, shiny new 4x4s in an area of prevailing poverty – our evident femaleness unexpectedly made us safer. Two (distinctly grimy) women on bikes with large panniers, in the middle of Colombia, claiming to have biked there from Caracas, Venezuela, simply did not fit any of their stereotypes. We could not be construed as a threat to their empire (in the way male cyclists might conceivably have been) and we certainly couldn't be considered a catch, either. They insisted we left our bikes with their trucks and join them for coca-colas in a café. They interrogated us in a bemused way. They paid for the cokes. And then they waved us away. If the trip wasn't an adventure by RGS standards, it certainly was by ours.

~

Part of loving the outdoors as a kid was, for me, that that's where most of the animals were. I loved animals, all animals: from the snails I used to collect and keep as pets to the large dogs I'd invariably toddle towards from a very young age. I was sure I'd be a vet when I grew up – a horse vet ideally – but, bad at physics, worse at chemistry and good at English, neither my teachers nor the vet I spent a summer shadowing were exactly encouraging. 'You'll never be a horse vet,' said Dick. 'A horse vet is the top job and they're almost always men. You'll be a hamster vet. You'll spend your time castrating overweight labradors and dealing with their ignorant owners.' I went to university to study English and randomly chose philosophy as my extra subject. I loved it and hated it in almost equal measure.

On good days, philosophy, like cycling, also transforms the ordinary. It questions all sorts of things typically taken for granted,

4

bringing normal life sharply back into focus – albeit through a strange lens. 'How do you know you exist?' 'What counts as 'knowing' anything?' 'What makes something right or wrong?' On bad days these questions seemed stupid, irrelevant and utterly exasperating. It wasn't until my final year, when I read a book called *Animal Liberation*[3], that I suddenly saw how philosophy could be more than an intellectual game – intriguing, infuriating or otherwise. 'Philosophy should question the assumptions of its age', wrote Peter Singer, the author. 'One of the assumptions of our age,' he continued, 'is that we are superior to other animals and entitled to treat them any way we see fit.' Or words to that effect. Singer argued that modern society systematically mistreats its animals – especially those in agriculture and in research. It was the description of how intensively farmed animals live out their lives as much as the argument that really got to me. Chickens in tiny cages so tightly packed together they could not stretch their wings. Pigs living their whole lives in barren, concrete pens in which they couldn't turn around.

I was disbelieving. Surely it couldn't be that bad. Then, learning more, I was outraged. I was in my twenties, I'd been either in school or at university more or less my whole life, I was an 'animal lover' and yet I didn't even know how the animals I was eating had been treated. How could my good Scottish education have omitted to inform me of such a thing? What *else* might be going on that I didn't know about? I gave up eating meat and I started to read around. It was a trail that lead to one disturbing discovery after another, profoundly disorienting my vague sense of things being basically okay with the world, and my naïve belief that I had a pretty good grasp of what was what out there. To be fair, I did know at least something about world poverty, courtesy of the Cranes' books; though the figures (about one billion people in a 'normal' non-famine situation are malnourished and without clean drinking water) never lost their capacity to shock. But I knew virtually nothing of the impacts of affluence.

Human activities – and particularly the activities that support rich, industrialised lifestyles – are having an astonishing impact on the other thirty million or so species we share the planet with, wiping out species at a rate somewhere between a hundred and a thousand times

---

[3] Peter Singer (1991) *Animal Liberation* (second edition) Thorsons

faster than the normal rate. The side effects of our ever-increasing consumption of resources keep relentlessly emerging, from decimated forests and other massively degraded habitats to polluted, over-fished oceans. We've knocked a hole in the ozone layer and scattered the world with a cocktail of pollutants. DDT has been found in the fat of Antarctic penguins, even though it has never been used on that continent. And yet, in terms of earth history, we've only just arrived. If you think of the time our planet has been in existence as equivalent to the distance of your outstretched arms, a single swipe of a nail-file would wipe out the whole of human history. Not to deny our extraordinary achievements, in this very short period as earth inhabitants we've managed to create one hell of a mess. And, despite all this mayhem, we aren't even meeting the basic needs of our own species!

The more I found out, the greater my sense of outrage and disbelief. That these things were happening, and that the whole world wasn't up in arms clamouring for them to stop. My focus widened from poverty amongst people and appalling living conditions amongst animals, to the environment and sustainability in general. I wanted to *do* something, but exactly what was never quite clear. Somehow, without ever really intending to, I became a lecturer. I taught environmental ethics, and did my best to be a mini-Singer. It wasn't going to save the world, but it was a start. In a small way I could raise awareness of the issues and, more importantly, ask questions; it was a chance to uncover and grapple, however safely and from a position of undeniable privilege, with the deeply disturbing dark side of our 'normal' Western lives. To question the assumptions of our age.

~

Towards the end of the nineties a 'new' environmental problem was becoming more and more prominent. Climate change. Scientists had actually been drawing attention to the likelihood that burning fossil fuels in enormous quantities would affect the earth's atmosphere for decades, but it took a while for this alarming news to filter down to essay-swamped ethics lecturers. As information about climate change unfolded and became more certain, I embarked on a familiar process of denial and disbelief. The implications for people – for our agricultural systems, our economics, our ability to meet our needs, our security and basic well-being – all seemed hard to exaggerate. The implications for other species, worse. Surely it couldn't be that bad. Surely if it were that bad we'd be doing something about it. Heck, it *is* that bad. Heck we're *not* doing (that much) about it! I went through a phase of wanting to stride through the land shouting, 'Wake up! This really matters and we need to do something! WAKE UP!' A friend told me she'd actually done just that, wearing pyjamas and carrying an alarm clock. I thought this a stroke of sheer brilliance but she said the reaction of colleagues in a car she'd walked over to had been typical: they'd wound up the window and driven away.

This of course *was* typical, in wider ways too. While the international scientific community was reaching an unprecedented and downright alarming degree of consensus that climate change was a real and urgent challenge, people all around were carrying on as normal. And normal, in the industrialised world, means a high carbon footprint. The nature of 'normal' is a large part of the problem. Which perhaps at least partly explains why, despite the deluge of information, poll after poll showed that significant proportions of UK and European populations simply didn't believe it was happening – or, if it was, that it was being caused by human activity – or, even if it was, that there was anything much they could do about it. The truth about climate change is, in Al Gore's masterful understatement, *inconvenient*. It requires us to change. Very much easier to deny it.

I brought climate change into all my lectures. But it didn't feel like anywhere near enough. And I was becoming increasingly frustrated at the constraints of working in an academic context. The world was facing a real threat, demanding urgent responses, but starting from the position that climate change was a problem and focusing on what to do about it was often considered a) biased and b) a bit too practical. It was not, I learned, my role as an academic to make climate change real, to explain its relevance, to debate solutions. It was not my role to inspire people to actually do anything about it.

∼

Meanwhile, 'almost anyone can have adventures in their lives if they want to' had become a mantra I uttered but didn't apply. The world of work was, inexorably, becoming more demanding – and more time-consuming. One day I realised I hadn't been on an extended trip for over a decade. It was time to get back on a bike. To cycle a long way, in mountains.

Not that it was quite that simple. I still had a job and a mortgage. And, while I was definitely in favour of a radical adjustment of my work/life balance, that didn't seem enough. I wanted to conjure up a trip that could also engage with climate change; a journey that would play some role in addition to being an adventurous holiday and a personal challenge. Using bike rides to raise money had worked reasonably well in the past but there's a limit to how many times you can ask friends and relatives to part with their cash for your latest good cause. Was there a way of using a bike ride to raise awareness instead? If I could pull off a trip that was long enough and challenging enough to give me some small amount of credibility in the world of 'real' adventurers – or at least those who enjoy hearing their tales – then perhaps I could use it to reach audiences beyond the university. I could use the journey as the basis of talks and slide shows. The bike ride could become a sort of Trojan horse, smuggling a climate change tale inside an adventure cycling tale.

Where? It had to have mountains. Ideally hot and sunny ones, at least for some of the trip. It had to have an adventurous ring to it. And now I was after some sort of climate change logic as well.

'Go back to basics,' a friend advised. 'What's at the root of climate change? What's really driving it? Go where the worst of that is.'

'Well, oil, I guess, in a word,' I said.

It was not a word that readily summoned a cycling route to mind. Nevertheless, the use of fossil fuels, especially oil, coal and gas, is undoubtedly one the main causes of climate change. The other main cause is deforestation, together adding up to an appalling double-whammy. Basically, we've taken carbon that has been stored under the earth for millions of years and burnt it, thus releasing vast amounts of additional carbon into the atmosphere. There, in the form of carbon dioxide, it acts as a 'greenhouse' gas, trapping additional heat from the sun in the earth's atmosphere, in much the same way as a greenhouse does. The temperature of the earth's atmosphere is, as a result, slowly but surely increasing, causing changes in climates around the world. At the same time, in our relentless search for growth, we're cutting down forests and degrading other ecosystems that would otherwise absorb carbon and act as natural carbon off-setters. Hence the double-whammy. On an immense scale.

Energy-hungry, high-consumption lifestyles have the highest carbon footprints by far. And suddenly, there it was, emerging from the overused atlas. The United States. It had it all. One of the most oil-intensive countries on earth, proudly featuring the vastly energy expensive 'American Way of Life'. The USA has only five per cent of the world's human population but produces nearly twenty-five percent of the entire world's greenhouse gas emissions. And of course, the USA in 2006 had President George Bush. Readily characterised as the arch-villain of the global climate change drama, Bush constantly questioned the reality of climate change and the role of human activity in causing it. He had steadfastly refused to sign the Kyoto Protocol and, under his administration, the US played a uniquely consistent role in derailing international climate change talks. The American way of life might be contributing disproportionately to climate change, but that was too bad. 'The American way of life [was] not up for negotiation' – at least, according to Bush.

But Bush had become deeply unpopular; and Bush was not the American people. To what extent, I wondered, would that most elusive of beings – the 'ordinary citizen' – agree with his views? What would they think about whether climate change was happening and what was causing it and what it meant and what needed to be done? Already aware of how easy it is to get into conversations if you arrive somewhere – anywhere – on a bike with large panniers, I imagined that, once started, conversations could readily be nudged in a climate change direction. Cycling in the USA offered fantastic opportunities for a random sampling of what citizens of one of the most oil-hungry, oil-dependent countries on earth thought about the climate consequences of this particular addiction – and the implications of trying to give it up.

And of course, the United States also had mountains. Hundreds and hundreds of miles of them. The Rocky mountains, stretching all the way up into Alaska. What if I tried to follow the spine of the Rockies, as closely as possible, from the Mexican border in, say, Texas, to Alaska? Texas to Alaska. It had a certain ring. The adventure logic was becoming clearer. And mountains had a climate change logic too. In a warming climate, one thing that many species can do is move – upwards or northwards. But species who live on mountains

9

are effectively trapped. They have nowhere else to go. Mountain ecosystems have been called 'the canaries of climate change', with ecologists predicting earlier and more drastic impacts there than elsewhere. I hated the thought that the mountains I'd been cycling through with such profound enjoyment all these years had, along with the animals who lived on them, quietly been suffering the early impacts of climate change all along. Was it true that mountain ecosystems now faced much more drastic impacts? If so, what did this mean?

Above all, I wanted to engage with what could be done. I didn't just want to record the negative impacts on places I loved. Given that climate change was happening, how should we respond? What were the solutions? What should we *do*? The American way of life was being fiercely defended, not least because it was profoundly threatened. And that, surely, would also mean that the USA had one of the strongest incentives to come up with answers. It offered the worst, but perhaps also the best. I knew enough about the problem. It was time to focus on solutions.

Slowly but surely, and with the help of occasional intake of a particularly inspirational Scottish liquid, a plan evolved. I would cycle through the States and into Canada, then on to Alaska. I would cycle from El Paso to Anchorage, following the spine of the Rockies as far as possible and talking to as many people as I could along the way. Since there is no obvious way of 'following' the Rockies on tarmac, my route would often take me across the Great Divide – the high mountain line that divides the fate of raindrops. Chris, a relatively recent (and hitherto largely non-cycling) partner, would join me about halfway. The first half I would ride alone. 'What are the solutions? How can we make ourselves and our ways of life climate friendly?' would be my guiding questions. With an atlas and a piece of string, we estimated the distance to be 4527 miles. At well over twice as far as I'd ever cycled before, and with numerous high mountain passes, it definitely qualified as a personal challenge. At an average of seventy-five miles a day, it would be two months of solid cycling. Then, to my astonishment and despite a cringe-making interview – in which I drew a complete blank when asked what I might tell people about Winston Churchill – I secured a Winston Churchill Memorial Trust

Travelling Fellowship.[4] The Fellowship transformed the financial feasibility of the whole enterprise, and the kudos did no harm either. Armed with both, I negotiated a chunk of unpaid leave from work and managed to carve out a blissful three months of time. Two months cycling, a month for interviews, diversions and rest days. It was, I thought, going to be a long but leisurely ride.

---

[4] Winston Churchill Memorial Trust Travelling Fellowship – apply for one here! http://www.wcmt.org.uk/

North
Pacific
Ocean

ANCHORAGE

CANADA

UNITED
STATES
of AMERICA

North
Atlantic Ocean

EL PASO

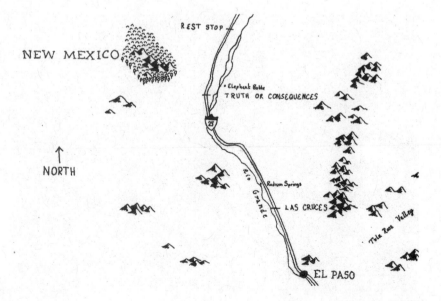

REST STOP

NEW MEXICO

Elephant Butte
TRUTH OR CONSEQUENCES

25

↑
NORTH

Rio Grande

Radium Springs

LAS CRUCES

Tula Rosa Valley

EL PASO

Chapter One
Too Hot for Cacti

'It is almost impossible to imagine how the world will avoid disastrous climate change impacts without a fundamental, and prompt, change in US policy.'

Elizabeth Kolbert [5]

'Climate change? Oh no, you won't have a problem with that until you go further north.'

US citizen in an airport queue, discussing New Mexico

I left El Paso on the 19th June 2006, at high noon. It was like riding into an oven. I was gleaming white and Rocky, fully loaded for the first time, was unnervingly heavy. Wobbling erratically around the hotel car park as a practice run, I wondered whether I could actually ride *anywhere* with this much weight. Not to mention the damage sustained to the bike on the flight over. For the first time, I suddenly had real doubts about the viability of this trip. Too far, too hot, too heavy, TOO MUCH! whimpered an internal voice. Don't be daft, I told it, it'll be fine. Then, mustering my courage, I headed out into the lunchtime traffic. The road out of town was uphill and infested with traffic lights, inflicting the maximum number of shaky hill starts. I wasn't convinced I could make it the two miles to the bike shop, let alone another fifty or so that day. And I didn't even want to think about Alaska. Drenched with sweat, I arrived at the Crazy Cat bike shop thinking I already deserved a hero's welcome. Instead of which a polite but not all that interested young man loaned me a high-pressure foot pump, told me he didn't think that cycling any kind of distance with four teeth missing from the front gear ring was feasible, and didn't ask where I was going. I skulked about in the cool interior pretending I might buy something – unlikely, given an unfortunate temporary separation between me and my credit card – until the air-conditioning got my temperature down to something

---

[5] Elizabeth Kolbert (2006) 'Can America Go Green?' *New Statesman* 19th June

functional. And then I headed off for real.

It felt amazing to be underway at all. 'Normal life' can be incredibly sticky when you try to leave it. On this occasion, it had required an immense effort to break free. Clearing the ground had somehow taken priority over training, and I hadn't been on a bike in at least a month. Weeks had flown past with no exercise more strenuous than lifting a computer mouse. On top of this less-than-ideal preparation for an endurance ride, mild asthma had turned into a stubborn, long-term cough. And, while I was undoubtedly a touch out of shape, the bike almost didn't make it at all. For many years I'd harboured the extravagant fantasy of having a bike hand-built by the exuberant Scottish bike builder, Charlie Ralph. Charlie specialises in custom-made machines for people who are, for example, very tall or, in my case, rather on the short side. My much-loved but undeniably elderly road-bike had recently been the source of considerable teasing from a group of friends on holiday in the Alps. This trip – further, harder, higher and altogether more ambitious – provided the ideal excuse.

Rocky, named for the Rockies we aimed to ride along, and painted a distinguished dark grey in keeping with the carbon-oriented nature of the mission, was due to arrive in March, for my birthday. This was postponed until April, just in time to get to know him before the Fred Whitton, a local challenge ride in May. Finally, on a windy day in June two days before I was due to leave for the States, Charlie arrived at my door in the Lake District with Rocky in the back of his car. 'There's just one small problem,' he said. 'It concerns the front wheel ...' He'd put the bike in the boot of his car ready to leave when his phone rang. Running in to answer it, he'd startled the cat, who jumped on the car, slamming the boot down on the front wheel – which promptly curled into an intriguing shape, a bit like a pretzel. In view of the time constraints, Charlie had brought the bike down anyway, and had then spent hours on the phone in the kitchen, ringing around every bike shop in Cumbria to see if a wheel of the right specs could be found. In the end he had to drive to Glasgow and back to get one. So much for bikes as a low-carbon commodity.

Rocky and I, then, were not all that well acquainted by the time we came to be navigating our way through Gatwick airport towards the departure lounge. Nevertheless, I felt a huge pang as I left him in his cardboard box in a cage marked 'oversize luggage'. Would we ever be reunited? A gentleman from San Antonio with silver hair, a yellow shirt and a large stomach, asked me what on earth I was thinking of, taking a bike to El Paso. He told me that it would be 115 degrees. He told me about 'retail kidnapping' in Mexico. (You get kidnapped; the kidnappers phone your family and ask for a DVD player/microwave/towel heater; the family take the DVD player/microwave/towel heater to the kidnappers, and receive you in exchange.) He told me under no circumstances to cross the border south into Mexico, and that, even heading north, while I might not be kidnapped, I would find little shade and should expect huge distances between the places where I could get water. Seizing the opening, I asked him whether climate change was a big concern in a place already so hot. This was not, he reassured me, a problem faced by southerners. 'Though it does,' he conceded, 'get cool in the evenings.' By the time I'd unscrambled my brain we'd been called to our separate check-in desks and I never saw him again. I decided the moral was probably to give up asking questions about climate change and use the more self-explanatory term 'global warming' instead.

~

Many hours later, I was reading my way through a stack of climate change articles, 35,000 feet above the north-eastern edge of Canada. Nothing I read was remotely reassuring, except perhaps that the 'greenhouse effect' at the heart of the issue is in itself a beneficial natural phenomenon. The average temperature of the earth would be about minus eighteen degrees and pretty uninhabitable without it. The problem, rather, is the vast quantity of extra greenhouse gases added to the atmosphere by human actions. I was fast learning that, when it comes to climate change, there are areas of rock-solid certainty, and areas of intense debate. The trick is to tell which is which – and not to fall for the age-old ploy of using the existence of the latter to cast doubt on the former. One of the certainties is that carbon dioxide molecules retain heat. We have released more of them into the atmosphere. Therefore the atmosphere is retaining more heat. If you can dispute any of those claims you should, as George Monbiot puts it in his book, *Heat,*[6] put yourself forward for a Nobel Prize in science. What exactly this warming atmosphere will mean for

---

[6] George Monbiot (2006) *Heat* Allen Lane, Penguin Books

particular climates around the world is one of the uncertainties. Some are getting hotter, some drier, some wetter, some may even get colder. Overall, though, atmospheric warming – aka global warming – has been likened to turning the heat up under a saucepan of water. The extra energy has to go somewhere. So as well as changing climates, it's expected to increase incidents of 'severe weather'. Storms, floods, droughts, hurricanes…

~

I arrived in El Paso, via Houston, at one in the morning western United States time – or eight in the morning British time – walking down the long corridor to the baggage claim with the accompaniment of the oddly incongruous sound of Vivaldi's 'The Four Seasons'. With a touch of bleary self-pity, I calculated that I'd been travelling for twenty-four hours and, apart from a snooze over Greenland, hadn't slept for – well, several days. Rocky didn't show up until after the last suitcase was wending its way soulfully round and round the baggage carousel and I was in the queue for lost luggage. A man walked through a hidden doorway carrying the battered bike box and everything else seemed suddenly irrelevant. We were here! Here in El Paso, Texas at one in the morning with the airport barometer reading eighty-five degrees! The friendly driver who squeezed the box into the back seat of his taxi asked me what I was up to and then told me I was crazy.

I woke to brilliant sunshine. The Holiday Inn Express, El Paso, is a tower block in a car park just off the interstate. My room looked across to a traffic junction and a vast advertisement for 'Amigos Bail Bonds' (available twenty-four hours). I'd decided to indulge in a hotel base camp for a day or so to sort things out before I set off. This proved to be a smart move, as there was a fair amount of sorting to do. All those articles to post back, for starters. And the fact that my wallet, complete with credit cards and driver's licence (ubiquitously required for identification in the States) had somehow stayed on the plane. Never believe those claims that replacement credit cards can be 'immediately expedited' to wherever you are in the world. It was going to take weeks. By great good fortune I'd bought $1000 at Gatwick Airport and this money had never made it into my wallet but was stuffed into a back pocket. I could survive for a good while on cash.

Meanwhile, Chris, already proving his worth back in Britain, arranged for new credit cards to be sent to friends in Colorado. I would pick them up en route, less than a thousand miles away...

Finally, all that remained to sort out was Rocky. I rescued the large cardboard box from the hotel office and took it up to my room in the elevator. The moment of truth! Would he be in one piece? A couple of deep chunks out of the sleek grey paintwork, despite the padding. Oh well. But wait, OH NO! Four teeth completely missing from the largest cog of the triple front chain wheel. Given how much foam and padding I'd crammed around the bike I could only imagine that the 'FRAGILE, DO NOT DROP' signs on the box had inspired the baggage handlers to hurl it with great force across the airport floor. Tool kit spread out across the eiderdown, I put the rest of the bike together and figured I could go past a bike shop on the way out of town. Though without a credit card I wouldn't be replacing large bits of kit. I would probably just have to cope until Colorado. At least it was the large ring – high gears – definitely easier to manage without than low gears. Later, to my astonishment, adjusting the saddle and handlebars in the hotel car park, all the gears seemed to work anyway. I spent the rest of the evening trying to fit all my stuff into panniers and writing a card to Chris while drinking his parting gift of a half bottle of champagne. Rocky, propped up against the bed, looked sleek and beautiful and ready to go.

~

I'd just crossed the Interstate not long after the Crazy Cat bike shop and was stopped at the side of the road figuring out my next move, when a man pulled up alongside in a large black truck. 'I'm a cyclist,' he said (from which I understood, 'I'm not dangerous') 'and you are looking at a map ...' I grinned, recalled the travel guide author's advice, and told him where I was going. 'Take this road,' he said, pointing on the map. 'It's only slightly out of your way but much prettier.' So I headed north out of Texas and into New Mexico on Highway 28.

The outskirts of El Paso turn into heavily irrigated farmland. Pecan orchards, a polo pitch (yes, a polo pitch), a field of alpacas, clipped out like bizarre, long-legged poodles. Beautiful horses: quarter horses, thoroughbreds and a few Arabs. Chattering sparrow sounds and lots of birds I didn't know the names of. Tiny, delicate doves; birds like

17

wagtails only with fatter tails; a vivid white egret, and later three humming birds in a row, hovering right above the road. The heat stayed
intense. I have cycled in heat before and relished it, but either this was
hotter (it was about 110 degrees when I left El Paso) or I was losing my
tolerance. (Getting older? Nothing to do with it!) Occasionally I crossed
the road to stand in the shadow of a tree or a stationary truck for a
couple of minutes. When I stopped I could really hear the bird song.
A couple of squirrels watched me from a hole in a house wall. The
water in my bottles was hot in minutes. And more or less gone by the
time I reached the tiny town of La Mesa, twenty-something miles later.

La Mesa did not have the cool café I'd been fantasizing about.
But at least it was there. Previous towns marked on the map had
barely existed beyond a couple of houses. And it did have a store. I
bought tortillas, Monterey Jack cheese and an unripe tomato and
stood outside in a strip of shadow pouring water down my throat and
occasionally over my head. Various folk coming and going said hello.
One asked me if I was married and why I was travelling by bike. I
was beginning to wonder this myself. Despite occasional godsends – I
never thought I'd be so happy to see a cloud go across the sun – I was
struggling by the time I reached Las Cruces, and seriously tempted
by the Comfort Inn and the thought of air-conditioning. Unfortunately I'd recently seen the figures for carbon offsetting motel rooms
– much higher than I'd imagined. Motel rooms needed to be seriously
rationed. And I had still only done about forty miles on a day when
I needed to do at least sixty. On the far side of Las Cruces my reward
for carrying on was several miles of pecan plantations, tall enough
to throw shade across the whole road. As the day wore on it became
slightly, almost imperceptibly, cooler. Then a road sign told me that
Radium Springs, my goal for that night, was closer than I'd thought.
Only ten miles left! I celebrated with a rest on a bridge over the Rio
Grande, sitting on the railings watching hundreds and hundreds of
swallows hunting above the coffee-coloured water. A sweet tailwind
swept me along the last few miles.

Radium Springs seemed to consist pretty much entirely of the Blue
Moon Restaurant and Bar. There was one truck outside. I went in. A
lone man and woman sat at the bar. The woman took one look at me
and stood up. 'Heck, sweetheart, y'all okay? What can we do for you?'

The friendliness soaked like water into my dry, tired self. I wanted to stay and soak up some more – and a beer or two – but she said the campsite was a few miles back down the road, so I figured I'd better go and find it first. Heading back, the tailwind was now a headwind, and the campsite was extremely elusive. I finally tracked it down beyond signs for the Leasburg Dam State Park. Two women with chihuahuas on leads assured me that yes, this was it, and yes, there were showers. I cycled in a squiggly sort of way along gravelled roads looking for somewhere I might be able to pitch a tent rather than park an RV. Finally, finding a sandy spot beyond the main camping area, I was struggling to keep hold of the unfurled tent in the rising wind when a woman approached bearing a large pile of leaflets. Elaine, the campsite host, tucked a leaflet detailing the campsite facilities under my arm and shooed me off to an official spot complete with shelter, bench and electric hook-up. It was even harder to pitch the tent there due to the rocklike ground which was interspersed with concrete. But Elaine was insistent. Maybe she had human male-related concerns in mind rather than the wind. Either way, I was too tired to argue.

Elaine chatted while I pecked at the ground with my tent pegs. She and her husband lived in the park all summer, she said, pointing to an enormous RV. (Not that theirs was larger than any of the other immense houses-on-wheels that squatted in clusters on the concrete landing pads.) Then they drove to Arizona for the winter. She said the park was famous for its cacti, but that the cacti were dying. 110 degrees was unusual even here, and it hadn't rained for nearly a year. So hot and dry that *cacti* were dying? No wonder I was feeling it.

'Do you think it's global warming?' I asked.

'Probably…' Elaine shrugged, and changed the subject before I had a chance to continue.

Finally, the tent more or less up, I headed for the shower. Bliss! In years of cycling I'd never reacted like this. My whole body felt overheated and yearning for water. Usually sun-proof, I now had blotches of vibrant red sunburn on the back of my left leg, ankle and both shoulders. My entire skin was dried up and my lips were cracked. After a single day. Back at the tent, I struggled to eat another tortilla, sent Chris a text message and crawled into the windy, flapping, hot tent. Lying naked on top of my Karrimat, I woke in the night and had to put some clothes on. What bliss to feel cool! Through the open tent door I could see hundreds and hundreds of hazy stars in the huge, dark sky.

~

We don't know for sure whether particular hot spells – like the one I'd inadvertently arranged to be cycling through – are due to global warming. But they are completely in line with the predictions. As these hot spells become more common, it seems increasingly likely that they are related to climate change. Twenty of the twenty-one hottest years since records began in 1860 occurred in the last twenty-five years. And hot places, in general, are predicted to get hotter. Deserts are predicted to spread. Not great news for New Mexico. Nor for those who depend on neighbouring 'bread-basket' states for wheat and other essential crops. Not great news for large parts of the African continent, either. In what's been described as a horrible accident of geography, the worst-hit parts of the world in terms of desertification, and all that means for failing agriculture, water supplies and conflict, will be (initially at least) places that already have disproportionate poverty. And which have done least to cause the problem.

We *do* know for certain that the average temperature on earth has increased by over half a degree. The Intergovernmental Panel on Climate Change – an extraordinary body that represents the consensus and expertise of over two thousand scientists from across the international scientific community – predicts rises of between 1.8 and 6.4 degrees Celsius by the end of the century. To put this in perspective, the difference in average global temperature between now and the last ice age, when vast tracts of Europe and North America were buried under ice about a mile thick, was at most about five degrees. Five degrees colder and we're covered in ice. Five degrees *hotter* would alter our climates almost beyond recognition. Even changes at the lower end of the spectrum will dramatically alter current weather patterns.

But – and here's the good news – catastrophic climate change may not yet be inevitable. Where we end up on that spectrum almost certainly still depends on us and on what we do. It especially depends on what we do over the next ten to fifteen years. The changes required are immense and urgent – we definitely need to get a move on. But we surely have to try. If we assume it is too late and simply do nothing (and no-one can know this for certain) then it's game over, guaranteed.

~

I woke just after six. For me, this was almost inconceivably early. It was beautiful. Rabbits, birds, wide landscape, distant dun-coloured hills, scattered with almost-green scrub. And cacti everywhere, in amazing, twisted, fingery shapes. A text from Chris. We had been together a little over a year. He had been unwaveringly supportive of this trip. Had helped research it. Had accepted the separation without question. Had joined in on my terms. It felt good to know he was out there. And it also felt good to be here alone, coping, enjoying the solitude, reconnecting with my old, independent self.

Back onto the Radium Springs road, the temperature was initially much gentler. Chris had asked, What does the desert *feel* like? I was just thinking, well, here it feels calm, peaceful ... when I passed a sign saying 'Peaceful Valley.' The Rio Grande flowed steadily alongside for a while, wide, almost khaki-coloured, a narrow strip of green on each side soon fading into the huge, scrubby spaces beyond. More beautiful horses. Fewer pecan orchards. Wilder... A drugs control checkpoint. I was waved on. Scattered houses. A large sign reading, *You got rocks?* followed by a phone number. After a while the road opened out into desert proper. Huge vistas of sandy, gravelly moguls. Immense flats, dried creeks, distant hills, everywhere dotted with khaki-coloured scrub.

The next few days fell into a pattern of sorts. I would get up uncharacteristically early. The mornings were beautiful: sometimes hazy, sometimes brilliant-blue-clear, always cool, and alive with wonderful birds. I'd get on the road as soon as I could but it was never long before the heat returned. After day two I realised I'd had it easy when the heat was joined by headwinds. Strong, hot headwinds. My speed would drop lower and lower until I'd be straining along at seven miles an hour, inwardly wincing when I failed to prevent my head from calculating how long it was going to take to get to that night's campsite.

Back in 1989 I'd spent two years as a postgraduate student in Colorado, and one summer had ridden south a thousand miles or so along the Rockies, ending just north of where I was now. That trip had been tight on time and I'd constructed it around a ninety miles a day average. After the Rhone ride, and some years before the

Andes, it was one of the first big rides I'd done. It had been utterly exhilarating to be out there alone and I'd revelled in the heat and the mountains. It was also exhausting. It had taken me all day and well into the evenings to keep the miles up and I was distinctly flattened at the end of it. For this trip, with a smug sense of learning from past over-exuberance, I'd revised my daily mileage ambitions down to a mere seventy-five. Seventy-five miles, I'd figured, would take me about three quarters of the day. I could then spend the rest of the day talking to people, doing some research and taking it easy. That first week, I'd planned to emphasise the taking it easy bit. I'd envisaged finishing my miles by mid-afternoon, setting up camp and spending leisurely evenings reading novels and recovering from the pre-departure frenzy.

But things were not going entirely as intended. Each day, something conspired to keep me cycling well into the evening. Sometimes it was the headwinds; sometimes my distance estimates would randomly revise themselves upwards. Sometimes it was punctures. One afternoon, fixing a tiny sidewall puncture by the side of the road in the blasting heat with absolutely no shade, a vivid memory returned of an evening in New Mexico all those years before. It must have been a few days north of where I was now, the only time on that previous trip I'd ever felt really vulnerable – fixing a back wheel puncture on a long, isolated road, vulnerability magnified a thousand times by having the bike upside down by the roadside. I remembered tensing as a solitary car approached. It drove on by. Absolutely nothing happened. The only danger was in my head and I'd never worked out why that lone patch of fear had suddenly disrupted my peace.

Now I just couldn't seem to keep a decent pace up. It was exasperating, and a little mysterious. A partial explanation was simple – fitness. But this didn't seem to fully account for it. Distance cycling is as much about stubbornness as strength and I didn't think my stubbornness had waned. That I'd been eighteen years younger on the previous Rockies ride hadn't even crossed my mind when Chris and I sat with the atlas in the comfort of our sitting room planning this trip. On the road in those first, long, slow hot days, the thought that my age – surely not! – might have something to do with my slowness sneaked into my head and niggled away at my confidence.

My head was one of the two main things I daily did battle with during that long first week. It kept informing me it was time to stop when most of that day's seventy-five miles lay ahead. My body hadn't settled into distance mode yet either. I couldn't quite get comfortable on the handlebars and, for some weird reason, the sole of my left foot really ached. And I was still coughing. I did, however, have one powerful weapon. Fourteen songs on a tiny recorder heroically copied there very late the night before I left by my wonderful, gadget-literate friend Jacqui. I would make myself wait until I was slowing almost to standstill in the mid-afternoon heat and then take out my precious black credit card-sized gadget, put in the minute ear-plugs, and switch on. I'd pull away to the unmistakable opening upbeat rhythm of Gnarls Barkley's 'Crazy' – fast becoming the trip's theme tune – gaze at the desert to the beautiful, wistful sound of Shooglenifty's 'Carboni's Farewell', and pound the pedals to KT Tunstall's wonderful lyrics. *You're or, or, or, or, orrrrr, the other side of the worrrrrrrrrld....* Somewhere in the middle of the sequence Jacqui had inserted the James Bond theme tune, which infallibly lent an aura of adventure to the most mundane stretch of road, instantly converting a hot, tedious slog into an urgent and thrilling mission – and restoring my sense of humour. I'd end with a rerun of 'Crazy' – *I remember when, when I lost my mind ... I must be crAAAAAAzy...* and then make myself put the little machine away so I didn't weary of the songs too soon. They always added several miles per hour to my speed.

It was typically around seven or eight o'clock by the time I crawled into a campsite, dead beat. One evening, on a day that had included vast straight stretches of road past the tiny town of Truth and Consequences, the last five miles to Elephant Butte (where do these names come from?) nearly reduced me to tears. It was the longest five miles I could remember. I could see nowhere to wild camp without dragging the loaded bike miles across rough ground, so I just kept going. The campsite, when it finally appeared, overlooked a huge, dammed lake glistening grey in the desert and buzzing with speedboats and jet-skis. I flopped for a few minutes and then steeled myself for the day's second main battle – with my tent. This time I managed to get it more or less erected near a tree, away from the official camping area, where the ground was fractionally less concrete. The light was fading by the time I hit the shower. Afterwards I sat by the tent eating an apple, and watching distant lightening race across the slate-grey sky. I left the core for a rabbit foraging nearby. A huge pickup truck towing a jet ski pulled up in one of the camping areas. Its all-male occupants were there to roar about on the water and I was trying to feed a rabbit! In my tired state I had an odd sense of different worlds colliding, and also a touch of hostility, almost certainly imagined. Their world was the one in which massively carbon-polluting forms of recreation were simply the norm – and critics were killjoys or tree-hugging environmental lunatics. And mine? Mine was the world of a person at odds with this 'normality'; appalled by its consequences; deeply critical and yet inevitably part of it too.

In bed by nine, I recalled the words of a friend who works in an outdoor shop. Dave is something of a camping-gear specialist. 'The Lazer,' he'd said carefully, when I told him what I'd just bought, 'is wonderfully light. But a little hard to put up single-handed in wind. And not ideal if the wind is high...' Just as I was drifting off, a high wind put in an appearance. You could hear it roaring in from the distance. It arrived with sudden ferocity, slamming into the tent. The tail-end collapsed onto my feet. At the same time, a posse of trucks roared up, their drivers yelling across the wind as they slammed doors and went to use the toilets. Getting out in my underpants to fix the tent seemed like a good way to attract the wrong kind of help. I lay still until the last set of truck lights arched across the canvas and revved off into the dark. Then I crawled out, tethered the tent to Rocky at one end (it was already tied to a tree at the other), pinned down the rest with rocks, and settled in for a windy night.

~

The good thing about low spots is that they make the high spots higher, and on bike trips the high spots are frequent. All sorts of ordinary events which are normally taken for granted soon begin to cause disproportionate joy. Like *not* cycling, even for a few minutes. Or drinking water. Or eating. Definitely eating. The tortillas and cheese I'd bought on day one were my main food all week, bungied on top of the panniers for ease of access. The cheese constantly melted and re-solidified, becoming puddle-shaped. I supplemented it where possible with a daily café stop, combining a bit of a rest, temperature restoration, water replenishment and food with an erratic injection of random extracts from United States' culture. In the

Pepper Pot café, a long room with ceiling fans and all the blinds down, I had a huge plate of huevos rancheros. The café walls were covered in ornate silver crosses, old LPs, photographs of tractors, and a 1963 newspaper headlining 'Johnson Sworn in as President'. The toilet walls specialised in pictures of lighthouses, carefully painted on pieces of wood. By the door stood a Christmas tree, covered in red, white and blue stars – all alight. The Buckhorn Bar, by comparison, featured benches with inset metal moose designs, reindeer antlers festooned with baseball caps, a piano with a stuffed mountain lion crouched on top of it, and a television playing continuous country and western videos. On each table, a photocopied GQ magazine front page inserted into the menu stand read, '20 hamburgers to eat before you die. Buckhorn burger voted #7 in America ...' Huevos rancheros was my mainstay in cafés throughout New Mexico. It has to be up there with the best vegetarian biking meals ever. Beans, potatoes, eggs, tortillas, cheese and chilli (green or red). Vast portions, of course; I would begin the meal with great relish and then about halfway through a feeling close to despair would creep in as I realised there was no way I could eat it all. Usually I'd get a doggy bag and keep it for later, strapped on my panniers on top of the cheese.

Drinking was also a major source of good feeling, perhaps even more than eating. In 110 degrees, this was not exactly an indulgence. Charlie had made space on the bike to fit three water bottles and I usually carried an additional couple of litres in old plastic bottles. It wasn't always enough. One morning when the hot headwinds were particularly relentless my minor road petered out. I'd heard bicycles weren't allowed on the interstate highways, and anyway they didn't sound too enticing. Now I didn't have a choice. I wheeled down towards Interstate 25, figuring that if it really were illegal to cycle there I'd be picked up by the police and with luck deposited a bit further north. But the sign at the junction, while banning pedestrians and motorbikes, declared bicycles to be legal so long as they kept to the hard shoulder. Happy to oblige, I crept cautiously onto the vast stretch of tarmac. Revelation! Not only was there little traffic, but the interstate ironed out most of the minor ups and downs, a benefit lost on its motorised constituents but of immense significance to tired cyclists. (I learned later that the interstates were built in this way so that fighter planes could land on them during the Cold War.) And by some logic that was beyond my grasp the headwind was much less fierce on the interstate than it was on the minor road, even though both roads went in exactly the same direction.

Miles later my glee at these discoveries began to fade as I realised I was not going to make it to the next town without more water. It wasn't exactly life-threatening; I could always flag down a truck. But the thought of doing that brought out an emphatic British reserve I didn't know I had. I became fixated with two large 'R's' on the map. Even in a semi-dehydrated state, I couldn't make 'R' stand for 'service station'. What else could it stand for that might have water? The last drip in the last bottle had gone miles back, and then I arrived at the best Rest Stop in the world. Pulling off the road, I was greeted by two men and a woman travelling to Las Vegas. With typical, if slightly scatty generosity, they handed me a bag of ice (first), then water and a doughnut. The Rest Stop had a water tap, toilets, a vending machine and a shaded area with tables. It even had a barbeque grill. A sign at one end read 'Dog Toilet', though various dogs came and went as they chose, and at the other, 'Beware of Rattlesnakes'. I settled at a table and made a cheese tortilla. The recent relief of my own immediate personal water shortage gave particularly vivid meaning to the predicated impacts of climate change on fresh water. About a third of the entire population of China, for example, depends on glacial meltwater for their drinking water. And if that source simply disappears? What will people do when water, something we literally cannot live without, is threatened? Perhaps luckily for my peace of mind, a truck driver wearing a white cowboy hat, immaculate white sleeveless vest, ironed cream jeans and cowboy boots climbed down from his cavernous cab and joined me. We chatted about the heat. I felt shyer than I'd anticipated, trying to bring up the subject of climate change in these brief exchanges. But when I did, I was quickly finding the weather to be the fastest route in. Like most people I'd talked to so far, the immaculate trucker said it was hotter than normal. And drier. And windier. He said there were big fires in Arizona, where the air was acrid with smoke.

'Do you think it's global warming?' I asked.

'Heck honey,' he said, 'I sure think it's Mother Nature.'

Mother Nature, natural cycles, sunspots... I'd already encountered numerous people who held roughly this view. Presumably, the consequences remain just as threatening whether global warming is caused by us or whether Mother Nature carries the can. But the Mother Nature view has one great advantage. If global warming is a natural phenomenon then we probably don't need to take on the responsibility of trying to prevent it. It's often held alongside the view that we're too small to make a difference anyway. Looking around at the vast gasoline guzzling trucks I could see how such a position might have an appeal. And at least the Mother Nature advocates had some conception of what global warming *was*.

I was just leaving when my mobile rang. Only two people had the number – Chris and the Office of the Mayor of Albuquerque. It was the latter.

'Dr Rawles!' said a strongly accented (to my ears) female voice, introducing herself as Rene. 'We are so glad you are well.' Thank goodness for phones that are not video-enabled, I thought, having just seen my blotched face and staring, still-dehydrated eyes in the rest-room mirror. 'The Mayor will be delighted to meet you at nine am on Friday as arranged. Does that still work for you? He has no other slot.' My date with the Mayor was the reason I'd been straining to keep up the mileage all week. Getting to Albuquerque by Thursday evening in order to be in a fit state to meet the Mayor on Friday morning was still going to be, well, a challenge.

'Of course,' I heard myself say, 'no problem at all. Is there anywhere to stay near the Mayor's office?'

'Oh yes,' said Rene, 'the Hyatt is very close. And there's also a Hilton.'

I collected Rocky, who was resting against the rattlesnake sign, and prepared to set off. 'Hmmmmm,' I said to Rocky and the hot blue sky, 'the Hyatt with no credit card. That should be interesting.' Clearly the Mayor's office was not in Motel Six belt. And I knew there were no campsites within miles.

As I left, a vast RV towing a Hummer pulled into the rest area, returning my attention to higher things and reminding me why I was cycling through this minor inferno in the first place. RVs do about five miles per gallon and the Hummer, basically a civilian tank, does about three miles per gallon – on a good day. 'Haven't you heard of global warming?' I wanted to shout at the short bearded man strolling towards the barbeque area. 'Wake up, you oil-addicted fool!'

Fortunately my British reserve kicked in again and I cycled silently away. The drivers of oversized vehicles were perhaps not best placed to see the issue with clarity. But one thing really did surprise me. An awful lot of people genuinely didn't seem to know there was an issue at all. How could it be, I wondered, that so many folk seemed barely to have heard of something that might fundamentally alter human society, if not remove us from the planet altogether – and that had been plastered for months if not years all over the European news? Here, I'd fast become accustomed to people changing the subject when I edged conversations towards global warming. When I dug a bit further the reason was evident. Despite all the concern about heat waves, in many cases they had, quite simply, never heard of it.

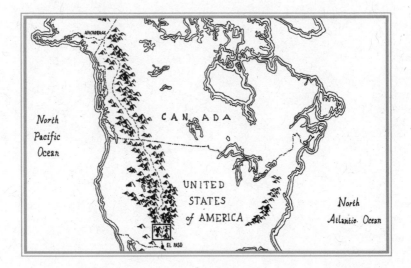

CHAPTER TWO
Wild Hogs and Chilli Festivals

'It isn't pollution that's harming the environment. It's the impurities in our air and water that's doing it.'

Governor George W. Bush

'They misunderestimated me...'

President George W. Bush

I set off from the Best Rest Station in the World in a much better mood, despite the Hummer. I cycled faster, for at least an hour. Off to my right was a huge area marked on the map as 'Bosque del Apache National Wildlife Refuge and Wilderness'. I wanted to be inside it, with the wildlife, but there didn't seem to be any roads leading there from the interstate. When one finally appeared I turned onto it, only to have it transform from tarmac to thick gravel within a mile. Back on Interstate 25, the hard shoulder became rough. I crossed over the bumpy rumble-strip – designed to wake up snoozing truckers – to a smooth strip of road just on the traffic side. Seconds later a vast truck hurtled past without pulling out even a millimetre and swept me straight back again. Point taken! I forgot the roughness in a glorious sweep down into San Antonio, past a mile long freight train with a mournful, evocative siren and a flock of tiny brown birds with white heads. And a road-runner. I'd never seen a road-runner before, but anyone who saw one, with that jaunty head and long legs, would somehow know that's what it was. When I left San Antonio, standing outside the café in the hot sun, looking back up the road to distant hills with cowboy music drifting out into the huge sky, I felt at peace with the trip for the first time.

The next morning, Chris and I managed to co-ordinate a phone call. I suddenly found myself pouring out a stream of doubts – about my fitness, about the heat, about my reserve around talking to people about climate change, about whether my slowness at this end of the trip would create too much pressure later on. About whether, for all my grand aims, I could actually make the trip mean something more than a personal challenge, which had, in the run up to leaving, begun to feel self-indulgent and, right now, wasn't even feeling like any kind of indulgence at all. Chris was endlessly reassuring. The trip will evolve. Its meaning will evolve. You have lots of time. You will get fitter and find ways of talking to people. You *are* talking to people! He told me that Carole at work had put up a big map of North America in the office and that the pin representing me was already a discernable distance north of El Paso. He told me he was sending various things to my friend Susan in Colorado and that he would try to sort out a hotel near the Mayor's office in Albuquerque. The conversation was just great. It put a whole load of things back into perspective which had been blown out of proportion as they endlessly ran and re-ran around my hot head. It also raised some big personal questions. I'd always done previous trips either alone or with a friend. Never with a partner. And certainly never with a partner at home acting as base camp manager, hunting down broken bike bits, posting replacement credit cards, phoning my Dad with updates, and sorting out hotels when I needed one. Was this *cheating*?? Worse, was it a threat to my treasured, lifelong, carefully guarded independence? The answer seemed likely to be, yes, in both cases. But right then, it sure as hell felt good.

The first gopher of the trip screeched at me as I cycled off for a short stretch on Interstate 25. Then I joined a quiet and beautiful side road. Farms, horses and, in this part of New Mexico, an increasing sense of people living on the edge. Lots of trailer houses, some in pretty battered shape. Scrapped cars. Once, a yard full of broken bicycles. A sign on a trailer-house fence read, *Please don't dump any more animals here. Mrs Olsen is ill and cannot look after them.* How, I wondered, would an increasingly disturbed, chaotic climate impact on these people? Would they cope better or worse for being on the edge already?

After a while I lost my small road and was deposited back on the interstate. Another wildlife refuge – the Sevilleta National Wildlife Refuge – was marked on both sides of me but again, I couldn't see how to get to it. One of the things I love about cycling is the way you are really *in* the landscape rather than isolated from it in the sound-proof tin box of a car. But so far I'd only really felt in the landscape when I *wasn't* cycling. Even in brief breaks, stopped in a sliver of shade somewhere, the birdsong would become vivid and half-noticed rustles would suddenly emerge as lizards. Now I wanted to be off the huge highway and immersed in this wilder country, hearing the birds, learning how to see all the animals that lived there. A fantasy grew in my mind. I would come across a park ranger who would say to me, Ma'am, can you ride a horse? Sure, I'd reply, and we'd saddle up two bay quarter horses and ride into the desert where he'd show me animal tracks and teach me the names of the birds and the plants....

Somewhere along the road I had another flat and some time later I went by a store on a corner with benches outside in the shade. I swooped by, thinking, I don't deserve to stop yet – and then spent the next half an hour thinking, You idiot! Two hours in the sun in a hundred plus degrees, and you can't stop for a lemonade? In my mind, the store became populated with friendly, interesting people, and had soon become a symbol of everything I needed to make time for on this trip. Conversation. Contact. Maybe it was a related intuition that prompted me, coming into Los Lunes for a late lunch, to cross to a café on the other side of the road – though I thought I was drawn by the sign advertising 'Deli and Salads'. The salad bar consisted primarily of grated cheese and shrivelled lettuce so I had huevos rancheros as usual.

As I was finishing, one of the three women who constituted the café's entire population came over. 'So, where are you biking to?' We got chatting. Her name was Thereze, and the café was hers, though she had a degree in Outdoor Recreation, and still coached softball. Before the café, she'd travelled in Europe, and liked Italy especially. Global warming? 'Sure, it's an issue,' she said. 'It's a *huge* issue. But people don't care. They're idiots. Our *President* is an idiot, straight up...'

Wondering how many people in New Mexico shared this view, I filled my water bottles at a tap in the washroom under a poster explaining how to deal with domestic violence. When I went to pay, the young girl behind the counter said, 'No, T's got it.'

T was not going to argue. She didn't even want to be thanked, turning away with a 'Have a good trip and be safe,' and leaving me with a treasured sense of connection and undemanding exchange.

~

The end of that first, long, hot week saw me cycling into Albuquerque. Outskirts and road works and busy traffic for miles and miles and then, with a bit of map-puzzling and a sanity stop on a bridge to watch the swallows, I suddenly arrived. Downtown! Some cities in the States don't really seem to have a downtown area, but Albuquerque certainly did. Swanky high-rise hotels and offices, huge pedestrian plazas and funky restaurants abruptly replaced the straggling outskirts. It had seemed judicious to clean up a bit before meeting the Mayor and I didn't want to be miles away in the morning. But the downtown hotels were not an option on my cash budget. Chris had somehow persuaded a hotel to let him pay for a room over the phone from the UK. Since they normally insist on seeing the relevant credit card, this was quite an achievement. Now, courtesy of Google maps, he guided me in with text messages, saying later it felt a bit like watching the little red dot move along the streets of Shanghai in *Mission Impossible*. 'You're coming to a junction. Take the next left!'

On the other side of the Atlantic I closed in, inexorably, on the target... The Doubletree Hotel. A zillion stories high and exceedingly plush. And just across the plaza from the Mayor's office. Leaving Rocky at the entrance I tentatively crossed the vast lobby, suddenly aware of my own griminess. Would they really let me in?

The response was impeccable. 'Certainly ma'am, your room is on the ninth floor.'

'Er, and my bike?'

'Oh, just take it with you.'

So Rocky and I rode upwards in an elevator, joined by various others who seemed equally unperturbed despite having to squeeze past the dusty panniers to get in. I laughed out loud when I saw the room. Number 916 was an absolute haven. Huge, lightly scented, discreet colours, immense bed: in short, altogether luxurious. I had one of the best showers ever, fixed a punctured inner tube while reclining on a lounge chair and then read about United States mayors propped up in the vast bed. Rocky leant against an immaculately papered wall and looked really quite at home.

The next morning, after a sumptuous eggs benedict breakfast, I walked across the sunny plaza to the Mayor's office. Eleven floors up, it was actually a whole suite of offices, open plan and scattered with sofas and enormous Chinese vases. Spectacular views across

Albuquerque and beyond beckoned from every sparkling window. I was greeted by the friendly Rene – slim, early thirties, dark hair – introduced to various people as 'The Doctor' or 'Doctor KR', given coffee and waved to a deep sofa to await the Mayor. I would have been willing to wait for some time. The Mayor of Albuquerque was, at that point, one of two hundred and forty-three 'Cool City' Mayors [7] across the United States who had basically said, the heck with Bush and the federal government; if they are not going to do anything about climate change, we will. They had simply bypassed Bush, and got on with the job of committing their cities to big reductions in climate change emissions, using the Kyoto Protocol as guidelines but often going well beyond them. From what I'd managed to find out so far, I was impressed. They were dynamic, they had clout and they were getting things done. They were focused on solutions. And they had some very clear ideas about what those solutions were.

I'd just figured out how to use the digital recorder (the same tiny machine that played host to my fourteen songs) and had rather nervously prepared a ton of questions. But Mayor Martin Chavez – short grey hair, very calm, focused, casual dress ('I'm going fishing later') – started by asking me about my trip. Then Barry – 'my energy man' – joined us. Then one of the Mayor's aides put her head around the door to say that someone from *The Albuquerque Tribune* was here. Before I knew it, I was being simultaneously interviewed by Cary from the *Tribune*, various unidentified people on the conference call system, and someone from the local radio station. The aide was mouthing, 'Tell them how important the issue is'; a dog barked in the background, and a photographer was snapping all of us. So my first recording of the trip was mostly of myself.

Finally, I got to ask the Mayor some questions. His vision was passionately held, (sort of) top-down, and focused on technology. Cleaner energy, greener fleets, energy efficiency. The Mayors were in a position to make it happen in their cities. They didn't need to wait for grass roots change from below and they didn't need permission from above. 'Leadership from the middle,' I thought, as Chavez talked. He was clearly having an impact on Albuquerque's carbon footprint. I asked him whether he thought his impact went beyond his

[7] More information about Cool City Mayors at http://coolcities.us/

city, whether the Mayors had influence at the federal level. His reply was beyond positive. It gave a glimpse of the world as an altogether different, saner place.

'Oh yes,' he said, 'the Mayors are certainly having an effect higher up. Environmental issues in general are going to be a major factor in the next presidential election. The USA will finally come fully on board in relation to global warming – and then it will lead the world. Then it will be a force to be reckoned with...'

The United States as a world leader in tackling climate change! That was really quite a thought, especially since the Bush administration was, at the time, still largely denying climate change even existed. But if it were, somehow, to become reality ... on the spot it was hard to think of any other single change of political position that could have a greater, more positive impact.

Meanwhile, back in the real world, I asked Mayor Chavez whether he thought that the gains in efficiency and other kinds of 'technofixes' he was harnessing would be sufficient. 'They're clearly crucial,' I said, 'but, well, do you think they will be enough? Do we need changes in our lifestyle as well?'

Chavez paused. 'Lifestyle changes?' Then he smiled. 'Yes, of course. But we don't need to go back to the caves.'

I was keen to get to the bottom of this enigmatic response. What lay behind the equation of 'lifestyle changes' with a return to stone-age living, even in jest? I suspected it might mean, 'Lifestyle changes? Not really.' Or even, 'Lifestyle changes? Sigh. You've just revealed yourself as an old-fashioned, unrealistic, back-to-the-ark, hippy environmentalist' – though this speculation was completely unfounded. I was just on the verge of formulating the single, laser-sharp question that would instantly uncover the truth when the Mayor was asked what he thought about my trip.

'Well, I think the Doctor is a ripple on a lake. A ripple that will turn into a tsunami...' I wasn't quite sure how to take this but before I could question his metaphor the Mayor indicated with a polite but emphatic, 'Is there anything else I can help you with?' that the interview was over. I was led away by the energy man to meet the exuberant hound, who turned out to be the Mayor's dog, Dukes.

I warmed to the Mayor even more after meeting his dog. Dukes – a delightful, sane, happy, black, grey and spotty retriever cross – was a rescue mutt who had gone on to star in the publicity for a spaying and neutering campaign, one of the Mayor's pet projects. Dukes brought a ball and dropped it at my feet. Throwing it seemed less than wise, but Barry grinned and said, 'Oh, just chuck it. If we break a vase we'll get the Chinese to send us another.' I assumed he didn't mean it. But I wasn't entirely convinced he was joking, either. Barry described himself as 'a Republican, but the greenest person in the building.' We went to his office and chatted about all sorts of things, including his reservations about biofuel – 'It releases huge amounts of carbon in the harvesting. It's not like we do it with a man and an ox. And it takes up habitat and agricultural land.' In relation to cars, he favoured hydrogen. And the energy for the reaction? 'Solar,' he said. 'We're not exactly short on sunshine here –' he threw a glance at my patchy arms – 'as you've probably noticed.' It was Barry who told me about the interstates and fighter planes, moving seamlessly from there to a discussion about his wife's gun (had she ever used it? 'Well, the time a burglar came through the bathroom window she would've') to his views about education, child-rearing and how ornery kids get if they watch TV while eating sugar.

~

It was almost lunchtime by the time I left the Mayor's office, packed up and left the Doubletree. I was waved off by the hotel staff, who had given me strict instructions about which roads to avoid at all costs. Back out in the Albuquerque lunchtime traffic, attempting to follow their directions with the words, 'I *live* here, and I wouldn't cycle on that,' ringing in my ears, I wasted at least an hour before realising that 'Cut through University,' meant, 'Take the road called "University"' rather than 'Take a shortcut through the campus.' I'd tried the latter and repeatedly come to a dead-end at the library. I finally ended up on the road I'd been warned off, only to find that it was the one I'd cycled in on. I had no wish to provoke fate by ignoring the advice of cycling locals but I guess they typically hadn't just come off the interstate. In between grappling with urban navigation, I thought about what Mayor Chavez had said. The Cool City Mayors were definitely on the case in terms of thinking about solutions. Their willingness to bypass Bush and just get on with it was inspiring. Leadership from the middle. An important bit of the jigsaw? How often do we feel too small as individuals to do anything – and yet how difficult it must be at the very top, too, as a president or a prime minister who is trying to deal with a climate crisis while also compelled to heed the short-term concerns of next term's electorate. The city or town, somewhere between the individual and the state, seemed to be a good size unit for change, for positive action, for putting solutions into immediate practice.

But what about the *kind* of solutions the Mayors were advocating? Of that I wasn't so sure. 'Technology' was, in sum, Chavez' answer to my question, 'How do we make ourselves and our ways of life climate friendly?' and I was troubled by his answer to my question about technofixes. No-one could doubt that gains in energy efficiency and other technological advances were crucial in the fight to reduce greenhouse gas emissions. Motor vehicles alone – an example high in my mind for obvious reasons – accounted for about forty percent of the USA's entire oil consumption. If cars across the US increased their efficiency by only one mile per gallon, the United States would save as much oil as the *total* it could possibly extract if it drilled (as it was proposing to do) in the wild and beautiful Arctic National Wildlife Refuge. Meanwhile, millions of cars across the States were chucking out vastly more CO_2 than they needed to – even to make the same journeys in the same cars! Improvements in energy efficiency were part of the solution, no question.

But Chavez' approach, and that of the Cool City Mayors generally, seemed to be focused on technological changes alone. I thought of the bearded Hummer-man who I'd so nearly verbally abused. A technofix approach could reduce his emissions by running his 'car' on a more carbon-efficient fuel. Such a move had already been made by Arnold Schwarzenegger. Schwarzenegger had taken up the environmental mantle, his campaigning earning him the nickname 'Germinator'. Shwarzenegger, the proud owner of five Hummers, had converted two of them: one to run on hydrogen and the other on biofuels. Maybe a Hummer could be made a bit more streamlined, too. But even a biofuelled, shape-shifted Hummer would still account for an awful lot of carbon. And then there was the sheer unnecessary-ness of the thing. Surely, even the Governor of California didn't really need to run around town in a tank?

In sum, Chavez' approach was inspiring; but it also left me

wondering. Could we simply keep our current lifestyle essentially intact, using clever technology to render it climate-friendly? Was it feasible as a solution to techno-fix not just Hummers, but the carbon consequences of our high levels of consumption in general – the carbon consequences of our throwaway, fast-fix consumer values? Energy consumption went up 80% in the thirty years from 1970 to the end of the century. Most analysts agree that, across the industrialised world, it needs to *come down* 80% by 2050. Could technology alone really take us all the way across that particular Great Divide – from where we are now to where we need to get to? If it couldn't, a deeper rethink was in order. Sacrilegious thought, but I couldn't help wondering whether we might even need to *give up* Hummers. And if we did, how much would we really lose?

~

The way out of town was lined with potential distractions. My eggy breakfast had been used up long since and there were numerous, tempting, university city-type places to eat. But I had it my head that I didn't deserve lunch until I was on the other side of town. Once I was thoroughly in the outskirts I stopped at a Taco Bell and, without great hope, asked what they had that was vegetarian. 'Would a seven-layer burrito be OK?' asked the young girl behind the counter. The seven layers turned out to include beans, guacamole, tomato and cheese. It cost a little over two dollars and was absolutely delicious. Just as I was leaving, my mobile rang. It was an old friend, Tom Buffalo, who'd got the number from Chris. I'd tried to contact Tom before leaving the UK but had apparently used an out-of-date number for an office in Alaska and he'd only just picked up the call. He was just about to give me his home number in Colorado when my phone packed in. There was nothing I could do. I cycled away, hoping Tom wasn't thinking I'd just been mugged.

The first few miles on the interstate were grim. It was vastly busier than further south and a real slog into the wind. I strained into the pedals while trying to avoid broken glass and tyre debris on the hard shoulder, or annihilation off the hard shoulder as huge trucks hurtled by, buffeting me with tail wind and noise. At last, I turned off onto Highway 14 – the 'Turquoise Trail' – and a big pull-up to another San Antonio. The Turquoise Trail National Scenic Byway is a gorgeous section of road between Albuquerque and Santa Fe – with a very dark past. Visitors are invited to 'drive back into history through the mining towns of Golden, Madrid and Cerrillos'. Drive a little further back and they might also witness Colonel Kit Carson marching Navajo people along the trail during their 'Long Walk' to incarceration at Fort Sumner. Carson had been sent to subdue the Navajo and move them to Fort Sumner on the Bosque Redondo Reservation. When they declined, he began a brutal campaign, destroying villages, livestock, crops and people until moving to the reservation was their only chance of survival. Eight or nine thousand people walked the three hundred miles to Fort Sumner. Hundreds died of cold and hunger. Less than a hundred and fifty years later, I struggled to think myself into Carson's mindset – into the worldview that would have made this seem like legitimate behaviour. How could that possibly have seemed like a normal, acceptable thing to do?

It wasn't only the march that killed people. Many more were to die later. The United States government decreed that the Navajo should engage in agriculture on the barren reservation. Some argue that this land was unsuitable for raising crops and that the Navajo did not have the right kind of farming experience. Others that, left to their own devices, the First Nations would have coped perfectly well; but that they were forced to change their farming methods by the new, white Americans – who scarcely knew the land – leading to failed harvests and damaged ecosystems. Either way, hunger followed.

From a modern perspective, the treatment of the First Nations seems astonishingly stupid and brutal. Yet the writer and farmer Wendell Berry, in his classic book *The Unsettling of America*,[8] argues that, however brutal, these events were just the beginning of a new and potentially catastrophic trend: a series of more or less forced displacements of people who knew and understood the land – and could support themselves sustainably from it – by people who didn't. The people who drove off and exploited the Navajo were, he points out, driven off and exploited in their turn, albeit by economic forces rather than military ones. And the same pattern can be seen across the world: small farms being displaced by immense, high-technology farming – by 'agribusiness'. It's done in the name of 'efficiency', of

---

[8] Wendell Berry (1977) *The Unsettling of America* Avon Books

course, but at what cost? Millions of people, often farming in a way that is actually more resilient and less damaging, displaced against their will. And immense problems in relation to food safety. ('It is one of the miracles of science and hygiene,' as Berry dryly summarises, 'that the germs that used to be in our food have been replaced by poisons.') Immense problems in relation to environmental pollution and soil erosion. ('How can it be "efficient" to damage, destroy, even lose, vast quantities of the soil that is the very thing that makes agriculture possible?' Berry asks).

And of course, modern agribusiness is fantastically energy-hungry. It depends on oil for its machinery, for its fertilizers and pesticides, for its packaging, and for the long-distance transportation of its produce. This was evident even to Berry in the 1970s: 'That we should have an agriculture based as much on petroleum as on the soil – that we need petroleum exactly as much as we need food and must have it *before* we can eat – may seem absurd. It is absurd. It is nevertheless true.' It makes modern agriculture – the source of the vast majority of our food – deeply vulnerable to changes in oil supply and cost. And it means that the systems by which we produce one of our most basic needs are contributing massively in terms of energy use, and hence CO_2 emissions, to climate change. The ultimate irony is that climate change presents a profound threat to these very same systems.

Not an easy train of thought. And one that raises that most fundamental of questions: how *should* we meet our needs? In particular, how should we relate to the land we rely on to do this? It's a question both deeply ethical and profoundly practical. Of course we need to eat and to do this we need to use 'nature'. But how do we distinguish between *use* of the land, of ecological systems, of people, of other species and other living beings – and *abuse*? How do we use the land in ways that are both sustainable and fair?

Far easier to be drawn back into the present, where the Turquoise Trail was turning into the best day's cycling so far. Big desert vistas, big blue sky. Hot, but not oven-like. Little traffic. At the top of a hill a car was pulled over on the hard shoulder and a couple were photographing cacti. I stopped. 'Hi!' they said, 'would you like a drink?' They handed me a huge glass of orange juice, introduced themselves as Luc and Denise from Vancouver, and told me that the flowering of the cacti, happening all around, was in fact a rare

41

occurrence. They took a photo of me, Rocky and a huge spiky plant festooned with rather straggly pink flowers and left me their number in case I should ever need help in Vancouver. Ravens flew alongside as I cycled off, craeking gently and occasionally tumbling in the hot sky.

Not long after, the road began an absolutely glorious, speedy descent. Rocky's top gears had not been in action for several days and, for the first time, I missed them. I pulled over and dug out my tool-kit, adjusting the limit screws that control the front gear mechanism. It made absolutely no difference. Ditto with adjusting the tension on the cable. I wasn't in the mood for indefinite fiddling to no effect. So we took off again, for miles of wonderful, long, swooping descents, the occasional tiny climbs quickly followed by more descent. Even with my legs spinning furiously it was fantastic.

~

The town of Golden hosted the first gold rush west of the Mississippi, in 1825, well before the gold rushes in California and Colorado. Now, in 2006, it barely existed. The town of Madrid, however, most certainly did. I cycled slowly down a long main street of decidedly funky-looking houses, many sporting anti-Iraq war posters, not something I had seen until then. A feisty atmosphere hung in the air. And the town was absolutely packed with people. Cafés and bars and sidewalks all spilled people onto the street, which was hung with banners proclaiming the 'Madrid Chilli Festival'. This was no quaintsy folk festival, though. There was the occasional chilli in evidence, but mostly there were rows and rows of machinery parts lined up on the sidewalk. At the far end of town was a huge open space, packed with trucks and an immense sound system, clearly gearing up for later with occasional fragments of music blasting into the hot air. I cycled slowly through, absolutely intrigued. What on earth was happening here? But I didn't stop. Friends of friends had offered a bed for the night and were expecting me in Santa Fe by eight. Given the late start, I was going to be hard-pushed to get there at any kind of civilised hour. But it was more than that. There's a sort of resistance to stopping I can get into when travelling. Partly a kind of shyness, partly a kind of laziness. It can be easier to keep moving – to skim across the surface of places and people – than to stop and engage. Leaving aside that this can make for an empty experience, finding ways to connect enough to chat about climate change was the very core of what I was trying to do.

On the other hand, engaging takes time and there wasn't a lot of extra time at my disposal. In this respect, one of several dilemmas at the heart of this trip was rapidly emerging and Madrid was a particularly acute example. Should I just *take* the time to stop off at unexpected chilli festivals and, if necessary, let Anchorage go? Or should I keep my focus on the final destination and keep moving, keep the miles up? At that point, I was feeling pretty stubborn about reaching Anchorage. I couldn't give up on it. Not yet. And so Madrid remained an intriguing opportunity – music, feisty people, what appeared to be a chunk of United States counter-culture at a big outdoor party – that I didn't take up.

On the far side of Madrid, the road kept dropping. It was already gone six in the evening. If the road goes up at the end of this descent as much as I've just come down, I thought, there is no way I am going to get to Santa Fe by anything like eight. Miraculously and mysteriously, given that Santa Fe is nearly two thousand feet higher than Albuquerque, it didn't. The road just levelled out around seven thousand feet. I'm not sure why, but I've always liked being at about that altitude – with all that heavy oxygen thinned out a bit, breathing becomes somehow easier. And I was feeling stronger than I had felt all week. It was a fabulous last couple of hours, racing to my fourteen songs, swooping downhill, standing in the pedals for the uphills, blasting the miles and getting closer and closer to arriving reasonably close to the hour I was actually expected. For the first time, I felt the exhilaration of being hot, sweaty and powerful, and dared to believe that my old, fit body might come back. The sun was setting as I hurtled (relatively speaking) into Santa Fe on Rodeo Road – which actually had a rodeo in full swing – and I would have made it for eight-thirty if I hadn't got lost. I spent an hour wandering around the suburbs of Santa Fe in the dusk with a mobile that wasn't working, increasingly aware of the late hour – and that my rear light had fallen off some time previously.

When I finally reached Jonathan and Mela, they had given up trying to phone me and were just going to bed. They waved away my apologies, gave me a plate of vegetable curry, showed me a luxurious bathroom and a fabulous bed under a wooden, wall-free roof-on-legs in the yard, surrounded by fairy lights. The bed was soft and delicious and I lay in it watching distant lightning and listening to the wind and the conversation of the neighbours next door.

Next morning, realising that the phone worked when it was plugged in, I commandeered the fairy lights' socket and turned it into a temporary office. I rang Tom and left a message to say I hadn't been kidnapped in Albuquerque. I left a message for a friend in Canada and sent Chris a text. Then I had a crumpet with *Marmite* (oh, what bliss!) and chatted. Jonathan was a builder – preferably with straw bales, though there wasn't, he said, much call for that – and they were doing up the house. The kitchen looked normal but everywhere else was a complete shell, except for the sumptuous bathroom. I asked them about the Madrid Chilli Festival.

'Madrid? That's a place that's a law unto itself,' said Jonathan. 'But I've never heard of the Chilli Festival.'

'Me neither,' said Mela.

I had said my goodbyes and was just about to unplug the phone and head off when Tom rang back. 'Let's meet up! How about today!' Tom was an old friend who I hadn't seen in twelve years. But he lived in Southern Colorado, about three hundred and fifty miles off my route. I didn't have time to bike it and there was no public transport. How would I get there? Tom, an aeroplane leaser by trade, was unperturbed. 'Easy, I'll pick you up in a plane,' he said.

'Tom,' I said, carefully, 'I'm on a climate change awareness journey. I can't take a lift in a plane!'

'No worries,' he said cheerfully, 'I'll bring a smaller one.'

Needless to say, this left me with another dilemma. I really wanted to see Tom and to meet his new wife, Rosalind. But I knew flying was hugely problematic from a climate change point of view. On a return journey from London to Manchester, roughly equivalent to the flight Tom was proposing, a three-quarters-full train would chuck about 30kg of CO_2 per person into the skies – whereas a similarly loaded plane would account for a whopping 96.5kg[9] per passenger. I wasn't sure how this compared to a small plane (the figures were for a Boeing 747) but I was pretty sure it wouldn't be good. Of course, the whole trip was underpinned by an even bigger dilemma as I'd just flown across the Atlantic to do it. And having just crossed the

---

[9] Comparison based on UK Department of Transport figures. See www.transportdirect.info 'Find CO2 emissions' under 'Tips and Tools'

Atlantic it seemed perverse to refuse Tom's lift. But for some reason, the prospect of it unsettled me. Up until now, I'd assumed I could justify my long flight. It wasn't as if I was going away for a weekend; I'd be away for three months. And the purpose of the ride made the flight worthwhile, surely. Now, faced with a much shorter flight, I was suddenly not so sure. My transatlantic flight would have emitted about a tonne of CO_2 per passenger. That's roughly what we should be aiming at per person *per year*. Hard, then, to make long-haul flights part of a personal, climate-friendly lifestyle. Yet assuming it's okay to fly, that it's necessary for whatever reason, is the norm. Flying is normal. I'd been assuming my own flight was somehow different, special, more important. But wasn't that precisely the problem? It was not a comfortable thought.

~

The airport was only three miles away, which left me time to visit the bike shop.

'I can't get the front derailleur to shift into top gear,' I explained. The shop was stuffed with bikes needing attention but I was on the road with big panniers. There seemed to be an unspoken ethic – I encountered it time and time again – that tourers who are actually touring get priority treatment in bike shops. Rocky was relieved of his panniers, lifted onto a stand and Luke, clearly the chief mechanic, carefully reset the limit screws, tightened the cable, tweaked the angle of the back derailleur ...

'You got a whole host of minor things adding up here, ma'am,' he said, and then, as I asked for a ton of inner tubes and the use of a high-pressure pump, he introduced me to *slime*. Slime is ... well, a slimy substance that, if injected into the inner tube, magically renders punctures self-sealing. Fantastic! Luke administered the slime, a shade of putrid lime green; I pumped up the tyres, and a well-adjusted Rocky and I cycled off in perfect time to meet Tom at eleven.

At the tiny Santa Fe airport we passed a building marked 'Million Aires', a couple of hangers, a very small reception area for routine flights – and arrived at the beautiful buff adobe building reserved for the occupants of private planes. It was a different world.

'Er, can I bring my bike in?'

'Of course, madam,' said the immaculate receptionist, handing me a glass of iced water. So Rocky and I waited in cool luxury, he leaning against the gift counter while I perched on a leather chair at a table next to plush sofas and a wood-burning stove (not burning) and wrote my diary until Tom arrived, grinning, hugging, and god-damning. Tom, pretty much the same despite the intervening years, put Rocky in the office, borrowed the staff car and drove me downtown for lunch.

Back at the airport, we squeezed Rocky into the tiny Cessna and took off over Santa Fe. Flying low, Tom insisted on following the road I'd be cycling on later. Since I rapidly get airsick in small planes – carbon payback! – I would have been quite happy to go by the most direct possible route. But it *was* amazing to see this part of New Mexico from the air. Cycling along I'd thought, yep, this is pretty desert-y, but I'd had no real sense of the scale. From above, I could see hundreds and hundreds of miles of dry land, scrub, empty watercourses. Wow! I really had been cycling through a desert! A regular scattering of tiny square patches were, Tom said, gas wells. By this time, the afternoon storms were building up into lurch-making bumpy clouds. Tom let me take the controls and only by focusing fiercely on the horizon and on keeping the wings straight did I avoid using the bin-liners we'd scrounged from reception. Much longer and they would have been critical, especially as the plane turned out to belong to a neighbour. In the nick of time we landed on a grass strip to be met by the beautiful Rosalind – tall, slim, big eyes, short grey hair, very striking and very welcoming. Tom and Rosalind had recently moved to this quiet part of Southern Colorado, bought a hundred acres, and were building a house. Meanwhile, they were living in a 'trailer', which turned out to be a beautiful, spacious white-painted house with a wooden deck and patio, under tall shady trees, looking out across hayfields to distant mountains. It was a lovely, lovely place.

I felt strongly inclined to spend the evening sitting on the deck under the trees, enjoying the view and the peace. But Tom and Rosalind were keen for me to meet their neighbours for dinner. When we arrived at John and Anne's, a few minutes away, it was just them and us. For some reason I had been imagining a formal, sit-down affair. Then a couple joined us, and then another. Then a group of kids piled out of a truck. Cars kept arriving. Soon the house was full of three generations of people wandering inside and out, drinking beers, cokes and margaritas. I chatted with a geologist specialising in hazardous waste who was retraining as a nurse specialising in anaesthesia. (An anaesthetist with a geological time-frame, what a thought! 'Let me put you to sleep for a hundred thousand years ...') His view on global warming was that climates have always been in flux and that this was just another flux. Even if it were happening, he added, talking about global warming isn't a good way to get people to act differently. 'It's too big and distant,' he said. 'Focus on the geopolitical situation and the desirability of energy independence. That'll get people's attention. That'll be much more effective.'

I chatted with a solar astrophysicist who'd been studying the sun's output since 1970. He promptly kicked Mother Nature into touch. 'We can't blame the sun's output for global warming any more,' he said. 'It is now *certain* that the output has been constant for the last thirty-odd years. And yes, I most definitely do believe that global warming is happening.'

Best of all, I chatted with Heidi. Small and slender, skin-tight jeans, beautiful boots, pink and white shirt and white cowboy hat above a long pale-blonde plait. Her large blue eyes had a calm, grounded sort of look. Wise, yes, but it was still extremely hard to believe that she was well past bus-pass age – or the Colorado equivalent. Heidi had a very large ranch in Utah – so beautiful, apparently, that more than one film star had offered to buy it. In the summer she rode the ranch checking on cattle and fences, sleeping out for five or six nights at a time and only coming back for the occasional bath. What an inspiration. Being a cowgirl was a long-standing fantasy of mine, though it had never sat entirely easily with being vegetarian.

That night in the 'trailer' I had a wonderful long sleep, disturbed only by the sound of something galloping along the deck outside. 'Darn!' said Rosalind when I mentioned it, 'That must be the racoon back.'

I was spoiled all weekend. Delicious food! Company! A bathroom! Rosalind and I sat on the deck and chatted and she shared some astonishing life stories that left me wondering how it is that some people seem to be dealt relentless challenges, and yet remain not just sane, but generous and apparently serene. Later, Tom and I visited Mesa Verde and the remains of a twelfth-century settlement. Tiny stone dwellings built into overhanging cliffs, curved and striped in beautiful pinks and oranges and buffs. We cut off the path and sat on a rock looking back across to the cliff-houses. The site felt deeply peaceful, though it must have been an intense way of living – such small spaces and lots of climbing to get in and out. Tom told me that it had taken eighty years to build, but was only inhabited for about a hundred years. Nobody really knew why they left, though Tom said he had heard a theory that the children got rebellious and took to cannibalism. Jared Diamond, in his book *Collapse*, [10] argues that the people of Mesa Verde, and other Anasazi in the south-west, had been brought down by a complex interaction of social and environmental factors; and that the environmental factors almost certainly included climate change. It had become drier, and their water source virtually disappeared. Their climate-change event would have been natural. Almost certainly nothing they could have done would have prevented it. Their catastrophe, however bad for them, had been small and local, I thought, looking at the silent, empty cliff-houses. Ours affects the whole earth. But they were gone, while we still had the option of turning things around.

Tom and I had been talking nonstop since Santa Fe, catching up on the last twelve years. Friends, work, travel, family. We talked about Hilary Clinton's chances of presidency and, of course, about climate change. Tom's view was that changes in the cost of energy would drive huge shifts in lifestyles in the next decade or so.

'Oil will peak,' he said, 'and become vastly more expensive, with all that entails.'

'Such as?'

'Such as jobs increasingly being outsourced internationally, leaving fewer jobs in the USA. Such as China becoming ever more powerful…'

He thought that the standard of living in the United States would drop, and that people would live more efficiently as a result. This would clearly have climate change benefits. But no way, in his view, would this be driven by individuals taking the initiative and acting on ethical and environmental concerns. 'It's economics, not ethics, that will change things,' he insisted. 'Economics is probably the *only* thing that will move us in the right direction, however inadvertently.'

I was not so sure. 'Once people know, once they really understand

[10] Jared Diamond (2006) *Collapse* Penguin Books

what climate change is and quite how bad its consequences will be, then they will care. How could people not care?'

'Kate, you're naïve,' Tom said, grinning, 'but I think you're great anyway.'

'Gee thanks,' I said. I hoped he was wrong. But Al Gore had said something very similar of himself: that in his early days as a climate change campaigner he'd been convinced that simply presenting the science would bring fellow politicians to his side. That he'd come to realise how naïve that was. How shocking he'd initially found it, hitting up against vested interests, barely disguised, the sheer power of oil and money. Economics driving hard in the wrong direction.

~

Back at the trailer, I asked Tom and Rosalind about the Madrid Chilli Festival.

'Madrid? That place is a law unto itself,' said Tom. 'But I've never heard of the Chilli Festival.'

'Me neither,' said Rosalind. 'Heck, lets go look it up.'

We Googled it. 'God damn!' said Tom, as we clicked on the first listing. Madrid, it transpired, had just been taken over for the film *Wild Hogs*, a motor-biking road movie starring John Travolta as one of four guys on bikes whose midlife crisis adventures included an encounter with the Del Fuegos, a mean New Mexican biker gang. The chilli festival I'd cycled through had not been a real festival at all, but part of a movie stage set.

We flew back to Santa Fe in Tom's plane rather than the neighbour's: a beautiful twin-prop turbo. Not so small. Rocky sat in the aisle quite comfortably, with seat belts gently constraining his panniers. The flight back was fabulous. Huge desert vistas, smooth and nausea-free. Somewhere near Ship Rock at the meeting of Colorado, New Mexico, Utah and Arizona, flying at twenty-one thousand feet, Tom took the plane off autopilot and let me fly (well, OK – steer). It was easy enough to keep on the compass bearing but of course you had to think about up and down as well... A plane like that climbs a thousand feet a minute, so it's unnervingly easy to drop or climb into somebody else's airspace. Tom even let me do the runway approach before taking over to the sound of air traffic asking if we'd seen the coyote on the runway. We could just see a tiny buff figure against the long asphalt strip, standing quite still in the sunlight until we were almost ruffling his hot, red fur.

I loved it. I loved the responsiveness of the machine and the subtle feel of the power it was taking just to stay in the air. I loved it as I also love driving – however much I try not to. This positive response to carbon-hungry machinery really didn't help with the unsettling realisation that the plane had already triggered. My own relationship with carbon emissions was a microcosm of the bigger problem. I had my own overly large carbon footprint, my own reasons for not wanting to cut it back, my own addiction to oil. And I'd scarcely thought about that at all.

I said my goodbyes to Tom on the runway. 'Keep in touch,' he said. 'Don't wanna fuss you, but, heck, let us know how you're doing. And hey,' he finished with a grin, 'if you ever really get stuck, I'll come get ya.'

I set off again from exactly where I'd left off, back past reception and Million Aires into the familiar world of hot New Mexican roads and headwinds. We were headed north, for Colorado, and I was now a climate change campaigner with a private plane backup for emergencies.

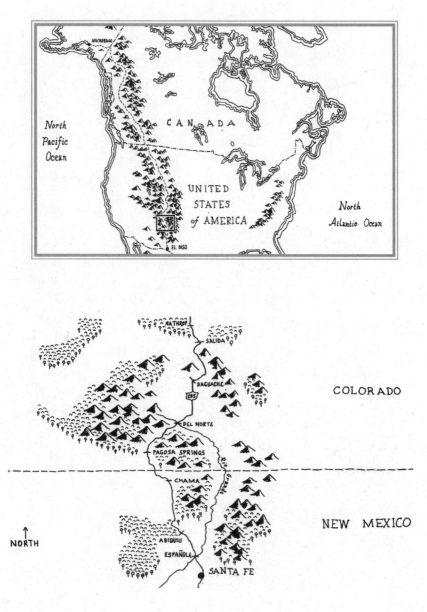

CHAPTER THREE
The Kindness of Strangers

'Rather than assume that Americans haven't done anything
about global warming because they are sceptical about the
threat, one could just as plausibly argue that they are sceptical
about the threat because they don't want to do anything.'

Elizabeth Kolbert [11]

Tom had warned me. 'The next hundred miles will be hot, long and
dull,' he said, after I'd declined to be dropped off at an airport a few
hundred miles further north. That would definitely be cheating. In
any case, he was wrong – at least about the dull part. When I finally
got away from downtown Santa Fe, out onto the main road north after
a three-shops-later new phone-battery, I had an absolutely glorious
fast run. Gorgeous heat, slight tailwind, big wide road; I cruised along
doing 25-30mph all the way to Española – the first European-founded
capital of the 'New World'. I stopped at the only obvious source of
food, disencouragingly called 'Dandy's Burgers'. Dandy's Burgers,
however, was not to be stereotyped. The menu featured a staggering
selection of vegetarian food. I sat down with a veggie combo at a
window where I could see Rocky and was soon joined by a man and
two boys in turbans.

'You having a good trip?' he asked, in a strong east-coast accent.
He was a cyclist too and, now living in India, was hoping to do
some touring with his sons while in New Mexico for a festival. The
Española Valley, he told me, had been colonised by the Spanish
when a certain Don Juan de Onate arrived with the conquistadors
in the late sixteenth century, brutally killing and enslaving the
resident and initially hospitable Anasazi people. By some leap of
historical logic Española was now home to the largest community of
ethnically diverse Sikhs in the world, and the destination for many
Sikhs on pilgrimage. That explained the vegetarian options. I found
out later that Española was also the epicentre of the 1950s fashion

---

[11] Elizabeth Kolbert (2006) 'Can America Go Green? *New Statesman*
19th June.

for modifying car suspension, hunching cars down until they only just cleared the ground. I had cycled straight through the 'Low-rider Capital of the World', officially broadcast as such by MTV. If only I'd known.

Back on the road I was just thinking that well-known hostage to fortune: 'At this rate I'll get well beyond my destination for today,' when the wind shifted, the road inclined uphill, and Rocky and I returned to our 7mph slog. The sky darkened, and the wind blew harder. At Abiquiu, where the painter Georgia O'Keefe lived and worked, I took shelter in the Tin Moon gift shop, looked at extremely tempting paintings and chatted to the Dutch owner, who also wrote the local walking guides. He told me that Abiquiu was a thriving artistic community and that abstract artists were especially talented in the area. And also that I could find various great sites for wild camping twenty odd miles further up the road – all with glorious views. 'Thanks,' I said, listening to the rain hammering on the roof. I blew a chunk of my remaining cash on a small silver raven for Chris and reluctantly left the shop. Outside, the rain was now torrential. And the air distinctly cold. Cold! I felt tired, despite having done only fifty miles, most of them easy. Another twenty miles and a wild camp or ... I rode back to the Abiquiu Inn and blew another wad of cash, sheepishly checking into the last of the cheaper rooms with a mixture of guilt and relief. I really should have cycled further and I really should have camped. But right then, I really didn't want to do either.

Grateful for the early stop, shower, warmth and time to catch up, I sorted through papers, threw a bunch away, left various messages and phoned Tom and Rosalind. Then I went across to the hotel office and followed up an earlier offer to use a staff computer. The advent of widespread wireless internet meant, for me, that writing the blog was more than a psychological challenge. Leaving aside that I never seemed to have enough time, practically all the motels and cafés I came across had long since dispensed with the idea of computers available for guests. Everyone travelled with a laptop. Except cyclists. Now, I sat at a computer on the front desk and deflected hotel enquiries while trying to update the eagerly waiting world about my progress. At Tom and Rosalind's I'd reluctantly written a rapid summary of the first couple of days. Unexpectedly pleased with the result, I'd hit 'send' and watched it disappear, to be replaced by a message saying, 'your session has expired'. My succinct, witty masterpiece was not in 'sent' and not in 'drafts'. It had vanished. Now I rewrote the same section from memory, hit send ... and watched it disappear. 'Your session has expired', the computer told me, mildly. 'Aaaaaaaargh!' I replied. Forget the days of heat, headwinds and long, long miles: from a blog point of view, I was still in El Paso.

~

The breakfast café next morning was beyond busy. The entire hotel was crowded with people saying things like, 'I need you to fly me out on the third so I can deal with issues on the ground in Mongolia.' A strong whiff of ego tainted the eggs. I talked to a friendly young woman in the checkout queue. The crowd was, she said, a film crew, working on a documentary about dinosaurs.

On the desk at checkout was a pile of lightweight, laminated brochures of New Mexican birds. Perfect! I'd been frustrated for miles, intrigued by the birds but not even knowing most of their names. Why should that matter? Some philosophers – and even some naturalists – argue that the ability to label birds and plants detracts from your experience of them. Knowing the name of the bird, so the argument goes, acts as a sort of barrier. You end up thinking, hey, this is a Lesser-Spotted New Mexican Diddly Thrush rather than giving your full attention to the creature actually in front of you. Clearly, I was in the opposite camp, an unreconstructed labeller. I bought a bird brochure. Then I went back to my room to retrieve Rocky, wheeling him out into the hot morning air. A group of women came over as I loaded the panniers. It was hard not to notice their striking range of shapes, from spectacularly thin to really quite large. They introduced me to Susan, 'our guide,' and told me they were on tour – yoga in the morning and Georgia O'Keefe in the afternoon. Somehow we moved from O'Keefe to Al Gore.

'His film is fantastic,' one of the women said. 'Really compelling. But most people are in another world. They aren't engaged with the issue at all.'

'Or they think, "heck, the government rubbishes global warming, why should I do anything about it?"' said another.

'Or they think that someone *should* do something about it, but the government, someone with power, not themselves,' said Susan.

'Why put it on individuals? That's what they think.'

I cycled off, stopping on the bridge just outside Abiquiu to look at the extraordinary rock vistas. Turning to take a picture of the fabulous desert vista in the other direction, the camera battery pronounced itself totally flat. Damn! I had just used a whole night's worth of precious I-am-not-in-a-tent energy availability recharging the cell-phone that rarely had any reception, but had completely forgotten the camera. The scenery was easily the most spectacular of the trip so far. The Chama valley. A wide, slow khaki river with a lush strip of green land around it, abruptly changing colour as it swept up into the extraordinary rock landscapes. Flat-topped mesas and huge buttresses rearing out of pyramids of loose rock. Stripes of cream against dark terracotta and salmon pink, all thickly sprinkled with scrub. And thousands of wheeling, chittering birds that my brochure allowed me to identify with confidence as cliff swallows.

I was just thinking, 'Goddamn! I NEED a way of recharging my camera battery,' when the Ghost Ranch Information Centre came into view, right by the road. I parked Rocky and went in. The receptionist proclaimed herself delighted to let me plug in my charger and suggested I look around. The centre was dedicated not to Georgia O'Keefe as I'd assumed, but to local natural history. I learned that the roots of aspen trees survive forest fires, lead the new growth and provide shelter for young conifers and habitat for hundreds of birds and insects. I learned that rattlesnakes give birth to fully formed snakes that hatch from eggs while still inside the mother, and gawped at a huge stuffed specimen that looked uncannily like a boa constrictor. A small display in the next room explained that the future of these species, and of the local ecosystems, depended on our decisions. It suggested that we should take responsibility for the way we use resources and that we should support nature conservation bodies. But there was absolutely nothing about climate change. Given that climate change is likely to have the biggest impact on New Mexican ecosystems since the last ice age, this seemed like just a bit of an oversight.

Just then the film crew turned up for lunch. 'Stay, honey, there's bound to be leftovers,' said Paula, one of the museum staff. But quite apart from the egos, I needed to get on. 'Well, if you're sure,' said Paula. And then, 'Don't think you're gonna get that far anyways.

Road's up ahead. It's gravel for miles.' Temporarily at a loss – there was only one road – I decided I'd deal with the problem when I got to it. I cycled off with my camera back in action and lots of good wishes. Paula even gave me her home phone number in case I needed rescuing. Paula and her colleagues weren't the people who had designed the displays. But somebody had. Why, I wondered for the next few miles, would an educational conservation site not even mention global warming? Was it possible that they didn't know about the implications of climate change for other species?

How hard-hit other species will be by climate change depends on how far up the range of possible temperature increases we travel, and that depends on what we do next. But climate change is coming onto the scene with biodiversity already badly compromised – by the impacts of industrial agriculture with its immense dependence on pesticides and artificial fertilizers and its massively disruptive impacts on local ecosystems; by the general encroachment of people and their cities and mines and roads on habitats; by global-scale resource extraction and pollution. Adding climate change to degraded habitats is a deadly mix. The current best estimates are that we risk losing a third – a third! – of our wild species by the end of the century.

My mind shied away when I tried to think about it. I wasn't sure if I simply couldn't comprehend the magnitude of the figure or cope with the awfulness of what the numbers meant. But for *conservationists* not to think about it seemed extraordinary. Perhaps it was some sort of failure of joined-up thinking; a sort of bizarre institutional carving up of roles so that an organisation labelled 'nature conservation' was not expected to take responsibility for something labelled 'climate change'. And that, I supposed (and many others have argued) was typical of our siloed thinking; of the way we tend to break things down into parts rather than look at the whole picture. It was normal. What, I wondered, as I cycled through the heat, would it take for all of us – organisations, governments, individuals, me, the yoga women's sceptical friends, George Bush – to break out of this normality? To look the big picture squarely in the eye? To accept that climate change was underway, that it was bad news and that we'd all, however unintentionally, contributed to bringing it about? To see the big picture and *act*?

~

Many beautiful and rather remote miles later, I stopped in an extremely small town, very hungry, at the solitary shop-cum-bar. The only substantial food on offer was burritos, and they were all chicken or beef. I bought a Twix, some gummy bears and a tiny packet of 'string cheese'. One of the three elderly men in the tiny bar asked me where I was headed.

'Del Norte,' I said. Del Norte was where my friend Susan lived. She was expecting me the next evening.

'Del Norte?' they said, almost in unison. 'You got two choices. Wolf Creek Pass or Chama Pass. Don't go over Wolf Creek. Chama Pass is way more direct. And easier.'

I thanked the men, filled up a water bottle from the tap outside and headed off, only to arrive minutes later at the roadworks. Paula had said they would be impossible to cycle through. Sure enough, the road surface had been completely removed, leaving a single lane inches thick with gravel. Just as I was thinking, hmm, what next ... an Official Road Works Truck pulled up and offered me a lift.

'Be a whole lot easier for us if you say yes,' grinned the man behind the wheel. Eight miles of deep gravel?

'Sure,' I said, and heaved Rocky into the back of the truck where he lay on top of a pile of road signs. Definitely not cheating. Crunching effortlessly over the thick porridge of loose stone, the driver told me his job was to rescue cyclists, remove other things that might obstruct the traffic, and put the marker barrels back up after the local lads knocked them down each night.

Then, 'Where you headed?' he asked.

'Del Norte,' I said.

'Del Norte? You got two choices, Wolf Creek Pass or Chama Pass.' And proceeded to offer the precise opposite of the previous advice.

I crawled into the town of Chama after miles of headwind, and dithered about. Chama was where the road divided. Wolf Creek to the left; Chama Pass, straight on. Decision needed. Left, straight on, or stop? I had hoped to be further up the road before I quit for the day but I was tired and I figured a few extra miles the next day wouldn't make that much difference. I could stop in Chama. But I couldn't really justify a motel and the campsites were somehow dispiriting.

I went into a gas station to ask about alternative campsites only to discover I wasn't a few miles, but *forty-nine* miles short of Pagosa Springs. Pagosa Springs, assuming I went left, was where I'd hoped to be that evening. Pagosa Springs should be the beginning of tomorrow! There was no way I could do an extra forty-nine miles on top of Wolf Creek Pass, or not if I wanted to arrive at Susan's before midnight and still capable of speech. By now it was early evening, and I was not thinking straight. I was tired and had eaten nothing but sugar all day. In the gas station the only edible options were junk food or beef burritos. Spaced out and starting to make stupid decisions, I bought a cinnamon roll (why only one?) and forgot to refill my water bottles. Then I tossed a coin, turned left, and headed for Chromo. Chromo was unlikely to feature a late-night vegetarian restaurant or indeed a restaurant of any description. According to the roadworks' truck-driver, Chromo was best described as 'a wide spot in the road'. But it was somewhere to aim for.

A few miles later I started to feel as if I was being rewarded for carrying on. The headwind eased, the road opened out, and the desert began to fall away behind us. The scenery was changing, almost exactly at the state border, from New Mexican desert to Colorado mountainscapes. Huge meadows, open spaces, big, big hills in the distance. Evening sunshine throwing long aspen shadows. Bird song. Shortly after crossing the state border, a sign told me I was also crossing the continental divide for the first time, almost imperceptibly, at around seven thousand feet. Quite suddenly I remembered passing the same sign on my previous trip, cycling in the other direction. Seventeen-year-old memories unexpectedly flooded back. A cowboy had been riding the fence-line alongside the road and we'd ridden together for a while, exchanging small talk and banter about whether he would swap his horse for my bike. A young, bay quarter horse for a then-almost-new, cream, steel, touring machine now in semi-retirement in my shed. Needless to say, the cowboy declined.

A couple of cyclists going the other way stopped to say hello. They told me the campsite at Chromo was shut and that there was nowhere else on the road. They were headed for Chama so they gave me their water – I was almost out by then – said they thought there was a water tap at Chromo I could use, wished me luck and rode off. Now I had water I could stop anywhere. I started looking for wild camping spots but the fields were fenced right up to the road and most of the smaller roads leading off it were gated and locked. I couldn't think it through. It was easier to keep going. I kept going, cycling more and more slowly until I was grinding along at little more than walking pace.

The sun had just about set when I crawled into Chromo. Chromo consisted of one shop and a tiny RV site, with a single RV and two Harley Davidson motorbikes in residence. I knocked on the RV door. A biker came out. He told me the site was technically shut but that I should be able to find Tom the owner in the trailer. I went to the trailer. There was no sign of Tom. I had absolutely no intention of going any further. So I put up my tent – on grass! Luxury! And then tried the trailer again. This time Tom appeared, a large man with a huge round face and curly hair who, peering out from behind the half-opened door, told me his grandmother had died in February and that the family were gathering to cremate her now. (Really? in June?) He said he was closed and that, even when he was open, he didn't cater for tents. No facilities, he said. Then he said to stay anyway, and abruptly closed the trailer door. By now it was dark, a spectacularly clear, cold night, the sky crowded with big, big stars. I decided to save my only food, the solitary cinnamon roll, for morning, and crawled into the beautiful warmth of my down sleeping bag, fully appreciated for the first time. I fell asleep to the sound of whippoorwill wingbeats in the dark and slept like a dead log.

~

I woke hungry. Propped on an elbow in the luxurious sleeping-bag warmth, I ate the cinnamon roll as slowly as possible. It was absolutely delicious. But it didn't seem to make much difference to the hunger pangs. By the time I'd packed up, though, the shop had opened. It was also run by Tom, and there was not much in it. I bought some crackers and cheese and ate them sitting on a road barrier just out-side Chromo, watching a herd of mules grazing in the early morning sunshine. A few miles later I passed a sign for a 'Native Animal Zoo' and was tempted to stop again. I would have loved to find out more about the native animals. I wasn't even sure what the native animals in this part of Colorado would be. But I'd never been a great fan of zoos. And, as usual, I needed to keep going.

From there to Pagosa Springs the ride was absolutely beautiful.

The air smelt of hot pine and sage, trees were still a novelty, and there were real mountains on the skyline. Pagosa Springs itself, though, was an abrupt entry into tourist-land. I sat outside a café-cum-gift shop with a huge plate of heuvos rancheros, a little stunned by the sheer quantity of people. Then I headed off up the valley towards Wolf Creek Pass. The weather, gorgeously hot but not too hot, began a rapid change. Clouds banked up and a distinct chill preceded the rain. A cold headwind arrived not long afterwards. The road began to climb. The climb went on and on. By the time I got to a sign that read 'Summit, eight miles', I was already tired. And my head was very much in the wrong place. I kept looking at the milometer, wanting the climb to be over. The last few, relentlessly steep miles I really could have done without. I reran the route of the Fred Whitton Challenge ride in my head to try to silence the whingeing 'are we nearly there yet?' thoughts. Then I worked through the alphabet in relation to Scottish towns, getting temporarily stuck on 'O' (sorry, Oban) and utterly stuck on 'Q'. Finally, five hours of solid slogging uphill at little over walking pace later, I reached the summit: 10,850 feet and still under the tree-line. An information board told me I was about to cross the continental divide – definitely not imperceptible on this occasion – for the second time. And also that it used to take Model T Fords *two days* to cross the pass, which made me feel a whole lot better.

Rocky and I swooped off down the far side past a series of highly tempting creek-side campsites, peaceful and inviting in the evening sunshine. The twenty-odd mile descent was beautiful, fast and bone-chilling. I rang Susan at the bottom. It was around 7pm and she was another twenty miles along the road. 'Shall I come and get you?' she asked. 'Be no bother.' Temptation! But I resisted and soon, cycling along a level road towards a chunk of rainbow in the sky, I was glad. I felt gradually normalised, neither grinding endlessly up nor hurtling madly, coldly down – just a smooth calm ride along a wide flat valley. I stopped to exchange stares with some mule deer and was bitten by mosquitoes, the first of the trip.

Susan and I had last seen each other in 1989. We had both been students at Colorado State University and shared an apartment for a while in Fort Collins. The apartment, I remembered, was unfurnished except for a tape deck and two mattresses. Now she had a husband, three kids, three dogs, four horses and a cat. And a wonderfully mad house. Because of my time at Colorado State, friends were bunched inconveniently close together on this ride. Three days after the break with Tom there was nothing for it but to take some more time off.

~

It was wonderful, catching up on the intervening years and getting to know each other again. We'd taken such different routes: Susan with a huge focus on her children, Chenoa, Liam and Lhasa – including home-schooling them – and me ending up with a university career almost by accident, remaining more or less single, resolutely unbroody. And restless, travelling intermittently and not meeting a potential partner – not a real partner – until just before this trip. What Susan and I shared was a love of mountains and deserts and a deep sense of outrage at the environmental impact of the industrialised world. She had been an environmental activist for years and talked a lot about how demoralized many people in the States were after Bush was elected for the second time.

'It wasn't just the outcome,' she said, as we sat in a Del Norte café one afternoon in a briefly childfree interval, 'but how it was achieved. One small example: Del Norte. A Democratic stronghold. The ballot box and all the votes were found, uncounted, in the janitor's office after the count was over.' She took a swig of coffee. 'Where do you go to indicate dissent when the democratic system has become so corrupted? What do you do when all possible avenues for voicing concern lead straight to a blank wall? Legal avenues, that is.'

I thought back to the shock and outrage of learning what we did to animals in farms and labs. I'd briefly contemplated joining the Animal Liberation Front, channelling that anger into action, legal or otherwise. One of the wisest women I knew, a lecturer at Glasgow vet school, had talked me out of it. 'If you go down that route you will lose your voice,' she'd said. 'You will be written off by most of the people who could actually make a difference. Keep your voice. Communicate the issues. In the end it's much more powerful.' I'd become so grateful for that advice, and for having taken it. But communication would be utterly pointless if no-one was listening. I wondered whether more environmentalists were switching tactics, driven to direct action out of despair. Susan said many she knew had lost both heart and energy and had pretty much given up. Temporarily, at least.

'This is the worst of times to give up!' I said.

'Don't I know it,' she replied.

Later, over supper with some of her friends, I voiced my surprise at the number of people I'd met, even in my short time in New Mexico, who didn't seem to have heard of global warming at all. Elizabeth Kolbert, an American journalist, writes about how unlikely that is given the information overload.[12] With global warming all over the news it is impossible, she argues, *not* to know about it. But given the extent to which ordinary Americans are dependent on oil, and cheap oil at that, they have very good reason to keep this knowledge at bay. Americans have the highest average per capita energy use of any country in the world, save for a handful of oil states. Their apparent lack of knowledge is, she suggests, actually denial. Her argument made a lot of sense, but I wasn't entirely convinced. I was pretty sure I'd encountered at least some genuine ignorance. I asked Susan's friends. '*Do* people really know about global warming, and what it means?'

'Well, the information is out there. But you have to know where to look to find it,' said Gary. 'Global warming isn't discussed in the local papers, or on TV. The news is dominated by Fox. And that means "the news" is Republican-controlled propaganda. For most Republicans, global warming is not happening. So it doesn't get reported. So no, I don't think it's denial; I think a lot of people really don't know.'

Later, when they had gone and the house was quiet, I realised how unsettled I was by what Gary had said. Could a media outlet as huge and as influential as Fox News really be so biased it would simply choose not to report on a threat capable of drastically revising human – and other – life on earth? Making the most of unprecedented computer access, I began to dig. A bit of Googling blew my naïve 'It couldn't, surely, be *that* bad' belief to smithereens. Fox News, described by one prominent journalist as 'a highly effective right-wing echo chamber' was, I learned, a twenty-four-hour cable network belonging to Rupert Murdoch. Aha. One of their main anchors, Tony Snow, had been a former speechwriter for George Bush senior. Aha, again. Fox's slogan was, I read: 'Fair and balanced. We report, you decide.' When I looked at past copy, though, headlines like 'Trees Cause Global Warming' or 'Junk Science: The Great Global Warming Race' made it all too

---

[12] Kolbert op. cit. See also her compelling book: Elizabeth Kolbert (2006) *Field Notes from a Catastrophe* Bloomsbury Publishing

clear that, even when they did report on climate change, buckets of bias were already built in.

Worse was to come. I was becoming used to having my innocent assumptions blown away, but a bit more searching revealed something on a different scale of shocking. The author of Fox's weekly junk science column, one Steve Milloy, had, I learned, a distinguished history of supporting the tobacco industry and, according to rigorously referenced research by George Monbiot, [13] had received large sums of money from both Philip Morris Tobacco – and ExxonMobil. ExxonMobil is the most profitable corporation in history, with annual profits of around $350 million. That's nearly a million dollars a day. They are the world's biggest player in the oil and gas industry, and one of the largest producers of climate change emissions in the world. 'If it was a country,' writes Shulman, an investigative journalist, 'ExxonMobil would rank sixth in terms of emissions.' [14] ExxonMobil emitted more CO_2 than Germany, Canada, the UK or France. ExxonMobil had some very big reasons for dismissing climate change. It had funded and supported phoney thinktanks with the deliberate intention of discrediting climate change science. And Steve Milloy, Fox News' 'junk science' man, was receiving payments from them.

It seemed Gary was right. For lots of people in the USA, information about climate change just wasn't being delivered. And it wasn't being delivered at least partly because of some very large vested interests in keeping the oil-hungry status quo. I felt I'd gone back in time, was back on the trail of shocking revelations that were derailing my sense of knowing what was what. Only this time it wasn't about animals. It was about money, oil and a great deal of power.

∼

Rocky had not been himself since the ride in the truck. Changing gears was again becoming an unreliable affair. In between opening the parcel from Chris, which contained a large packet of yoghurt-covered banana chips as well as my new credit card, catching up with

[13] George Monbiot (2006) *Heat* Allen Lane, Penguin Books

[14] See, for example, 'Smoke, Mirrors and Hot Air: How ExxonMobil uses Big Tobacco's Tactics to Manufacture Uncertainty on Climate Science', published by the Union of Concerned Scientists in 2007. Shulman was the lead author.

blog-writing, sending emails, riding Susan's horses and being talked into watching *Pirates of the Caribbean* with the kids, I cycled across town to Gary and Patti's house, the unloaded bike darting across the road in unpredictable ways and feeling almost as if it were levitating. 'Normal' houses suddenly looked dull after a couple of days at Susan and Kevin's. But Gary and Patti had a fantastic collection of bike tools, which more than compensated. 'Squirrely,' said Gary. 'That's how it feels when you take the panniers off.' It was a perfect description. Squirrelyness was not, however, my main concern. Between us we checked the derailleur alignment (out), tuned the front wheel (kinked), fiddled with the index gear adjusters (erratic), and removed the spring-loaded barrel adjuster at the front of the gear cable (squashed). And chatted about the Tour de France.

I left Susan's, reluctantly, on the 2nd July, with a handmade card from Chenoa featuring me on a bicycle with long yellow hair and flowers for hands. Inside was a five-dollar note, taken from her savings. Even I was moved. I told Chenoa I would buy an especially good lunch with her money. And that next time we met I was sure she would be an eco-warrior. 'She already is,' said Kevin. I finally cycled off just before eleven with Susan, Kevin, Chenoa, Liam, Lhasa and Bingo the dog all watching from the road and, 'Stay just one more day! Come rafting with us!' ringing in my ears. I felt a mix of emotions which were rapidly becoming familiar. Great warmth and happiness at reconnecting with a wonderful friend and spending time with lovely people. Gratitude for the access to other people's views on climate change that these friendships were able to open up. And a sort of poignant sadness. We lived on different sides of the Atlantic in a world where frequent flying should probably become a criminal offence. When were we likely to see each other again?

I rode back through Del Norte, turning onto Highway 112 and then, after about an hour, onto Highway 285. Highway 285 heads due North in a long, utterly straight line all the way to Saguache about forty miles later. It was a beautiful morning. Blue sky, warm but not hot, easy riding on a long, flat road. Huge irrigation systems like the skeletons of enormous aeroplane wings filled the air with a rhythmic hissing as they sprayed water across wheat, barley and crops I didn't recognise. Where the irrigation giants didn't reach, flat dun-coloured land with short tufts of prickly-looking grey-green grass stretched away towards distant scrubby hills. Behind them was a long line of mountains proper; the Sangre de Cristo range, named for the colour they turn when the setting sun sets them alight with vivid red. The mountains were hazy with fire smoke. Once I saw a rabbit scudding away across the plain and later, a hare. The hare ran at high speed, ears sharply upright and highly visible, white with black tips. It still must have been in its winter fur. When it stopped, it folded its ears across its back and instantly vanished, camouflaged in the patchy grass.

Occasionally I stopped for a bite of yoghurt-covered banana chips or the fantastically sweet Tootsie Roll that I'd been told I couldn't possibly visit the States without eating at least once. Mostly I bowled along at sixteen, seventeen, eighteen miles an hour thinking, this is the life! A car with bikes on the roof drew alongside and the people inside asked if I had enough water. We chatted briefly before they pulled away, leaving me smiling. Cyclists looking out for cyclists. It felt good. In fact, there seemed to be a sort of two-wheelers' fraternity out there on the road. Motorbikers as well as cyclists would typically wave me (what I took to be) a friendly two-fingered 'V' salute as they roared past. They were usually helmet-less and sometimes spectacular, like the woman on a Harley Davidson who grinned and waved, a mass of curly black hair streaming out behind a wide red headband.

Clouds were building up grey over the hills and I was cycling towards lightning when I finally pulled into Saguache. Intrigued by a museum sign that read 'JAIL', I left Rocky leaning against the wall and went in, to a rather reserved greeting from two elderly women who relieved me of three dollars and then left me to wander. Numerous small rooms were bursting with an eclectic mix of furniture, clothes and household goods from the early twentieth century, plus a rock collection, a few Indian artefacts and an enormous array of guns – including a tiny 'ladies' Colt that had, I read, belonged to a Mrs Evans – who had foiled a stagecoach hold-up with it. There were old saddles and spurs and a collection of different kinds of barbed wire. I had never really thought about the historical significance of barbed wire but the sudden availability of cheap fencing had apparently revolutionised ranching. And a collection of scrapbooks telling stories of the women of the valley;

a tantalising glimpse of past lives I didn't have time to follow.

Inside the jail proper was an extraordinary metal pen, with sliding bolts operated by a huge lever. In this grim metal cage were four bunk beds, crammed into the tiny space.

'Nobody ever escaped,' grinned the two women, visibly pleased at my astonishment. 'If you stop again on your way back, we'll show you more…'

'I'm flying straight home from Alaska,' I explained.

Alaska! So far away. 'Well, thanks for stopping this time,' they said, and directed me to the Oasis café which, joy of joys, did meals 'for the smaller appetite', a size that easily catered for the appetite of the average ravenous European cyclist. I had a bean and potato burrito courtesy of Chenoa's $5 and wrote my diary while the rain hammered down outside.

I set off into a more or less dry but overcast afternoon. Never trust the locals when they say you'll have a tailwind. Gary and Patti had both said that Salida, my aim for that night, would be an effortless ride. 'It's mostly flat. Poncha Pass is an easy climb. The wind is bound to be behind you.' Just as I was thinking that thought that I should've known better than to let into my head by now – at this rate I'll be there early – the tailwind veered into a headwind and suddenly I was slogging along at eight miles an hour, seven miles an hour, six miles an hour. Aaaargh! Soon we were inching across a strange flat plateau dotted with tent trailers. Looking back I could just about make out the hummocky white shapes of the Great Sand Dunes National Park, bizarrely pale below the grey mountains.

The whole way to the top of Poncha Pass was a relentless headwind batter. I thought about my colleague Liz, who would be sea kayaking in the Outer Hebrides with our students about that time, and wondered if she was straining into a similar wind. On my side of the Atlantic, the good news was that Poncha Pass wasn't really a climb at all. I kept expecting a steep section but it never arrived. Then, out of nowhere, there was the summit sign. I stopped and looked back. The evening light on the trees was spectacular against a dark grey sky. The view and the birdsong, suddenly audible as I stopped, lifted my spirits. A prairie dog scolded as I rolled away and a bird of prey lifted off close by. The bad news was that it was now the wrong side of 7.30pm and the headwind was even stronger on the other side of the pass, turning what should have been a long, sweepy, whizzy descent into a six-mile-an-hour grind. Mountain passes are one thing; at least you choose to go over them. But headwinds that make you struggle to go downhill feel downright unfair.

~

The next morning, under a gorgeous blue sky, I coasted into Salida and the Absolute Bike Shop where, with my new credit-card freedom, I bought an array of lightweight back lights and not one but two barrel adjusters. And got a Tour update. A veritable galaxy of erstwhile stars had been thrown out of the race for drug-related offences. But Floyd Llandis, the post-Lance Armstrong American favourite, was riding strongly. He was, indeed, to win. Little did we know he would promptly be stripped of his title for drug use, too. Right next to the bike shop was a café with a highly tempting aroma of fresh coffee, a signboard advertising 'Full vegetarian breakfasts', and seats outside in the morning sunshine. I'll just go and sort the phone, I thought, and then come back and treat myself to breakfast. Second breakfast. The phone I'd started the trip with no longer had any reception at all. Apparently I needed a different provider. Text messages were my main way of staying in touch with Chris. And also my dad. Dad and I had not always seen eye to eye on the virtues of long-distance bike trips. On the Andes ride he had practically disowned me. I should be spending the summer finishing my PhD, he had fumed, rather than fooling about on a bike. This time he'd come up to London the night before I left, and bought me dinner at the airport Hilton. He was, Chris said, following my progress and even ringing if there was too long a gap between messages. I was keen to keep the good feeling between us about this trip. So I set off across town – old shop fronts, a bookstore, more cafés, elderly houses with wooden porches and verandas in leafy streets – for the phone shop.

The Verizon cellphone store was a new building on a busy main road. Nick, a young, ginger-haired man with a surly Australian cattle dog that occasionally crept out from behind the counter to snarl at his customers, told me I had definitely come to the right place. Verizon has great coverage across the States, he said. We can take automatic payments from a credit card for three months. And there is even an aerial for improving reception in mountains that is magnet-mounted and will readily sit on a handlebar stem. Perfect! Nick, fielding the dog ('Yes, she's a harmer,' he said, looking at her lovingly) took a multitude of details, made phone calls, entered data. Then, on the verge of owning this magic phone, there was a glitch. The computer declined to accept my postcode. Nick called multiple helplines. But there was no way around it; the company could not accept a European credit card. Nick was temporarily stumped. Then, 'You know what? Go up the road to Walmart and buy a Tracphone and a phone card. You can register on the spot. Come back and use the landline here to do it.'

I cycled off to Walmart, did my bit for consumer culture, bought a phone and a phone card with hundreds of credits, and pedalled back to Verizon to spend a good fifteen minutes feeding code after code into the handset.

Just as we were finishing, I asked how to send international texts. 'International texts?' drawled the code-issuing voice. 'Heck, no, we don't do that.' The voice gave me my last code and hung up.

'That's nonsense,' said Nick. 'They do for sure. You just need to register. You can do it online.' He looked at my face and then said, 'I'll do it.' But when he had to enter my credit card details ... it wouldn't accept the European postcode. 'You know what?' said Nick. 'You can buy a prepaid credit card. From the gas station.'

I cycled to the gas station, which sent me to a pub, which sold me a card for $10, and showed me how to put $100 credit onto it. Back at Verizon, Nick rang the Tracphone people with the new card number. 'Oh no, we don't take those prepaid cards,' said the new operator.

'But the last person I spoke said you definitely did!' said Nick. 'No, don't put me on hold! Just give me a supervisor...'

By now even calm, cheerful Nick was bordering on apoplexy. Just as he was about to give up and smash something, a tall blonde woman in her fifties came over and introduced herself. Daphne had big blue eyes, a strong face and a peaceful border collie called Magpie. She had overheard the last part of the saga.

'Use my card,' she said. 'You can pay me the cash.

'Really?'

She smiled. 'Really. I've travelled a lot,' she said, 'and been helped out many times. Nice to pay back.'

Daphne and I chatted while Nick sorted the payment. When I mentioned global warming, she said she'd had a bad car crash and now wouldn't drive anything smaller than a truck. 'I need to look after my body,' she said, 'I'm a ski instructor. But I've been working on "light-footing" it. If I coast the road home and anticipate the lights right I can cut my gas by half. Gotta be worth doing.' Finally, at about 5pm, Nick got an international facility (in Daphne's name) on my phone. I reached Chris' answerphone. He phoned back. We exchanged texts. It worked!

I thanked Nick over and over. He'd spent all day helping me get sorted on a phone he hadn't even sold me. I would never have managed it alone on a payphone. By this time, hunger left me barely able to get a sentence out that made sense. So I cycled back to the bike shop café, and had dinner instead of breakfast. A bowl of white bean soup and a sandwich later, I began to feel human again. Just as I was leaving, Nick turned up. 'I thought I'd find you here. You left your back lights in the shop! No, I didn't come out of my way. I live three blocks away. In fact, you can camp in my garden if you like. And come with me to a friend's birthday party...' He wasn't at all offended when I declined.

I left Salida to *begin* the day's cycling at 6.15pm. Of all the late starts and days that felt resistant to progress, this one took first prize by a mile. It felt very, very good to be moving. A couple of hours later, I pulled off at a big campsite near Nathrop with the light fading fast. A friendly woman charged me $20 and directed me to a site with softish ground next to a couple who had, she said, climbed a four-thousander that day. 'They're very nice,' she said, 'but completely wiped out. They'll be good and quiet for you.' It felt odd to be on such a large site. But it was also fascinating. Most of the tents were in a field below mine – rows and rows of trucks like some sort of truck convention, each with a large tent pitched behind it. Each tent/truck had a blazing open fire with people sitting around it, eating, drinking, chatting. I wandered about, thinking that someone might invite me to join them for a beer. Lots of folk said hi, but there were no beer invites. Maybe after such a short day I just didn't look thirsty enough. On my field, aside from my tent-dwelling, hill-walking neighbours, all the campers were in RVs. A number of these were decked out with red, white and blue decorations and one even had red, white and blue lighting around its patch. I ate a bagel and sent Chris a message. Then, toasty warm in my glorious sleeping bag, I actually managed

70

to read for a while, the first time on the trip. I'd just started Annie Proulx, *That Old Ace in the Hole*, and was instantly swept off to a neighbouring world. The campsite was almost silent by ten. The cell phone challenge had been more tiring than my normal seventy or eighty mile days. Soon, I slept. And slept. And slept.

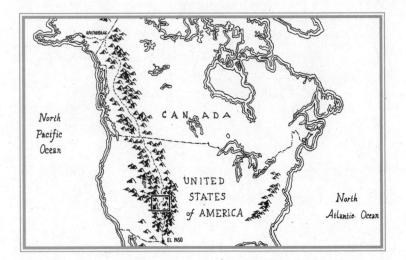

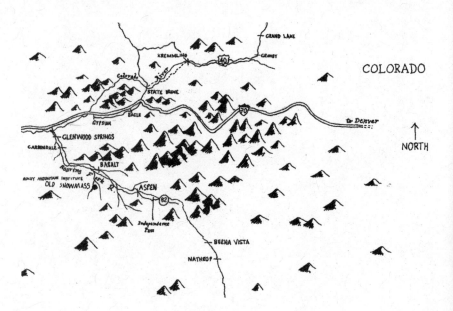

CHAPTER FOUR
American Dreams

> Why care about the Earth when the droughts, floods, famine
> and pestilence wrought by ecological collapse are signs of the
> apocalypse foretold in the Bible? Why care about global climate
> change when you and yours will be rescued in the rapture?
> *Bill Moyers* [15]

July 4th! I half-woke, drifted back to sleep, and eventually coaxed myself into consciousness. I ate a bagel and chatted to my neighbours. They had just climbed Harvard, a 14,000-plus foot peak, and had been hoping to do Yale. On the other hand, they said, wincing stiffly around their tent, perhaps they would just have breakfast in town instead. This had been their first ever hill-walk and they were definitely suffering. 'But the dog loved it!' they said, cheerfully. 'And it was fabulous up there ...'

'I'd be interested to know what you think about global warming,' I said bravely, the connection between mountain ecosystems and global warming appearing, in my mind, to make this a logical follow-up.

'Global warming?' they said. 'Yep. So, how far are you planning to cycle today?'

A large man from the red, white and blue-illuminated RV asked me the same question. He chatted about the merits of different 4x4s while I stroked the two miniature chihuahuas whose leads were looped around long lines attached to the massive house-on-wheels. They whizzed up and down the line, barking, like tiny fluff-balls with teeth. I wanted to ask their owner about global warming, too. But looking at the man's friendly, enquiring face, I lost my nerve. It felt a bit like bringing a judgemental alien from a hostile planet in for tea with your grandparents. A man with a Siamese cat on a lead apologised when the cat took fright as I leaned down to greet her. 'She sure hates people,' he said. I don't blame her, I thought; me too. Looking across the quietly busy campground, I corrected myself. I didn't hate people. I hated the way we were all, however innocently, living

---

[15] Bill Moyers (2006) *Welcome to Doomsday* New York Review Books

lives that wreaked swathes of havoc across the planet, with our RVs and 4x4s and astonishing levels of consumption and plane flights and central heating and air conditioning and all the stuff we buy and don't need or hardly use or just throw away… How had we all been duped into thinking this was normal and this was okay? It was normal, but it wasn't okay. None of us were setting out to trash the planet. We somehow just hadn't realised what all these resource-hungry activities added up to: its vast environmental cost. And we certainly didn't seem to have clocked what this would mean for our own health and wellbeing, let alone for our kids and for other species. What it already means in parts of the world where climate change and collapsing ecosystems are ending ancient ways of life, creating refugees, causing mayhem.

I left just after eight, cycling into a glorious blue morning and determined to make the most of it. After yesterday, I needed to catch up on the miles. I cruised along a steady, easy-going road with the massive craggy bulks of the fourteen-thousanders ranging alongside to the left. These were the 'Collegiate' mountains: Princeton, Yale, Columbia, Harvard, Oxford. Youngsters by mountain standards at around 65–100 million years old, their heads reared above the tree-line and tiny patches of snow still glinted white in their gullies. Somewhere beyond this range lay Independence Pass, my goal for the day. The pass climbs to just above 12,000 feet before dropping down into the Hunter-Fryingpan Wilderness and, beyond that, the famous skiing town of Aspen. Buena Vista, the town just ahead of me, sat at the mountains' toes around 8000 feet. A 5000-foot climb in the sunshine to Independence Pass on Independence Day sounded good to me.

~

Coming in to Buena Vista I decided to stop for some non-bagel-based food – and to stock up for later. I locked Rocky to a bench outside a supermarket, and got seriously carried away. I bought a huge bag of cherries, two nectarines, a tomato, some sliced Monterey Jack cheese, a packet of tortillas, an avocado, some organic salad leaves and a banana. And a bag of bagels. At the checkout, the man in front of me insisted I use his saver loyalty card. 'He just saved you ten bucks,' said the woman on the till, and I still managed to put $26 on the blasted prepaid Visa card. Outside, Rocky had fallen over. With the panniers in place it was a struggle to lift him. Then I made the whole outfit even heavier by bungie-ing the bags of food on top of the regular load. Then I sat on a bench outside the store in the sunshine and ate the banana. By now, it was nearly ten. Crowds of people were lining the self-proclaimed 'historic main street'.

'We need to get out of here before we get caught up in the parade,' I said to Rocky, standing on the pedals and wobbling out onto the road. Then I caught myself. 'This is ridiculous!' I said to the sky. 'It's July 4th! I'm in Colorado, USA, on Independence Day!' I stopped, turned around and cycled back into town, where I leaned Rocky against a signpost and joined the crowd.

'Is everyone here for the parade?' I asked a woman with a whippet standing next to me.

'Yep,' she said, 'it's just about to start.' Her name was Diane, and she'd recently moved to Buena Vista from Boulder, a few hundred miles further north. 'Buena Vista is more conservative – five churches to every pub – but more peaceful. Water is a big issue though,' she said. 'We have a saying. "Whisky is for drinking. Water is for fighting."'

It was a good saying, I thought. Wars had already been fought over oil. Water is even more vital; and climate change has alarming implications for our water supplies. It must therefore have some pretty alarming implications for conflict, too. Not so far away, the Rio Grande was already the subject of a longstanding quarrel between Mexico and the United States over water rights, profoundly impacted by, amongst other things, extravagant water use north of the border. (Are lawns made of non-native, water-hungry grass really crucial to quality of life?) With climate change, these conflicts were only set to increase. Diane agreed.

'No-one can live without water. No-one.' She worked in a bank and bred alpacas in her spare time. 'If you decide to spend longer here, come and stay. I have a spare yurt. Just out of town.' I would have loved to. But, as usual, I couldn't really afford to stop. I was already stopped when I hadn't meant to, after a day when I'd barely made any progress at all.

Meanwhile, the parade was gearing up. Streams of people, horseback riders, wacky vehicles, a penny-farthing bicycle, old tractors, candidates for Sheriff. A motley collection of decorated cars and floats, ranging from the Hillbilly Music Reunion to the League of Women Voters, trundled past to clapping and cheers, throwing sweets to the crowds as they went. Diane clapped loudest when the Democrat's car went by.

'There are at least four Democrats in town,' she said, 'and there's three of them.' Kids and dogs scrabbled for the sweets in the sunshine. There was a slightly manic atmosphere of goodwill and celebration. It was impossible not to grin.

Diane asked about the climate change views I'd encountered so far. I told her about the people who didn't seem to have heard of climate change at all. I told her I thought even those who knew and cared about the issue often considered it a matter for someone else to deal with, rather than something they could tackle in their own lives. She agreed, pointing to a convoy of festive, decorated trucks. 'There's one of the biggest problems right there. People don't want to give up their big cars. And gas is still so cheap.' As the parade tailed off, Diane gave me her card. 'Don't forget,' she said, as she left, 'just ring if you decide to stay.' I knew I'd enjoy more of Diane's company, not to mention the yurt and the Alpacas. In fact, she felt like a kindred spirit. But I wasn't going to stop. These bittersweet glimpses of potential friendship and offers of hospitality and human connection that I knew I was going to pass by were becoming more and more familiar.

~

A woman I half-recognised greeted me. 'I was in the Verizon store yesterday,' she said. 'Did you get your phone fixed?!'

Good heavens, I thought, I am becoming known in Colorado. By now it was well past eleven. Twin Lakes, at the foot of Independence Pass, was about twenty miles away. I decided to forget the pass for the day. There was no point going over it in the afternoon clouds. I could have an easy day and time in a campsite to write and relax. A July 4th holiday! I cycled off in very good spirits; a gift of a day, friendly people, a wide road, big mountains, and bigger mountains just around the corner.

Lakes View campsite was a mile off the main road, and that mile was all uphill. It was worth the climb. The campsite was quiet and spacious and, while I couldn't see any lakes, it had views across the valley to the mountains. Writing up the journal on a bench beside my tent, I was visited by a hummingbird and a bird that looked like a tree-creeper, making a sound like a blue tit as it collected pine-cone seeds. And the park ranger, who said there was less wildlife than there used to be, but that with binoculars you could see elk and mountain goats on the distant hill-side. I collected firewood, ate cherries and a delicious tortilla – with organic salad – and wrote some more. Time flew by. As the light faded I was still almost alone on the site. I felt deeply peaceful. I could have sat there for days.

Next morning, I woke thinking, 'I have definitely bought the wrong sleeping bag.' My wonderful top of the range down extravagance was evidently meant for infinitely colder climes. I had sweated so much in the night that the down was drenched and flattened into useless clumps. Outside, a cloud inversion gradually burned away in the early sunshine and coal tit-like birds sat in a tree close by, watching as I sleepily sorted my stuff. I scattered the birds some crumbs, and worked on Rocky's gears. Then, deciding I could not eat another single cherry and not wanting to ride over Independence Pass with an extra pound of fruit hanging from my panniers – or throw them away – I walked across the site towards the sound of voices. A couple in a tent-trailer were camped near the toilet block. 'Excuse me,' I said to the man, who was fetching water, 'would you like some cherries?'

The man looked at me oddly. He pointed over to a heavily pregnant woman sitting outside the trailer in a pink jumpsuit. 'Ask my wife,' he said.

The woman gave me an even stranger look when I explained my predicament. It turned out she had been fantasizing about, yes, cherries, for which she was craving. She had just finished telling her husband how desperately she wanted some when I appeared! As I filled up my water bottles at the toilet block I heard her say, 'Well, it's a little disconcerting, actually ...' I had to admit I felt rather the same.

I freewheeled back down the hill to the main road, heading towards Independence Pass. The ranger had said it was about a twenty-mile climb to the top. Spruce trees crowded the road under a blue, blue sky, and I cycled to the sound of an unseen river. Flowers whose names I didn't know scattered the ground at the edge of the trees with vivid colour. Yellow, white and dark violet were predominant, but spikes of deep orangey-red flowers occasionally broke through alongside tall purple orchids. The trees stretched far up into the mountains, gradually thinning out to reveal their bare, grey heads. It looked like someone had thrown a green bristly rug over the mountains that, with time and much scuffing, had worn away on the summits. For hundreds of miles this huge vista towered grey and green, flecked only rarely with streaks of old glinting snow.

The climb was great. Long, but much, much easier than Wolf Creek. Starting first thing instead of two-thirds through a lengthy day undoubtedly helped. But the road was easier too – occasional flat sections rewarded the steepest climbs, and the scenery was more compelling. My head was in a positive place. I might even have been getting fitter. Birdsong, surprisingly absent in the campsite, ricocheted around the trees and once I glimpsed a cat-sized ginger animal with a round head and a thin tail. The word 'marmot' came into my mind, but whether for any good reason I wasn't entirely sure.

As we climbed higher, the verges got steeper, until they were falling spectacularly away from the road on the downhill side. Slowly we came level with the tree line. And then we left the trees below us. A vanload of people with binoculars stood at the side of the road, staring intensely across to the far mountainside. I'd already passed them once. The second time I couldn't resist. I stopped and went over. 'What have you seen?' I asked. They were Amish people on holiday from Ohio, and they were looking for elk. The women all wore white caps and the girls, black ones. The men sported beards with distinctive trim-lines – very straight and very tidy. The Amish holiday makers crowded around me, asking lots of questions and wanting to take my name.

'El Paso to Anchorage! That's astonishing!'

I told them I was interested in global warming.

'Nothing we can do about it,' said one of the men, emphatically.

'Well,' I said carefully, 'what about the fact that we contribute to it?'

'We do?' he said, sounding genuinely surprised. 'How?'

'By burning fossil fuels, for example,' I suggested.

'Oh, like that. Well...'

He was interrupted by a colleague. 'See, as Christians, we believe that God will look after things. When He's ready, the world will end anyway. It's not up to us to sort it out.'

'What about the environmental damage we know we're causing?'

I persisted.

'Well, we do think about that. Education is key. And we never drop litter...'

I was keen to explore this tangle of views but they were suddenly keen to get away. As they waved their goodbyes, I thought a fair summary would be that taking action against global warming was not a priority for this particular Amish community. I was not even convinced they really knew what it was. And yet the Amish, Berry argues, are amongst the most effective, low-impact, small-scale farmers still surviving in the modern world, with a real sense of connection to the land, an intelligent discerning resistance to certain forms of technology and strongly community-oriented rather than profit orientated values [16] ... making this group's views on climate change all the more intriguing.

Clouds were massing around the tops and, for the last couple of miles, the rain came and went. I wondered what it must be like to really, truly believe that God could, if he or she chose to, sort out climate change for us, and that we shouldn't try to do anything about it ourselves. Despite the fact that we've caused it in the first place. And what must it be like to believe that God will, at some point, simply end the world? I could barely get my head around it. But these were views that had, in various forms, been extraordinarily influential in the United States. Jonathon Porritt reports that, according to regular opinion polls, at least *a quarter* of Americans believe we are living in the run up to 'rapture' – when God will whisk the true believers off to heaven before destroying the planet. And this, he goes on, means that millions of rapture-anticipating Christian fundamentalists in the United States believe not only that there is no point in tackling climate change, but that environmental destruction is to be positively welcomed as a sign of the impending apocalypse. [17]

From a European perspective, these views might seem extraordinary. They certainly seemed extraordinary to me. In the States, they were almost commonplace. Not just that: these were views that

---

[16] Wendell Berry (1977) *The Unsettling of America* Avon Books

[17] Jonathon Porritt, (2005) *Capitalism as if the World Matters* Earthscan

had informed the positions of many of the religious political right. They were views that had, apparently, exerted a truly frightening influence on United States climate change policy. According to Porritt, 'just under 50% of congressmen [were] backed – politically and financially – by the religious right.' Certainly, for whatever reason, Bush's anti-environmental actions were legion. By 2006, the Bush administration had overturned or weakened vast swathes of the United States' environmental policies. And his administration systematically undermined international climate change negotiations. Vested oil interests were clearly part of the story. Could the refusal of one of the most influential countries on earth to co-operate on climate change solutions really also be driven, even in part, by the belief in rapture? The thought that Bush or his advisors might personally see life through the distorting lens of this astonishing metaphysics did not bear thinking about. Surely, we would not end up letting climate change rip because a small group of men with a great deal of power thought the world was going to end anyway?

~

The summit was a car park with portaloos. And the Continental Divide sign. I parked Rocky against it to take a photograph and a tall slender man with a long moustache offered to take one of both of us. His wife and son came over to chat.

'El Paso to *Anchorage?* Honey, you sure are crazy.'

'Global warming??' The woman in the group looked at me hard. 'That is giving me goose-bumps when you say it,' she said.

'Why goose-bumps?' I asked.

'Because you are doing something that is going to be really important.'

'I doubt it!' I laughed. But it was still good to hear. I left Rocky by a shed and walked over to the viewpoint. 12,095 feet, and mountains all around. These mountains were not pretty, or even especially majestic. But they had a certain silent power, with their grey heads and green flanks and flicks of snow. And they certainly were big.

Many people greeted me. 'We saw you earlier!' 'How far are you going?' 'Where next?' 'Why?' A man from Texas begged permission to take my picture. 'I've never met anyone doing something like that before,' he said. And a threesome discussed my route, the men telling me how illogical it was, and how much more direct it would be if I missed out Fort Collins.

The less-than-always-convenient location of my friends had significantly impacted on my route choice. And so had potentially interesting climate change projects. Independence Pass itself was a rather monumental detour in order to visit the Rocky Mountain Institute, famous for its innovative approach to reducing greenhouse gas emissions. The Rocky Mountain Institute specialised in solutions. As I prepared to head downhill towards it, the rain resumed and, almost as an afterthought, I put leggings on over my shorts. But not overshoes. I rolled off the summit to distant thunder and soon the rain become torrential. The road was pot-holey and slick. I rapidly became cold – especially my feet, which were drenched in minutes. Stupid! The road went down and down until finally, stiff, wet and really chilled I reached some lower, warmer air. The outskirts of Aspen followed soon after. Vast houses and an airfield dedicated to private planes.

Aspen itself was horrendous. Or at least, that's how it seemed to me. On the plus side was the Aspen Institute, which seeks to foster 'values-based leadership' and has an annual environment forum. But the rest of the town appeared to be a monument to consumerism, excess wealth and status based on possessions. A woman on the summit had warned me. 'Aspen has become one big shopping mall,' she'd said. 'And there are women with *high-heeled shoes!*'

It came as a shock to the system after the last few days, and especially after the solitude and peace of the high mountain campsite the previous evening. Consumption in *itself*, I thought as I searched for somewhere to change, isn't automatically a bad thing. We have to consume a certain amount in order to live. But modern societies in general, and North America in particular, seemed to have moved far beyond consumption in order to meet basic needs. The American Dream – which I'd understood to mean that everyone, if they worked hard, should be able to achieve a decent quality of life – had been subverted into a crazy parody of itself: into consumption for its own sake. Consumption had become consumerism: a system that exhorts us to consume vastly more than we need and that somehow manages to convince us we're neither successful nor happy without it.

On the other hand, there are plenty of people who claim to

enjoy vast quantities of shopping and plenty more who say, and why not? From what I'd been reading, there were some pretty compelling retorts. For a start, the current situation is massively inequitable. 2.8 billion people still live on less than $2 a day and the rich, according to the Worldwatch Institute, [18] spend more on perfume and makeup in one year ($32 billion) than it would cost to eliminate malnutrition and provide clean drinking water across the whole world. Then there are a few minor side-effects to our high levels of consumption. Like global climate change. Like mountains of waste. Like life-threatening quantities of pollution. Like growing resource shortages. High-consumption lifestyles don't just have a huge carbon footprint: they have a huge environmental footprint more generally. High-consumption lifestyles – our lifestyles – are, in short, utterly unsustainable.

The World Wildlife Fund offers a most compelling summary of this, pointing out that, if everyone on earth lived like the average North American, then by 2050 we would need five planet Earths. [19] As my favourite bumper sticker says, *Good Planets are Hard to Find*. To cap it all, high levels of consumption don't even seem to be a particularly reliable route to happiness. Indeed, you could reasonably argue that billions of dollars are spent on advertising designed to make us *unhappy*: discontented with what we currently own, and endlessly wanting more. This is perhaps the most bizarre aspect of all: study after study showing that, after a certain point, increasing wealth and consumption isn't actually increasing our quality of life. [20] The more I read, the more I realised that the consumerist version of the American Dream was not just utterly unsustainable. The American Dream, even for those who were living it, was often the ultimate rat-race trap. For people as well as planet, this version of the American Dream was surely becoming a nightmare.

---

[18] Worldwatch Institute (2004) *State of the World 2004*; *Progress Towards a Sustainable Society* Earthscan

[19] See the regular, and extremely helpful, WWF Living Planet reports. Available at: http://wwf.panda.org/about_our_earth/all_publica-tions/living_planet_report/

[20] See, for example, the New Economics Foundation: http://www. neweconomics.org/programmes/well-being

'So we, the rich, are consuming more and more in ways that make it harder for the poorest to meet their basic needs, and that is having an unprecedented effect on our environment – including changing the climate – without even making ourselves any happier!' I said out loud to the Aspen outskirts. Not that it was fair to scapegoat Aspen in particular. This was clearly a continent-wide, if not western-world-wide phenomenon. If everyone on earth lived as an average western European, we wouldn't need five planets – but we would need two or three. In Aspen, though, I really got it. On a deeply emotional level, the things I'd read about consumerism and multiple-planet living really hit home. The consumerist values everywhere on display in Aspen's plush shopping malls – packed with expensive, glittering goods that nobody really needs and flanked by private plane runways – seemed vivid and crass. I had a strong desire to get the hell out of there. I took off several soggy layers of clothing and scooted out of Aspen as fast as I could.

~

The road out of town ran through a gorgeous, fertile valley. The Roaring Fork, a free-flowing, un-dammed river raced alongside and the rocks glowed a strong red in the weak, returning sunshine. The valley was beautiful. And absolutely battered by traffic. I rode fast with cars and trucks screaming past me, feeling wound up and fired up. This crass, materialistic culture – all external appearances and possessions – and all these bloody cars. This is what we are destroying the earth for! As if to confirm my train of thought, a stretch Hummer roared past. A *stretch Hummer!!* I imagined a conversation with its occupants. 'Excuse me, but, given the reality of global warming, do you think a stretch hummer is an appropriate choice of vehicle?' 'The hell with you, lady, who do you think you are? I have God-given rights as an American citizen to freedom of choice!'

At last, I turned off the main road onto a quiet back road that I thought should take me to Old Snowmass. I was just checking the map when a police car drove past. It stopped, turned around and came back. 'Are you lost?' the sheriff enquired.

'I'm not sure. Does this road lead to the Rocky Mountain Institute?'

'Sure does, ma'am,' he said with an enormous friendly smile, before wishing me luck and driving on. I arrived not long after.

83

The Rocky Mountain Institute was set up in 1982 by Amory Lovins. It pioneers work into improving fuel efficiency, in all sorts of ingenious ways. Lovins is probably the most brilliant advocate of the view that we can keep our current high-consumption lifestyles basically intact, dealing with their environmental impact through advances in technology and design. He had agreed to meet me and talk about his work. Unfortunately, we had failed to converge on a date. While I was in Colorado, he was in Europe. Instead, his colleague Nathan Glasgow welcomed me in. We sat on enormous sofas and chatted, Nathan politely ignoring my rain-swept, road-grease-spattered and generally unsavoury appearance. Nathan was a cyclist himself. He told me that Independence Pass had been a stagecoach route and that it was closed for most of the winter.

'There's a fantastic bike race over it two days before it opens,' he said. I had to admit that 'fantastic' would not have been my first choice of words at the thought of racing over that pass. Though I guessed it would be a rather different experience without panniers.

Nathan could not have been more helpful. 'We can make enormous gains through simple energy efficiency alone,' he explained. 'Take the military. We don't always think about it, but they use a lot of large transport trucks. Well, first we work on efficiency. Taking off roof chimneys, for example, and streamlining the shape. Across an entire fleet – that makes a big difference. Then we would want to change the fuel they run on. The goal? To get the USA off oil completely. It's all set out in our book, *Winning the Oil End Game.*'[21] Nathan was totally optimistic about the potential to deal with climate change, and certain that this could be done in a way that enabled businesses to make more, rather than less, profit. He was also convinced it could be done without major changes in lifestyle. Lovins (who had said of himself, 'I'm not an environmentalist, I'm a cultural repairman') clearly shared that view. The Rocky Mountain Institute was, it seemed, a close conceptual cousin of the Cool City Mayors' approach to climate change. Indeed, it was doing everything it could to research their kind of solutions, to make the technofix dreams a practical reality.

Lovin's own house was a little distance away. It was open for self-guided tours. The super-insulated building had no central heating

---

[21] Available online at http://www.oilendgame.com/

system, despite the minus forty Colorado winters. It was so well insulated that it only lost about 1% of the heat it gained from sunlight, and from the people and computers in the building. 'I can offset this tiny loss,' Lovins had written, 'by playing with my dog (who generates about 50 watts of heat, adjustable to 100 watts if you throw a ball to her) or by burning obsolete energy studies in a small wood-stove on the coldest nights.'[22]

Inside, the house was gorgeous. I was especially taken with the huge conservatory area – said to have produced twenty-eight crops of bananas – complete with indoor pond. Multiple signs read, 'Hi, I'm Hedgemon the Hedgehog. Please keep the doors shut.' Hedgemon, the signs explained, was responsible for insect control. Almost every wall was adorned with pictures of orangutans. These intelligent, highly social, endangered creatures had, I learned, been amongst the many victims of the profoundly misplaced attempt to mitigate climate change by burning particular kinds of biofuels – leading to rainforest destruction on an even more massive scale than usual. The whole house spoke of a compassionate, intelligent, intriguing occupant – who was, frustratingly, due back late the following day.

I had to make a decision: camp nearby for a couple of days or keep going. I was inspired by Lovins' focus on solutions and the breakthroughs he'd achieved. Yet I was still not convinced the technofix/ efficiency approach was sufficient. I could see that efficiency had to be part of the solution; even that technological breakthroughs were exciting, a cause of optimism, to be embraced. But could technology really deliver the consumerist version of the American Dream across the whole world? Could it turn our multiple-planet lifestyles into single-planet ones, magically rendering a high consumption lifestyle environmentally feasible for six to nine billion people? *Could it* take us across that particular Great Divide? And Aspen had thrown another question sharply into focus: whether this lifestyle was really so great anyway. Was consumerism really our best achievement, our best shot at leading a good life? Did we actually *want* the consumerist version of the American Dream? Lovins' approach seemed to suggest that, with the right approach to efficiency, we could all drive Hummers – maybe even stretch Hummers. I was moving towards the view that, however far

[22] Amory Lovins (2005) 'More Profit with Less Carbon' *Scientific American* September, 2005

technology could or could not take us, we needed a profound change in values, a rethink of what quality of life actually means. I very much wanted to know what Lovins might say to all this. But the number of days off I'd already taken was weighing on my mind. And I was committed to another stop with friends in Fort Collins a day or so ahead. It was one of the hardest calls of the trip, but I decided not to wait.

Back on the car-infested wet main road I blasted to Old Basalt as fast as I could. Old Basalt was unexpectedly quaint. But not a campsite town, and not cheap – as I discovered on enquiring about a room at the Green Drake Motel. The woman at reception – perhaps a little older than me, short blonde hair, black and white striped shirt – was loquacious in her astonishment when I explained my appearance by explaining what I was up to.

'Oh my God! I've never heard of such a thing! You are so brave! The cheapest rooms have gone but I could give you a ten-dollar discount. I am going to put this in the computer. "Woman travelling ALONE from El Paso to Anchorage. By BIKE." Oh my God, I want to see your legs!' I asked her what she thought about global warming. 'Global warming? Well, I'm glad somebody is doing something.' (I think that referred to me.) And then, in a sudden sideways lurch of a kind I was becoming used to: 'Yesterday, I saw that Enron man having lunch. And now he's dead!'

I winced at the price despite the discount. I could not afford to do this too often. In fact, I couldn't really afford to do it all. But I badly wanted to try to marshal the day's emotions – exuberance on the Pass, anger in Aspen, optimism at RMI, scepticism about the optimism – into some kind of coherence. And I was wet and cold. It was a good call. The shower was awesome – hot and skin-blasting – and the room was three flights up with views of mountains across the town roofs and a dangerously attractive bookshop. I washed some clothes and studied the map, figuring I was about three or four days away from my friends Bill and Steph, who lived just outside Fort Collins. I wrote and wrote, trying to unscramble the day. And then I treated myself to a chapter of *That Old Ace in the Hole* [23] sitting up in the huge, clean bed.

---

[23] Annie Proulx (2002) *That Old Ace in the Hole* Fourth Estate

~

Carbondale, my first stop the next day, appeared to consist of one main street, along which I found two bike shops. I borrowed a high-pressure foot pump, and begged a Tour de France update. Then I rode on in blistering traffic towards Glenwood Springs. I kept thinking I was back in New Mexico. Small hills like oversized quarry spill-overs speckled with green scrub crouched a little away from the road. The hills constantly changed colour, from a pale, gravely grey to dark salmon, and back to grey. The bike-shop at Glenwood Springs had a stack of cards in the same series as 'New Mexico Birds'. I left with 'Animal Tracks', 'Colorado Wildlife', and 'Colorado Trees and Flowers' and had a sandwich and blueberry smoothie outside the rather soulless 'Sacred Places' café.

Glenwood Springs was the point at which I turned east, heading back in the general direction of Fort Collins after my rather westerly detour over Independence Pass. Unfortunately, this appeared to involve a hefty chunk of miles on Interstate 70. Acting on a tip from the bike shop, I followed signs for a bike trail along the Glenwood Canyon. It was extraordinary. Past a string of hotels, the trail suddenly emerged into the steep-sided canyon, at the bottom of which ran the Colorado River – splashed with bright yellow rafts full of kids shrieking in the wavy bits – a railway track, Interstate 70 and the cycle path, all running side by side. Interstate 70, part of Eisenhower's vision for Modern America, had evidently been a stunning feat of engineering, cutting through the canyon with numerous tunnels and becoming a major part of the United States' road network. The cycle/pedestrian path was not much less impressive, complete with information signs, regular rest stops and toilets. It was also not very wide, rather twisty and definitely more dangerous than the interstate, on account of the cyclists – who tended to drift at random from side to side – and the occasional knots of walkers that would suddenly emerge around corners, completely blocking the path. But it was still good to be off the main road.

An hour or so later, the track climbed out of the canyon and joined a small road running alongside I 70. The valley opened out to the pale hills and scattered scrub. Every half mile or so I'd be followed by a black bird, flying alongside with a scolding 'tscuk, tsuck, tsuck' and clearly trying to see me off its territory. I'd calmed down since Aspen, and the upset and anger was waning. But it had left me thinking. Right then I was thinking that we humans needed to find a way of reining ourselves in. At the moment, by far the biggest factor controlling how much energy we use and what we use it for, is wealth. If you are rich enough, you can fly your personal plane to Aspen and then drive your Hummer to the mall to spend the whole day shopping. And any criticisms – let alone threats – to this 'freedom' would be ferociously resisted. Freedom of choice. It is given such high priority. But how have we come to prioritise our freedom of choice as consumers over protecting our one and only planet? Is it really more important that consumers should be free to pursue the option of a stretch hummer than that everyone should have a climate conducive to life?

~

Back on the busy I 70 I stopped several times to watch little dun-coloured animals, with brown eyes and slender tails. When disturbed they raced to their burrows where they stood on their hind legs like meercats, shouting a high-pitched warning cry. There were hundreds of them, living in a hinterland of sandy soil between the roadside and a bank of signs reading 'Warning! High Pressure Gas Pipeline'. Initially startled by the bike, they often stood by their burrows and watched me when I stopped. What must it be like, I wondered, to live in a community of these animals, right next to this road?

At Gypsum, I bought three plums from a man with a stall, who also gave me a peach for free – 'for eating now. Too mushy to sell,' he said, 'but still delicious.' As I slurped the peach, he told me he'd once gone to Alaska for a holiday and had stayed eight years. 'It was wonderful,' he said. 'Then I came back south and met her.' He pointed to a sulky looking woman reading a paper and picking at her long fingernails. 'Never made it back. I envy you. Not the biking. The Alaska bit.'

At the tiny town of Eagle, I stopped again. There was a market in the single main street. A stall manned by a woman from Yorkshire was selling clothes from Asia. There was some pottery, almond toffee (with free samples), and a bread stall. I bought half a multigrain loaf and ate samples of garlic bread, cheese bread and spinach bread. And a totally delicious chocolate chip cookie I really didn't need. 'Are you staying for the music?' asked the woman who'd sold it to me. 'It's a band from Denver. Playing free in the park about six thirty. Everyone from the town will be there ...' Oh no! I thought. Of all the things that could delay me, live music outdoors was one of the most tempting. But it was already clear that this was one of those days – there were many – where seventy-five miles measured with string on the map and the reality on the ground were significantly different. I'd already done seventy-five miles. But I was well short of where I'd thought that should take me.

I carried on. I would stop at the campsite marked just shy of Wolcott. I overshot it. Some young, very polite men in the Wolcott Yacht Club (yacht club? In the middle of the Rockies? Did I dream that?) directed me back a couple of miles to a site that was simply marked on the road as a picnic table. I rolled off the road with relief. The site was beautiful. It sat between the Eagle River on one side and the road on the other. I could still hear the road traffic. But I found a spot right by the water. A family of geese were paddling slowly upstream along the far side. I sat on a picnic bench in the sun, magpies scratching and chattering around me, and identified my small brown creatures as prairie dogs. Clouds of silver insects danced above the bushes. The setting felt somehow appropriate. Wasn't this, in the end, what this trip was about? Trying to fight for the river, the geese and the prairie dogs; fighting to keep some space for them, in between the roads? After a while I put the tent up. Then I wrote my diary until the mosquitoes started to bite. Snug in the tent behind the mosquito net, I watched the river and read Annie Proulx. It was not long before I was asleep.

I woke just after eleven to the sound of a revving car engine and loud music. Very close. Oh oh. I could just imagine a posse of drunken lads coming down to the river for a late liquid picnic. It was not an appealing scenario. My tiny tent seemed almost designed to provoke drunken humour. If they realised there was a woman by herself inside it ... I silently pulled on my leggings, and a fleece. Is it logical to reach for your clothes when you're feeling threatened? I suppose so. I sat in the dark, listening to the sounds of car doors slamming, voices, music, and visualising a nightmare visit by drunken yobs. Yet something didn't quite add up. Then I realised. The music. Would the drunken yobs of my imagination really be listening to Tracy Chapman? As quietly as I could I unzipped the fly sheet and looked out. The first thing I saw was a very large woman in a white tank-top and shorts, and then a man carrying something heavy in a long, rectangular bag that looked somehow familiar. A tent! They were campers! Campers arriving late and not all that sober, but a couple of campers nonetheless. Not a pack of lads. Tracy Chapman's heart-wrenching voice thudded through the darkness. 'Sorry. All that you can say...' I resigned myself to a noisy but safe night. It was a strange night though, with various cars coming and going, their headlights flaring across the tent as they passed in the darkness. Once I looked out again after engine noise had recurred in my dreams and thought I saw a mini four-wheeler, like the one the park warden at Twin Lakes had used, driving away. A park warden at 3am? Perhaps I was dreaming or perhaps by then I was hallucinating. I woke again to shouting. The late campers were most definitely arguing. I lay in my tent sleepily wondering what I should do if it turned violent. Try to intervene? Lie low? The fight gradually subsided into stillness, and we all drifted back to sleep.

~

It was nearly nine before I got going next morning, delayed by a chipmunk who'd emerged from some fallen wood just as I was ready to leave. I rolled a half-eaten plum towards him/her and took photographs as he/she paused to eat it. Back at Wolcott I turned north, heading for State Bridge, and a long climb up into big, beautiful, deserty country. The sun was out, the sky was blue, the traffic fell away and I rode upwards for hours through huge vistas and fantastical rock formations. Five miles of swooping descent dropped me back down to State Bridge. The original bridge, financed by the State of Colorado in 1890, had been built so that wagons could cross the Grand River. Now I stopped and watched rafts shoot below me before I rolled down into State Bridge itself. The tiny town, sitting at 6,700 feet and right by the side of what is now known as the Colorado River, consisted of one shop and a lodge/restaurant, currently closed. In the shop, the only half-edible food was a Snickers bar, and water was available exclusively in tiny plastic bottles. I would have needed hundreds of them. I sat in the sun besides a sign saying 'Parking for Harley Davidsons only' and waited for the lodge to open instead.

A cheerful ginger-haired young woman let me in about ten minutes later. I sat on a high stool looking out across the road to the river, perusing a dream menu stuffed with vegetarian options. I finally settled on a breakfast burrito, only to be told that breakfast was not available on Fridays. I had nachos with beans and guacamole, sour cream, cheese and jalapeños instead. And gallons of water. A young man with blonde hair and a rather spaced-out manner sat down next to me. He asked me where I was headed, and told me he lived in his car and did a lot of mountain biking. He said I should stay to the west in Wyoming, in order to avoid the Indian reservations, which he described as 'rough'. He told me that grizzly bears were becoming aggressive in Montana and that the mosquitoes would eat me alive – 'I mean *literally* eat you alive' – in Canada. He suggested that I might want to change my plans and travel to Alaska by ferry. Then he told me that he didn't think the Rocky Mountain National Park – squarely on my route – allowed cyclists on the roads during the summer months because of all the traffic and the lack of hard shoulder. And that, were I allowed in, I would almost certainly be run over. Then he wandered off.

A couple arrived, on motorbikes. They ordered a margarita each, and a burger and chips to share between them. They were a striking pair. Arthur was black, and wore a red headscarf over his dark hair. Jodie was pale, tall and thin, blonde hair shining under a black bandana. They were from Mississippi. Global warming, they agreed, was being talked about a lot more in Mississippi since Hurricane Katrina. No-one knew for sure whether Katrina had been caused by global warming, but it was a 'Category 5' storm, exactly the kind that climate change scientists warn we should expect more of. People were indeed expecting more extreme weather, Arthur acknowledged.

'What are people *doing* about it though?' I asked.

'Preparing for the worst,' Jodie said.

'Anything to try to prevent it?'

'Nope. Lots of people think it's just natural cycles. Me,' (this was Arthur) 'I'm not intelligent enough to try to sort all that out.'

Neither of them thought many people believed that they might have contributed to *causing* the extreme weather – nor that they could take action to help prevent it worsening. We're so disconnected, I thought. Not just the people of New Orleans; all of us. Disconnected from the environmental consequences of our actions and lifestyles. Disconnected from feedback. If we were dumping waste upstream in a river we drank from, the links between action and consequences would be obvious. We'd get the feedback loud and clear. Yet the links between dumping waste in the atmosphere and chaotic weather further downstream somehow weren't being felt. The feedback was there all right – but it wasn't getting through.

The waitress brought over a second round of margaritas and asked if we were staying for the music. A band from Denver. Grateful Dead-type music. Free camping. 'There'll be six to seven hundred folk here...' she said. I found out later that State Bridge Lodge was a major music venue, with music and parties, famous across the States, almost every weekend. It seemed I was doomed to cycle into almost irresistible temptations on a daily basis. But I had been looking at the map. The miles ahead were nagging at me. I wanted to get to the town of Estes Park by the following evening. That involved crossing Trail Ridge Road, the biggest climb so far. To have a reasonable chance of doing Trail Ridge Road in a day, I really needed to get to Granby that night. On the main road, it was about fifty-two miles in a big triangle, north-west and then east to Kremmling, and then another twenty-seven to Granby, on top of the meagre sixteen or so I'd just done. Ninety-five miles! No music nights for me, then. The good news was the short cut. A minor road ran directly north-east from State Bridge to Kremmling. This little road looked more like twenty-five or maybe thirty miles. Significantly less than fifty-two, anyway. But it was white on the map. The legend said these roads were 'improved'.

'Is this road paved?' I asked the waitress.

'No. But it's oiled gravel, so it's hard,' she said. 'Has some bumpy bits but mostly it's okay. Definitely shorter. You'll be fine.'

~

I set off around noon, rather reluctantly. I was full of nachos and I felt like chatting. The road surface was indeed hard, but it was patched and streaked with loose gravel. When a car or, especially, a truck went by, I ate dirt. But it felt fantastic. High, remote, open mountain vistas stretched out from the glinting Colorado River, rapidly falling away below as we climbed. It turned into one hell of a twenty-five or thirty miles. The road climbed and dipped and climbed again and this, and the rougher surface, made it slow, hard going. Then it rained. Dirt spattered all over us. My legs were instantly coated with wet grit and

Rocky's gears began to crunch and slip. A van-load of people towing a trailer of river rafts asked if I wanted a lift. I passed the turn-off to Radium Springs and came to the point where the map showed the road arching up to touch the river once more. What the map didn't show was that the road was actually hundreds of feet above it. A last long climb and we came out onto a beautiful, high, grassy plain. Distant mountains and a top of the world feel. I stood and gazed and grinned before a long descent and an unexpected final pull upwards for a mile or so on rough surfaces back to the tarmac road, just to finish the whole thing (and me) off.

At Kremmling I searched out a café and ordered a pile of oatmeal and raisin cookies and a latte. I'd been experimenting with giving up coffee and this was my first latte for months. I needed something to whizz me back to life. I sank into a deep armchair surrounded by photographs of mountain bikers and a fantastically lean, strong-looking female mountain-runner, apparently the café owner. The hot coffee tasted wonderful. I felt dazed. The short cut had definitely been a short cut in terms of miles. Whether it had been in terms of time and energy was more debatable. I could have sat in that armchair a long, long time. But by now it was five-ish, and Granby was still about twenty-seven miles away. Back outside, I emptied water bottles over Rocky's gear mech and chain. We both looked as if we'd been mountain biking. Legs, feet, panniers, frame, bottles – all coated with grit. The front gear-shifter refused to shift onto the top ring and all the gears were crunching. In my head, I broke the remaining distance down into smaller bits. Only twelve miles to Parshall. Most of that is downhill. The Colorado River was back alongside. We were in a high valley, with rounded hills on each side and big mountains glimpsed in the distance. It began to look somehow familiar. Had I cycled this way before? Where was it that my friends Pauline and Josh had lived? On the previous trip I'd cycled in the other direction from Drake, through Estes Park, up over Trail Ridge Road and down to Granby where Josh had offered to come and fetch me. But I hadn't been able to get through on the phone so I'd just kept going. I'd ended up doing a hundred and thirty miles, the last two up a gravel track, to find that my friends had gone to bed, not imagining I would arrive that day. Fortunately, they'd left the door open and Josh came down in the night to find me utterly asleep on the sofa. How the hell had I done a hundred and thirty miles on top of a big climb, with panniers? The more I thought about that trip, and the ninety mile per-day average, the more I began to respect my younger, fitter self.

Meanwhile, my older self was struggling to maintain a seventy-five mile-per-day average, and struggling even harder not to admit I was struggling. A Union Pacific train about a mile long pulled gradually past, grinding and squealing. A fantastic way to travel, I thought, inching effortlessly across the United States at about fifteen miles an hour. A herd of horses took off as it passed, then clustered back around piles of hay, shifting restlessly from one to the other. Suddenly, a black Golf cabriolet with its roof down pulled over in front of me. Two young guys, one with a black hood pulled over his head, grinned out at me.

'Do you want a ride?' the hood asked. Of the various rides I'd been offered, and intuitively felt certain to be safe, this was not one of them. But it didn't feel threatening, either. Amusing, if anything.

'Thanks for asking,' I grinned back. 'But I'm fine. They drove off. The driver's arm appeared above the hood, his hand jerking into a 'v' sign. I chose to interpret it as friendly and waved back. They passed me again a bit further along the road, and didn't stop. But I did get a wave.

An hour or so later, I was definitely flagging. In fact, I might as well have got off and walked. I stopped, and put my music on. The effect was instantaneous. Jaqui, I thought, with utter gratitude, you are a total star! How long, I wondered, would these songs retain their ability to transform my mood and speed me up? I pedalled off to 'Crazy' and sang as I cycled. And suddenly there was Granby on the horizon, coinciding with a black, black sky. In front of both, a headwind pushed through, as if to hold Granby and respite at a distance for just that bit longer.

~

The next morning was overcast. Fourteen miles along the steadily ascending road I decided to have a second breakfast at Grand Lake before beginning the climb over Trail Ridge Road for real. A sign read: 'This is a quiet little drinking town with a hunting, fishing and snow-mobiling problem.' For all the humour, Grand Lake was depressing. The main street, as far as I could see, consisted entirely of tourist shops. In fact, Colorado in general seemed to have become one big Lake

District, full of people driving to look at beautiful scenery. Perhaps it was like that when I'd lived there previously. But I remembered it as quieter, wilder, less developed and with much less traffic.

I chose the friendliest looking café – the Fat Cat – and had an all-you-can-eat buffet. An extremely accommodating chef made me a couple of veggie wraps to take away while I ate my way through scrambled eggs, potatoes and vegetarian gravy, followed by a cinnamon roll, a pile of strawberries, a slice of melon and two glasses of orange juice. Fantastic! 'In my next life, I will be a tourist,' said the woman on the till as I paid. Somehow we got onto the subject of brown trees. I'd noticed that some of the forests looked as if it were autumn. But it was not autumn. And they were evergreen pine forests. Apparently the culprit was a beetle which burrows under the bark and kills the tree.

'Where have the beetles come from?' I asked.

'They've always been here,' she said. 'But our winters used to be much colder. Minus fifty or even sixty degrees. Killed them off. Now it's not so cold, they're surviving all year. Thousands of trees are dying. It's very sad. And a huge fire risk...'

I cycled back onto the main road feeling low. Colorado, the wild mountain state of my dreams and memories, was full of tourists. And the forests were dying in front of our eyes. I had a sudden, powerful sense of there being just too many people. When Columbus set sail there were about 500 million people in the whole world. At the beginning of the 20th century we numbered about 1.6 billion. Now in 2006 we had reached 6.7 billion, and rising. Too many people, everywhere. Too much impact, everywhere. Impact isn't just about numbers of course – the carbon footprint of an average US citizen, for example, is about ten times that of the average citizen of India. But, as David Attenborough puts it, 'all environmental problems become harder – and ultimately impossible – with ever more people.' [24] Our sheer numbers exacerbate every issue and make solutions vastly more difficult. And meanwhile, our presence is increasingly felt across the whole planet. Were there any wild, undamaged, uncrowded places left anywhere? Maybe they were ahead of me. I cycled across the Rocky Mountain National Park boundary. Nobody tried to prevent me. Suddenly I came across a melee of cars and people, abandoned

---

[24] David Attenborough quoted at http://populationmatters.org/

at random in the road, their occupants crowded along the roadside. A car crash? I stopped and walked over, half-expecting to see a car rolled off the road. What I saw was a moose and her calf, calmly grazing. People had left their vehicles, still with keys in the ignition, in the excitement. Everyone seemed so thrilled to see these enormous, gentle creatures. Leaving aside the fact that we were all – including me – scrabbling to photograph them, to capture and own them rather than just watch them – it had to be grounds for hope. People clearly responded with love to these creatures. I couldn't believe they would be indifferent to the immense changes that threatened them, if only they really knew. Yes, this chaotic clutter of cars and people was surely a reason for optimism. I grinned. And then became aware of a stinging sensation. I looked down to see my legs entirely covered in mosquitoes.

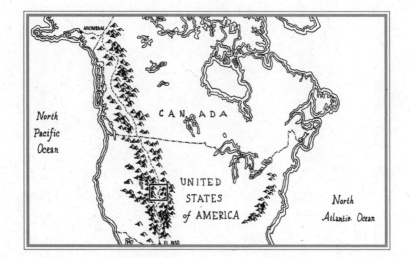

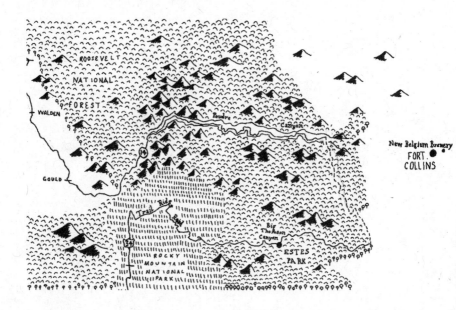

CHAPTER FIVE
Big Hills and Small Beer

'I have learned that, beyond death and taxes, there is at least one absolutely indisputable fact. Not only does human-caused global warming exist, but it is also growing more and more dangerous, and at a pace that has now made it a planetary emergency.'

Al Gore [25]

'Global warming is just your particular pet passion.'

Bill Olsen [26]

The final big pass, for now at least, turned into a bit of an epic. Trail Ridge Road, one of the most spectacular roads in the world in terms of mountain scenery (allegedly). At the foot of the climb, it started to rain. The climb was not steep, but it was relentless. I inched slowly upwards. Occasional glimpses of an abrupt drop to the valley below broke through the clouds. Mostly, though, the scenic highlights were wisps of light cloud superimposed on the darker cloud that was the entire sky, the entire horizon. In fact my entire world, for most of that day, was grey cloud studded with green, green, sodden trees. The rain got harder. After a couple of hours I stopped to try to imagine the view. A large dark blue truck swerved across the road and jerked to a halt right in front of me. The window opened just enough for the man inside to bark out a question.

'Have you been over this pass before?' he asked, in a voice dripping with scorn and incredulity and a sort of outrage.

'Well, yes, actually,' I said, 'though a few years ago now and from the other side.'

The man in the nice warm truck shook his head. His whole manner somehow suggested that he didn't think women should do *anything* alone; and that a woman cycling by herself clearly just

---

[25] Al Gore (2009) *Our Choice* Bloomsbury

[26] Bill Olsen (2006) personal communication – and still a friend despite it!

didn't know what she was thinking of. And, sooner or later, would need rescuing – probably by a man like him. (As it happened, I nearly did. But he wasn't to know that.) 'Well, I wouldn't go over it now,' he snorted. 'It's bad up there, really bad.' And with those words of encouragement, he revved and was gone.

Later, a man with a cowboy hat leaned out of a truck coming down the pass and yelled, 'Hard core!' I'd just stopped to put on waterproof overshoes and, whatever my external appearance, was not feeling remotely hard core on the inside. But the complement cheered me up. Then a man watching bighorn sheep through huge binoculars shouted a warning. 'When you get to the Continental Divide sign, it isn't the top. You've still another two thousand feet to go!' I reached the sign and sheltered behind the toilets while I put on all the clothes I could. Leggings, more waterproofs, another layer under my jacket. Then I gulped down a veggi wrap from the previous café-stop. It was delicious – and soggy in seconds. Time to move on.

Just as I thought it couldn't get any wetter, the rain picked up a notch. It was driving wet. The climb went on and on. Soon I couldn't see further than one snow marker pole ahead of me. It was like being in the rain equivalent of a white-out, now with accompanying headwind. And still the road kept rising. I was definitely tiring, and kept stopping to slump forward over the handlebars for a breather. But I knew there was a visitor's centre at the summit, and the thought of warmth (I distinctly remembered standing on a hot air outlet just inside the door last time around) and a huge mug of hot chocolate, kept me going. When I finally got there, the visibility was so bad I overshot it and had to go back. The car park was strangely empty. I cycled right up to the large glass doorway. A small sign had been taped onto it. It read, 'Closed early, due to bad weather.' I stared at it in disbelief. Then, digging through wet layers to my watch, I was startled to discover it was well after five. I needed to get a move on. But, even after the visitor centre, which I'd remembered as being right at the top, the road kept rising. By now, I had two main fears. One was that I had somehow pedalled into the cycling equivalent of the Ancient Mariner's doldrums and was doomed to spend the rest of my life on this mountain, struggling along at two miles per hour in the cold rain, on a pass that went upwards forever and had no summit. The other was that a park ranger would stop and ask if

I was okay and I would burst into tears. Then he/she would make me accept a lift. And then I really would have cheated. I began to hate the road for going up so interminably. It seemed so excessive, so absolutely unnecessary. By now, I was close to losing the plot. I was stopping every few minutes to rest, and found myself talking to the road (always a bad sign). 'Just go down. Please. Just go DOWN!' My breath was making an odd rasping noise that I didn't seem to have much control over, and my face ached from the wind and cold and from trying not to whimper out loud. I was close to hyperventilating. I needed to get a grip.

At last, many, many hours into the climb, I reached an unmarked kink in the road that really was the summit. Twelve thousand feet and absolutely no view! But the road, thank goodness, was definitely heading downwards. I stopped and fixed both of my new back lights onto the panniers as best I could, with a view to minimising the chances of someone accidentally taking me out from behind in the gloom. I was utterly relieved to be heading down, but now had a new dilemma. I was drenched and cold. Should I go down as fast as I dared? This would get it over and done with quicker, but be a lot colder. Or should I slow down and take longer? I went as fast as I dared, arriving at Estes Park in the dark, after twenty-five miles of cold, wet descent, way beyond drowned rat. It was definitely a motel night.

I stopped on the town outskirts to sort myself out and a kindly passerby wiped my glasses for me. Sight at least partially restored, I started motel hunting. There were lots of them. They were all full. I widened my range, and finally, at the distinctly posh-looking 'Brynwood on the River' the receptionist took pity on me. She had no rooms, but would help me find one. Her kindness nearly reduced me to tears. As I stood and dripped in the elegant hotel lobby, she rang motel after motel until, grinning, she announced a find – the Discovery Lodge on the other side of town. Yippee! Back on the road, traffic lights silently changed colour in an almost empty street running with black rain. A short ride later, still dripping and shivering, I checked into Room 307, and straight into the bath. My friend Bill pointed out later how ironic it would have been to get hypothermia and frostbite on a global warming trip. Very funny.

~

Next morning, I had a breakfast date with Larry Gamble, chief planner for the Rocky Mountain National Park. I quizzed him remorselessly as we ate our eggs. He told me that he thought wolves would soon arrive in the park from Yellowstone. He said that the impact of nitrogen from farming and the acidification of water were causing problems for a range of wildlife. I asked about the pine beetles. Were they getting a hold because of the milder winters? Larry said he thought it had more to do with bad forest management.

· 'Fires aren't allowed to go through any more,' he said. 'So the trees are denser. This means they're stressed. Because they're stressed, they can't resist the beetle attacks.'

'So it isn't a global warming issue?' I asked.

'No, I don't think so,' Larry said, carefully. 'But these factors will all affect the trees' capacity to *respond* to global warming. So even if global warming hasn't caused the beetle problem, it will affect the trees in the end. And of course the projected impacts of global warming across a whole range of other species are really dire. We're going to lose unthinkable numbers of species. I don't think people realise that. Nor what it means.'

I told Larry about the people watching the moose. 'Couldn't we use people's love for the park, or for fishing, or for watching moose, to inspire positive change?' I asked. 'Make connections between things people do that contribute to global warming, and the threat this poses to the things they love?'

'Give me an example,' Larry said.

'Well,' I suggested, 'if the park could explain that oil burned through driving, say, contributes to global warming, and that global warming will cause massive problems for the creatures they've driven to see, perhaps people would be inspired to drive less; or to trade in their big trucks and SUV's for something smaller.' Build on the connection, nurture reconnection instead of disconnection. A small start, in this case, but a start nonetheless. I was full of coffee-enhanced enthusiasm for the idea, but Larry seemed less than convinced. I was haunted, later, by the conviction that I wasn't communicating well; that the issues might not have had a good hearing, simply because I had been their spokesperson. Or maybe it was just a stupid idea; maybe these people would be outraged at the thought of changing their mode of transport; maybe they loved driving in their big, comfortable cars far too much to change and definitely more than they loved other animals. Maybe they were only there to take in the sights and to look at the animals as they might watch a TV show or a zoo display. Maybe they were acting out an ironic form of *disconnection* from nature and their presence in the park actually had nothing to do with reconnection, either with the animals or with the consequences of their lifestyle choices. Or maybe they *did* know about their own impacts and just didn't care and I was just being naïve again. And yet I couldn't quite accept this. Would people care if they knew or did they know but just didn't give a damn? A significant part of me still couldn't help but err towards the more optimistic view of humanity.

~

Back in Room 307, Bill rang to say that there were flash flood warnings, loose rock on the road and a storm forecast. He was coming to get me and I wasn't to argue. I didn't. It was still raining, and I felt distinctly fragile. I sat in the beautiful (expensive) room, appreciating the ability to whack the occasional way-beyond-one's-real-means extravagance on a credit card (I would have paid thousands) looking out of the picture window to the still shrouded mountains and trying to figure out what exactly had nearly done for me the previous day. Downright whimpering! And the strange, choking breath. I'd been at almost exactly the same altitude a few days before (and many times previously) with no hint of altitude sickness or anything like it. Yet Trail Ridge Road had to have been the hardest day's biking I'd ever experienced. According to the milometer, I'd only ridden 63.8 miles. Objectively speaking, doing the same climb plus twice the distance on my previous ride must have been harder. But it hadn't had anything like the same impact. In the end I put it down to the rain. I've always functioned better in heat than cold, and especially wet cold. Give me a choice between extreme heat and a cold rainstorm and I'd choose the heat any day. It makes me wonder why I still live in the UK.

There was a loud hammering on the door. 'Scruff! You in there?' It was Bill. 'Scruff' had been my nickname in the old Fort Collins days when I'd been included in a wacky, good-humoured group of mountain bikers who called themselves 'Scum' and specialised in glorious, long, remote rides usually involving lots of mud and ending in an immense, chaotic meal at 'Das Haus'. I'd lived in Das Haus for a

103

year or so, with Bill and Steph, and two Brazilian friends, Marcia and Gunars. We were all graduate students at Colorado State University and truly lived up to the 'work hard, play hard' cliché. It had been one of those eras that, even at the time, I'd known to be amongst the best of my life.

Bill was still at least a foot taller than me, and still rangy and bearded, though no longer chewing tobacco. Many huge hugs later, I heaved Rocky into the back of Bill's truck – still yellow, though not the same one – and we drove down Big Thompson Canyon, Bill regaling me with stories of a recent flash flood that had swept away whole chunks of road, amongst other things. He and Steph now lived in a small, open plan, wooden house, a little way up Poudre Canyon, just outside Fort Collins. Steph looked much the same too: slim, blonde, big olive eyes, beautiful smile. The rest of the day vanished. Chatting and drinking beer and catching up on the decade or so since they'd visited me in England. I still have a photograph, sepia tinted by Bill, of me and Steph grinning and drenched with rain, Steph's long hair plastered against her face on a walk up towards the Fairfield Horseshoe in the English Lake District.

~

The next few days vanished, too. Bill had set up a computer for me on the dining room table, so we could all work at once. Bill and Steph were battling with one of Steph's more urgent graphic design projects. I fought to catch up on my rapidly backlogging email inbox and worked endlessly on the blog. Initially, I'd deeply resented the blog. In fact, I'd rather blown a fuse when Chris suggested I should write one. One of the things I'd been looking forward to – yearning for! – was a chunk of time away from damned computers and email. The last thing I wanted was to commit myself to regular computer-based duties. Now, to my surprise, I found I was relishing the challenge of trying to summarize days of cycling and extract the most interesting incidents from the miles and miles of road and wind and mundane encounters. I would reread my journals and then put them aside, writing the blog from memory, at speed. What came out of this process often took me by surprise. I was becoming addicted to it.

The sun returned, and Bill declared a day off. He drove Steph and me back up to Estes Park so we could cycle the section I'd missed. We started from the door of Room 307 Discovery Lodge and rode out of Estes Park on a glorious blue-sky day. The mountains behind towered above the town, glinting silver in the sunshine and clearly indicating quite how stunning the views would have been up there, had I been able to see them. The downpour had, it turned out, marked the end of a year-long drought, so it seemed churlish of me to complain about lack of scenery. But it had been seriously wet – wet enough to make the news, and not just on Trail Ridge, or even in Colorado. Part of the road from Socorro, New Mexico, was under four feet of water and roads were closed in Albuquerque. The Rocky Mountain news told of flash floods near Westcreek, narrowly escaped by, amongst others, one Charlotte Ferguson.

> 'Ferguson, 68, said she scrambled up a hill near her home Saturday morning as rescue crews prepared to bring her across the rushing creek. "I climbed the hill with my .38 and my curling iron," she said, noting that the gun was for protection against bears and the curling iron was with her simply because she had forgotten to put it down.'

You really couldn't make it up.

Steph and I took off down the canyon. Pannier-free bikes in the sunshine, miles of downhill, the river brown and white alongside, curling and folding around the rocks. It was like a live thing: a huge brown snake, with constantly changing white markings along its back. I crossed my first thousand miles with Steph, in the sunshine, on that holiday of a ride. Bill photographed the milometer. We all whooped out loud. It was a magic moment, though almost as daunting as it was cheering. A thousand miles was less than a quarter of the total distance to Anchorage. This ride was already erring on the challenging side, and there were 3,500 miles still ahead.

After miles of swooping, Steph and I turned off the Thompson canyon road, heading across country. The road became more undulating and rather more like work, especially for Steph, who was on a mountain bike with knobbly tyres. A man on a carbon racing bike pulled alongside and introduced himself as Brook. He was out for a day ride, having moved to Colorado from Austin, Texas.

'So, do you know Lance, then?' I joked.

'Sure I do,' he said, 'I've worked with him. He's an ass.' Lance Armstrong, in my view, was the best cyclist on planet earth. He could be a total ass every day of the year so far as I was concerned.

Brook was positive about climate change. He said he thought the USA was coming out of a thirty-year sleep.

'There was a lot of focus on environmental issues in the seventies,' he said. 'Then it all vanished. Now we're waking up again.'

'Waking up?' I asked.

'Yes. Waking up. For sure. My mom is a staunch Republican, and even she believes in global warming.'

~

That evening, I dived back into the blog backlog. Eventually, Bill put a beer in my hand and forced me to stop. The evening proceeded along what used to be familiar lines. Bill cooked pizza. Another 'Scum' member – Sugarbear, now a father with cubs – showed up as a surprise. Beer was consumed all round. Big discussions ensued. Bill and Steph had been amongst my closest friends in Fort Collins, but we never had seen eye-to-eye on, well, most things that would come under the heading of 'politics' or 'environment'. On climate change, our disagreements were particularly acute. Bill emphatically did not believe in it. Or at least, he did not believe that the change in the average global temperature was in any way related to human activity. He was a firm believer in sunspots. Global warming was due to variations in the sun's output. Period. Never mind that everything I'd read clearly demonstrated that current temperature changes simply can't be explained without factoring in human impacts; that our contribution to global warming is an area of certainty in mainstream climate science. For Bill, it was Mother Nature alone. And, if global warming was caused by the sun and not by people burning oil then there was no need for people to stop burning oil. Long live trucks and cheap fuel!

I found these disputes, even with friends – perhaps especially with friends – truly frustrating. I wasn't a physicist or an atmospheric chemist but I was pretty sure I had a reasonable grasp of the basic science. And the basic science was based on undisputed premises and inexorable logic. Molecules of carbon dioxide retain heat. If you put more of them in the atmosphere, it will warm up. We are putting more of them – and other greenhouse gases – in the atmosphere. It is warming up. There is a striking visual representation of this in Al Gore's film: a graph of atmospheric temperature over millions of years, its spiky peaks and troughs tracing across an entire wall like a giant cardiogram. [27] And then, in a different colour, he added the graph that traces changes in atmospheric CO_2 over the same timescale. The correlation is utterly alarming. It is almost completely exact. These are not Gore's own graphs, of course, but those presented by the IPCC, amongst others. And it's not just the correlation that is alarming, but the so-called 'hockey-stick' shape: the way both graphs shoot up towards the sky when they reach the 'present time and beyond' end of the time axis. Very, very much more CO_2. Very, very much more heat.

At the end of the day, though, my position on climate change was inevitably based on trust. As a non-scientist, I had to believe other people's data. The key question, then, was: who is it most reasonable to trust? On the one hand, we have an international panel representing thousands of scientists, whose research echoes the experiences of millions of people across the world already struggling to deal with the changes the scientists delineate in the abstract. On the other hand, a minority of climate change deniers, most of whom turn out to have links to oil companies. Except Bill. Bill was a forester. He had absolutely no links to Exxon whatsoever. His position, as far as I could tell, was based on a sort of naïve radical stubbornness. Bill was one of the kindest, most generous friends imaginable. And he drove me nuts.

There was only one thing that mad me madder than Bill's views on climate change. That evening, it was a position held by everyone but me. Bill, Steph and Sugarbear were unanimous that my concern with global warming, and the environment generally, was just 'my passion'. Global warming was my personal pet interest, on a par with other people's passions, such as RV ownership or downhill skiing. By now, I was trying hard not to choke on the pizza.

'Surely all sorts of things are much more than "personal passions,"' I spluttered, fighting hard for my corner. 'Suppose I were an anti-child pornography campaigner, for example. That wouldn't just be my personal passion. It would also be about core social values – values

---

[27] *An Inconvenient Truth* (2006) directed by Davis Guggenheim

that any civilised society needs, in order to *be* civilised. Same with global warming. Protecting the environment we all depend on is – or ought to be – a core value of *all* societies.' I was warming up to my theme. 'It's insane to say that concern for the environment is just another special interest. It underpins all interests! If we don't look after the environment, you can forget all other special interests. Forget the economy, let alone RVs and skiing. Forget society! How can there be a healthy economy or a healthy society without a healthy environment?'

Unfortunately, beer was fuddling their logic (and just possibly mine) and I made no headway. Before I could regain control the conversation had shifted to 'What if there was an infinite life pill,' and how, among other things, infinite life would affect the bacteria responsible for tooth decay.

~

Bill, despite his fundamental disagreements with the nature of my cause, had done his best to make it a success. He and Steph had arranged all sorts of trips. While Steph sweated with her design work, Bill and I drove north to visit an Excel wind farm just across the border in Wyoming. It was a stunning site. The huge, almost silent blades turned against a hot blue sky on a vast rolling plain grazed by buffalo. Ken, the site manager, knew each of the forty-five turbines and their various mechanical glitches individually – and introduced us to several of them. 'This is number twenty-nine,' he said, while I climbed inside and looked back out across the plain. 'Bit of an oil leak in the gear box on this one.' On the horizon, a herd of antelopes were silhouetted against the huge sky. Ken told us how much effort went into keeping the windmills running. 'Maintenance is expensive,' he said. 'I often need to hire a crane. The parts are dear. And heavy.' A gear box alone weighed about five tons, and the machinery was surprisingly delicate. Number fifteen was a case in point. A mouse had meandered into its electrics, shorted them out, and then remained part of the circuit for days, causing $50,000 worth of damage. It was unusual to hear stories about wildlife's impact on windmills.

'What about the windmills' impact on wildlife?' Bill asked.

Ken agreed this was an issue. Birds, and especially raptors were, he said, their biggest concern. 'They used to use them as lookouts for hunting. When they see prey, they just dive. They don't look up. The blades kill them.' Ken's windmills had been designed with no perching places and deliberately placed below the ridgeline where the raptors tended to hunt.

'Amendment 37' in Colorado required energy companies to produce ten per cent of their energy from renewable resources by 2010. In 2006, less than one per cent of US energy came from the wind. Ken was optimistic this would rise to ten or fifteen per cent in a decade. A good thing? As a source of energy, wind power undoubtedly has a lower carbon footprint than fossil fuels, and it doesn't leave a legacy of highly toxic, long-term dangerous nuclear waste either. Windmills are, despite their evident eccentricities, relatively low-tech and could, at least in principle, be run and controlled by local communities as a source of local power. And, as I well knew, wind was not in short supply in these parts. Harnessing the wind for energy could certainly be seen, at least potentially, as part of the solution.

On the other hand, given the way our energy grids are currently structured, any power generated by wind simply feeds into the main grid. It doesn't, in fact, power local communities and so it doesn't, in fact, help connect those communities with their own power consumption and the need to make choices about where energy comes from, how much it is reasonable to use, and what the real-life consequences of using energy are – whether they be climate change or windmills in your field of view. And we would need an awful lot of windmills to come close to replacing fossil fuels. The writer Paul Kingsnorth has argued that this is a typical of a horribly distorted form of environmentalism: wild open landscapes being covered in vast machines in order to fuel our high-consumption lifestyles in a 'cleaner' way. [28] A technofix that doesn't tackle the value questions. What do we really need energy *for*? What are our priorities here?

And yet, as we drove slowly off the site through a large herd of buffalo, it seemed to me that these machines, beautiful in their way (at least in small numbers) *could* be part of the answer, part of a different story about what we value and how we power our lives. We almost certainly need to use less energy. But, even with massive gains in conservation and efficiency, we will still need energy. Unlike nuclear

---

[28] Paul Kingsnorth (2011) 'Confessions of a recovering environmentalist' *Orion* Jan/Feb 2012

or oil or other sources that could not conceivably be controlled locally, and that have immense carbon footprints, wind power is at least compatible with a different, more localised, more joined up, more connected-to-consequences, lower impact approach to meeting our energy needs.

Back at Fort Collins we headed for my favourite visit of all. A wind-powered brewery. With or without reservations about wind power, New Belgium Brewery was an inspiring 'solutions' story. It began after a bike ride through Belgium prompted the owners to experiment with their own beer brewing. From selling the results out of the back of a car, the brewery now employed two hundred and seventy-five people in Fort Collins, and was hugely successful. Back in 1992 the staff, believing it a less harmful source of power, had voted unanimously to switch to wind energy and to absorb any extra costs themselves. The plant was still a hundred per cent wind-powered and its delivery fleet ran on biodiesel. There were constant ongoing innovations to improve energy efficiency.

'For example,' explained Bryan, who was showing us around, 'these merlins.' The merlins were beautiful steel vats in a gorgeous high-beamed wooden building. The beer was heated there as part of the brewing process and the merlins spread the beer over a bigger surface area. Less depth of beer meant less energy was needed to heat it. Such innovations were not simply decreed from above: the brewery had strong views about engaging staff with the rationale behind these changes, and everyone was involved and consulted in the search for new ways to reduce environmental impacts. They had fun too – after their first year, employees were given a 'fat tyre' bicycle (the name of one of their most popular beers) and many rode to work on them. Bryan had worked at the brewery for nine years, despite being a journalist by training. 'It was only meant to be a summer job,' he said. 'I still love it. The atmosphere, the sense of shared purpose. The values.'

The tour of the building was followed by a serious tasting session. Bill, Bryan and I sat at a table lined with glasses, and compared notes – all in the interests of global warming research, of course. Sometime later, Bill and I left with a free six-pack each, in a distinctly cheerful mood. What a great place! Leadership from the middle, it seemed, was not confined to mayors. New Belgium Brewery was another example. A business saying, heck, let's just get on and do it. A business taking

110

the lead on solutions, and modelling a rather different way of *doing* business. Not reducing all values to economic growth and efficiency alone but valuing the environment; valuing meaningful work; valuing a sense of contribution and community. The brewery was not just successful in terms of reducing its climate change impact. It was successful in becoming an employer people really wanted to work for.

~

In terms of businesses rooted in environmental values – or indeed any positive values – you couldn't get a much greater contrast between New Belgium and our next stop. Wal-mart. Wal-mart was to drastically change its position over the next few years, but back in 2006 it was regularly pilloried as one of the worst offenders on environmental and social grounds, with low wages and violations of environmental regulations – water pollution, air pollution, storage of toxic materials – in numerous states. Unfortunately, it was my best option for downloading photographs onto CDs. And I had to keep buying cards to feed to the Tracfone. Bill was on fine form. He swiftly accosted a shop assistant.

'Could you tell us where the Tracfone cards are? And what do you think of global warming?'

'Global warming?' replied the young woman. 'Hard core! Well, I think it's totally scary, ice caps melting and all that. What do I *do* about it? Well, my flatmate and I try not to waste stuff. And we have a garden. We're planting trees and flowers. Not that the flowers make a lot of difference. I drive a car and it doesn't have a windmill on the roof or anything. But it's not a Hummer...' We chatted on, Bill expertly unravelling the tangle of ideas and picking up on her leads. He was not remotely shy. I should have hired him.

'See you!' Bill hollered across the shop as we finally departed, heading for Jax and some more biking errands. Jax was a real institution, packed with camping and hunting equipment. Rows of rifles jostled for space with crossbows, fishing rods, snares and other ways of killing things. I picked up some mosquito repellent, and questioned an assistant about pepper spray.

'What do you want it for?' he asked.

I told him a bit about my trip. 'Bears and boys,' I summarised.

'Well, typically, they'd be different sprays. But,' he said, with a kindly smile, 'here's one that'll work on both.' I paid at a checkout next to a display of automatic rifles. My high-strength mosquito repellent and dual-purpose mace spray felt positively benign.

'Hope you don't have to use it!' said the man who'd served me with a grin and a wave as we departed.

We drove past Das Haus on the way back. It was surrounded by trees and I didn't recognise it. In downtown Fort Collins, the main streets had all been smartened up and were full of bookshops and restaurants I didn't remember. I recognised 'Old Chicago', but only by name. And Lee's Cyclery seemed somehow in the wrong place. We bought takeaway sandwiches and salads at Avogadros and drove back for a late supper.

~

The next day, I'd fully intended to leave. I sorted my kit and worked through a pile of jobs – emails, phone calls, things to send back to the UK. A journalist arrived from the Colorado State University Alumni magazine and interviewed me. Bill and I worked on Rocky in the gaps, swapping the broken-toothed gear wheel for the one Chris had sent over and then trying to get the whole gear system back into synch. Never in my life had I encountered such a highly strung gear setup as Rocky's. I never really did figure out what, exactly, upset it. I suspect many things upset it. By lunchtime, Rocky had new teeth, my panniers were more or less packed, various parcels were ready to post and almost all my emails had been responded to. But the blog was only just past meeting the Mayor in Albuquerque. Bill and Steph ganged up on me. 'Think how much you'll get done if you stay and write!' 'If you go first thing tomorrow you'll soon catch up on the miles ...' I wasn't going to get over Cameron Pass before dark, and the blog was weighing on my mind. I stayed. Bill and Steph dealt with their design crisis and I wrote and wrote, finally giving in when Bill put a beer in my hand about seven in the evening and announced we were going for a walk up the canyon.

'These are Ponderosa Pines,' said Bill. 'Smell them!' I put my arms around a tall, slim tree and took a deep breath. Amazing! The bark had a strong, vanilla-like, practically edible smell. Ponderosas also, he swore, came in butterscotch and chocolate flavours. We walked up to a clearing in the trees and watched the sky change colour. Then

112

back to the house for lasagne and finally up to a flat spot in their garden where we lay and watched the stars, their huge fluffy ginger cat sprawled next to us on sun-loungers under piles of blankets. We talked UFOs and Big Foot and Bill told a story about a cyclist on Cameron Pass who'd heard a strange padding noise behind him and looked over his shoulder to see a mountain lion. He was wearing a duffle bag that saved his life. The cat tackled him but got the bag and was shot off by a passing motorist. After that the conversation degenerated. We sat up way too late talking nonsense and watching shooting stars.

I finally left Bill and Steph six days after I'd arrived at the foot of Trail Ridge Road. In fact, between Bill, Steph and Susan, I'd used up rather a lot of the rest days allocated for the entire trip, the significance of which was to become rather more real later on. For now, I couldn't imagine that I could have just dropped in. It had been so wonderful to catch up. And Bill and Steph had been way beyond generous hosts, setting up visits, providing computer and washing machine, helping with the bike ... in between feeding me a constant stream of blueberry pancakes, French toast, pizza and beer. No, it had been good to stop. Now I would just have to cycle faster, further. As if she had heard this thought, Steph wished me goodbye and good luck with a multicoloured necklace which had a tiny buffalo woven into the beads for strength and stubbornness. Bill offered to cycle with me for the first ten miles and ended up coming to the top. It was a fifty-mile climb up through the spectacular Poudre Canyon to Cameron Pass in glorious sunshine, Bill struggling to find a gear low enough to allow him to ride at my creeping, pannier-loaded speed. It took us all day and we parted company on the summit – a mere 10,000 feet – Bill for a two-hour descent in the dark with no lights and me for a shorter swoop down to a campsite just beyond Gould, grinning and mulling on generosity and friendship.

~

I just snuck into the campsite. People in front of me were turned away, but the owners looked at Rocky and relented. They found me a tiny patch in the busy site – one without an electricity hook-up: not exactly a hardship. Different campsites seemed to have different qualities that endured as individual campers came and went. This one had hundreds of humming bird feeders and was characterised by friendliness. As I pitched my tiny tent, a woman came out of a nearby RV and introduced herself. 'I sleep there,' she said, pointing to the RV's back-end. 'Just in case you need any help in the night.' I didn't. I slept like a log.

The humming bird feeders on the way to the shower block next morning could have delayed me for hours. Tiny, scraggy little birds, some green with buff throats, some with vivid red throats, all with long, delicate beaks, they made a constant fierce whirring and often fought ferociously, the tiny birds darting and hovering mid-air like that dubious character in the early scenes of Star Wars. Various camping neighbours stopped to say hello. One set offered me a lift to Walden. When I grinned a 'Thanks, but that would be cheating,' he grinned back and said, 'Good girl!'

It was a gorgeous ride. Wide hay meadows, trees, distant snowy mountains, the smell of sage. For a couple of hours, I revelled in that feeling of effortless riding in hot sunshine with beautiful views that is one of cycling's enduring highs. At Walden, the 'Moose watching capital of Colorado', the main street was closed off. A (very small) craft fair was underway. I had a veggi-burger in a huge wood-lined café hung with moose-heads, and chatted to a young man touring on an ancient bicycle with a very loose crank. He was headed across Trail Ridge. I doubted he would make it. There was nothing I could do. I was carrying a reasonable tool kit, but not a crank key. Not long after, I met a cluster of cyclists from Essex, England, also on a three-month tour. Their panniers made me and Rocky look like lightweights. They were fantastically loaded, front and back. One man was even carrying a full-size foot-pump.

'It doesn't actually weigh all that much,' he said. 'And you'd be amazed how many friends we make because of it!'

A thought occurred to me. 'Do you have a crank key?' I asked.

'Of course!'

'Maybe you could look out for a young man on an old black bike. Just ahead of you.' I explained the situation. I often wondered if they'd ever met up.

North of Walden, the road stretched long and straight. Chipmunks scooted across the road, their tails held vertically like exclamation marks. Just as it had in New Mexico, the scenery changed almost exactly at the state border. The vistas got wider, and the mountains fell away. The sun burned hotter in a huge blue sky. I was leaving the mountains of Colorado for the hot, high plains of Wyoming.

CHAPTER SIX

Headwinds

'We have to get beyond the artificial division we've created between the human community and the rest of the planet.'

Thomas Berry [29]

If Colorado was characterised by big mountain passes, Wyoming was memorable for headwinds. Hot headwinds. Learn to love the winds, I told myself. Not always easy. I was heading almost exactly due north. The country became more and more deserty, with sage scrub growing out of pale sand. Ahead of me, Interstate 80 was visible for miles, trucks in a long line threading across the flat landscape. There were no mountains in sight at all. I stopped at a gas station for water just before a section on the main road. A man on a motorbike said, 'Judging by your legs, you ride that bike *a lot*,' and then (rather pointedly, I thought) that the hot springs nearby had free showers. I stood outside in a sliver of shade eating a bagel. A man in what looked like a Boy Scout uniform asked me where I was going. 'No shit!' was his reassuring response when I tentatively mentioned Alaska. He and his partner were retracing the journey of the Donner party, one of the last major wagon trains of 1846. The Donners had taken an ill-advised 'short-cut' and become stranded in snow storms while crossing Wyoming. They'd eaten their horses, their dogs and, eventually, the dead people in their party. In a hundred degrees, it was hard to imagine freezing to death in the snow. But I'd seen the huge snow barriers along the side of the road and could only imagine that Wyoming did winter as uncompromisingly as it did summer.

'I'm doing a bit of research about global warming,' I said.

'Heck, you're in the right place!' he laughed. 'It's HOT!' He told me he thought global warming was definitely happening, but that he based this on science rather than on experience. 'Changes in weather are too incremental to really be sure,' he said. 'Science says it's real though. I try to do the small things I can. Drive less. Dry my

---

[29] Thomas Berry, quoted in Derrick Jensen's powerful and thought-provoking *Endgame Volume II: RESISTANCE* Seven Stories Press (2006)

clothes in the sun. We all need to do those small things. But beyond that, you have to go higher up. To the refineries, for example.' And then, apparently seriously, 'Be careful who you talk to. This is Dick Cheney's state.'

I laughed. Dick Cheney was then the vice-president of the United States – a figure who would not, presumably, put private interests above public good. For sure, Cheney had previously made a fortune as the chief executive of Halliburton. And what did Halliburton do? Well, it was one of the world's largest oil services companies. But still... Even as I tracked this train of thought, I could sense naivety rearing its head again. Oil consumption has to be reduced if we're to bring climate change under control, so Cheney clearly had reason to deny the existence of climate change – even to oppose those trying to tackle it. And Cheney, it seemed, was not shy of conflict. He had been a key member of the pressure group 'Project for a New American Century', whose self-professed aims were 'to shape a new century favorable to American principles and interests' – on the grounds that American leadership was good both for America and for the world[30], even if military strength were needed to persuade the world of this. Project for a New American Century had been advocating military action against Saddam Hussein as far back as 1998, with securing a major supply of oil openly stated as a key justification. Messing with Dick Cheney on the subject of oil was evidently not something to be undertaken lightly.

I was beginning to glimpse the Bush administration in a different light. Not just 'an idiot', as Thereze had suggested, but part of something much more sinister. Something deeply corrosive of the democratic process; something that would play to the sheer power of vested interests, apparently allowing those people whose (immense) short-term wealth depended on oil revenues to completely put aside the longer term interests of their own fellow-citizens, not to mention the world. Allowing them to deny outright the reality of the threat they were implicated in causing. And not just deny it, but fund the systematic broadcasting of 'information' about its nonexistence; to fund the publication of 'research' that set out to 'disprove' the link between oil and global warming, just as previous 'research' had

---

[30] See http://www.newamericancentury.org/

118

been funded by the tobacco industry to 'disprove' the links between smoking and cancer. What chance, I wondered, did Susan and her allies have against this kind of brute wealth and power? Could it be brought to heel?

~

The first chunk of interstate was fine, though very busy. Enormous trucks blasted past, truck after truck. For a while the headwinds were so fierce that every few minutes I had to stop cycling and brace into the wind so as not to be knocked backwards. Huge sheets of cardboard flew back past me at high speed across the scrub. Then a truck would go by and I'd be blown forward in a brief blast until the truck-wind died and the real wind retrenched and hurled me backwards again. It was one of the few times I took my helmet off the panniers and put it on my head.

Next morning my snot was bloody and I had a bad feeling behind my left eye. I took an aspirin. 'Just get on with it!' I said to myself, as I cycled sluggishly up out of Rawlins. I was headed for the 'empty quarter', a huge section of vast Wyoming plain with few human-inhabited stops. I was feeling distinctly apprehensive about the coming day. First, the distance between places I might get water appeared to be on the long side. Second, the obvious place to head for that evening was Jeffrey City. Cyclists I'd met earlier had said that Jeffrey City was a ghost town. 'Literally, a ghost town,' they'd told me. 'It was really frightening.' I had no idea what they meant, but it didn't sound good. They'd also said that the headwinds had given them such grief they'd hitched for ninety miles. And they had been travelling in the opposite direction! How could we *both* have headwinds? Clearly Wyoming winds did not obey normal laws at all.

Still quite high – about seven thousand feet – it would nevertheless have been an overstatement to describe the landscape as rolling, let alone hilly. Occasionally the road would incline fractionally upwards for about ten miles, and then it would slope cautiously down again. More angular than rolling, and only just off flat. After one such incline, a huge expanse opened out in front of me. The Great Divide Basin. Silver-grey sage-brush scattered across pale sandy soil for hundreds and hundreds of miles. The traffic came in pestilential pulses, backed up by a convey system for some nonexistent roadworks

I'd cycled through earlier. It was irritating the hell out of me, though I knew that really it was uncertainty that was getting to me. I tried confronting it head-on. 'What's the big deal?' I asked myself. As long as I had water, I would surely be able to find somewhere to camp. The idea of getting to the end of the day mildly heat-stroked, with no way of cooling down until it got dark, battling with mosquitoes while searching for somewhere out of sight of the road that I could actually reach with my skinny tyres and then hoping that the landowner wasn't going to give me a hard time for trespassing, was not appealing. But it wasn't exactly life-threatening either. That was my bottom line. I often appealed to it as a way of trying to keep things in perspective. If it wasn't life-threatening or seriously health-threatening, then what the heck; ultimately it was an experience, not a disaster. That's what I told myself.

A cyclist appeared over the horizon. He stopped, and introduced himself as Richard. He'd started that day in Jeffrey City. Jeffrey City! The ghost town!

'So, there's somewhere to camp there?' I asked.

'No,' said Richard, 'but there is a hotel.' A hotel! 'Well, it's pretty basic. Not a lot of services. If you can make it to Lander, I would. I definitely would.' Given that Lander was about a hundred and thirty miles from where I'd started the day, this seemed unlikely. In any case, there was no need. Jeffrey City had a hotel! And I'd been anticipating tumbleweeds and a dried-up water faucet.

~

The stretch of Wyoming I'd been apprehensive about turned into one of the best days yet. First, it proved to be thirty-three miles to Lamont, not the forty-four I was expecting. Eleven saved miles can feel like a continent. Lamont appeared on the horizon as a scatter of shapes, one of which resolved into a huge sign that read, 'Grandma's Café: OPEN'. A line of trucks outside, and all men inside, like the Old Dog Café in Annie Proulx's novel. [31] I was served by a large woman with brown ringlets who was friendly in a you-are-outside-my-known-world-but-that's-no-reason-not-to-be-civil kind of way and ate my cheese toasty (the only thing that wasn't a burger) on a round table by a window hung with red and white curtains with a strawberry print, next to a

---

[31] Annie Proulx (2002) *That Old Ace in the Hole* Fourth Estate

picture of a wolf in a snowstorm. Grandma herself appeared later and looked at my attire – shorts and sleeveless biking top – with evident disgust. She didn't return my smile, but pointed to the sink when I asked if I could fill my water bottles, and nodded when I thanked her. Outside, there were signs for the 'Chief Washakie Trail'. I wondered who Chief Washakie was, and what he might have done to bequeath his name to the trail and indeed, to an entire town up ahead.

The second unexpected bonus was that the pass over the Continental Divide proved to be lower than Lamont rather than higher, and the climb I was expecting never materialised. Third, the scenery was extraordinary. The immense, high, flat vista was as powerful in its way as the mountains had been. I felt as if I was riding through a desert. In a sense, it *was* a desert. Yet I saw as many animals there as anywhere, chipmunks scooting across the road, antelopes and mule deer grazing on the scrub. And there was hardly any wind. When a headwind began to pick up I found myself singing (tunelessly) to it. 'Easy, little, wind, easy...' The wind dropped away. There was virtually no wind for the rest of the day.

I was indulging in an unlikely-to-be-fulfilled fantasy about ice-cream as I approached the tiny village of Muddy Gap. Muddy Gap consisted primarily of a gas station. I was greeted by a friendly attendant who said, 'Ice-cream? We have homemade Italian Gellato!' I browsed their unexpected collection of books while eating a double scoop of Muddy Gap Mud and Strawberry. The attendant was ex-air-force and had travelled widely in Europe and Scandinavia. Now he was studying local history, and working in the gas station shop. The books included three volumes of diaries and journals written by people who'd crossed this area in wagons in the nineteenth century. I could feel Rocky's back wheel groaning as I looked at them. I asked the attendant, whose name I never learned, about Jeffrey City.

'Yes, there is a motel. Not many rooms functioning yet though. And there is an RV site. But ...' he made a 'dodgy' sign with his hands '... if I were you, I'd head for Sweetwater Junction. Another twenty miles. If you can. The Mormons have a museum and free camping by the river. A place called Sixth Crossing. It's a nice spot.'

I thanked him and went outside, where I met a Glaswegian who'd trained in Outdoor Education in Wales and was now living in Boulder, about fifty miles south of Fort Collins. We would undoubtedly have discovered shared acquaintances had we talked longer. He was on his way back from camping in Montana with his three sons and a yellow Labrador called Angus.

'These guys are really into global warming,' he said, pointing to the sons.

'What do you think we should be doing about it?' I asked them.

They gave me a strange look. 'Stopping it, of course,' was the unanimous reply. Of course.

I was well underway before I realised I hadn't asked the historian-attendant about Chief Washakie. From Muddy Gap, it was a glorious ride. The temperature had dropped a little – I'd guess about ninety – and, without the wind, cycling became a joy again. I stopped at Split Rock a little further on. Arapahoe, Sioux, Crow and Shoshone tribes had all lived on these plains until the westerners arrived and, to quote the sign-boards, 'tragic conflict ensued'. In the direction I was travelling, Split Rock could be seen for a day, and for two days further as you left it behind. It had been used as a navigational aide by the pioneers crossing the plains in covered wagons, the Mormons – fleeing persecution with their possessions in handcarts – the fur-traders and the Pony Express, amongst others. The information board included a photograph of an old advert for Pony Express riders. It read, 'Wanted! Wiry young men, not older than eighteen, must be expert horsemen and prepared to face death daily. Orphans preferred.' I walked up into the rocky outcrop, with juniper and sage growing magically out of rock-cracks and scenting the hot air. It was a beautiful spot. I wanted to stop there and just sit, looking out across the huge plain scattered with faint trails, the Sweetwater River winding in the distance. It was an intensely powerful place - and incredibly moving to think of people crossing those plains in wagons, let alone pushing handcarts.

I rode away, looking back at Split Rock. I kept having to stop to take photographs. The landscape was unlike any I'd ever seen. I felt excited by it as I had many years previously, in the good old days before I'd understood the link between air travel and climate change, flying across vast stretches of Australia where the earth was a shade of red I'd never seen before.

~

I arrived at Jeffrey City about five. It was a former uranium-mining town, though the mine had long since shut down, but the bar had, a notice said, been open continuously for seventy years. The motel was off the road, in a line of dark sheds, below a sign with a black bowler hat. It didn't feel unsafe, though it wasn't exactly inviting, either. But I was intrigued. All the bad things I'd heard about the place sorely tempted me to stay. On the other hand, there were several hours of daylight left, there was still no wind, and I was feeling strong. It made more sense to keep going. I cycled reluctantly on, past rows of derelict sheds, a sign to the RV site, a single house with sprinklers on a faded, patchy lawn, and a closed liquor store. Not long afterwards I met a couple on bikes, heading for Jeffrey City. They'd heard rumours of rum goings-on but didn't care – it was a cheap place to stay with a shower. Two more cyclists, also heading for Jeffrey City, appeared over the horizon a couple of hours later. It was now on the late side. We exchanged banter. They claimed they'd heard of murders. I told them there were cyclists already there. And that I was seriously tempted to turn back, so we could all have a cyclists' night in the bar. They said, 'It could be a cyclists' massacre!' I said if I read of their demise in the paper, I'd remember them fondly. 'Worry more if you *don't* read about us...' And then they left, grinning and waving. I never did find out what, if anything, had happened to give Jeffrey City such a bad name.

I rolled down into Sweetwater Junction at the end of an eighty-seven-mile day. As promised, there was the 'Sixth Crossing' campsite by the river, with one empty caravan and hundreds of rabbits in residence. A horseshoe of sites, all on grass, with shaded benches. I chose one with a cluster of worm-stalking robins, parked Rocky against the bench, and walked to the river. There were clumps of tall purple flowers like lupins; tiny, almost tame rabbits, and a huge white bird a bit like a gannet. And there it was, that calm, satisfied, in-the-moment serenity. Here I am, I thought, with the birds and the river, completely here and nowhere else, at peace at the end of a great, great day.

I put my tent up, and ate a tortilla. A truck arrived. Its occupant introduced himself as Brett. 'I should warn you,' Brett said, 'that about thirty Mormons are about to arrive. They're re-enacting a handcart journey. We're doing backup. You might not have the quiet night I'm guessing you're hoping for.' We chatted. Brett described himself as an ex-baseball player, drinker and womanizer, now living a saner life having found Jesus. The handcart re-enactment was, he said, a really powerful experience, especially for the kids. 'Teaches them how lucky they are ...' He was based in Utah, where he built expensive houses. 'I get to work with a lot of assholes,' he said. 'There are a lot of rich people in Utah, many of them Mormons. Double incomes, even, though the Church doesn't really believe in women working.' I heard an inner voice counselling, *Don't even go there*. I didn't. He said that environmental issues were over his head. Plus the Lord knew we were making a mess of things, and would either sort it out – or not. 'Unlike some of my colleagues,' he added, with a familiar abrupt switch of topic, 'I don't think someone will go to hell if they don't believe, so long as they live decently.' (I think he was hinting that I might be okay.) 'When Jesus comes down again,' he explained, 'which will be soon, bad people will go to hell, and then there's different layers of glory for good and goodish people. Adulterers who've repented, for example, might get to the first layer.' Brett said that personally, he wasn't even thinking beyond layer one. He'd be more than happy there. And he didn't think he'd like the higher layers' inhabitants. In between summarising the Mormon worldview, he'd fished a huge air mattress from the truck and was inflating it, or trying to, with an automatic air pump that whined like a gigantic mosquito. He'd left the working party early on the grounds that he'd done a full day's work and had had enough. 'The other guys will be pissed at me,' he said, 'some of them at least. But I don't care. I've done my bit.'

There was no sign of the remaining thirty Mormons. I hauled a bench in front of my tent so I wouldn't be accidentally run over and turned in. I was just dozing off when they arrived. It was elevenish. I heard Brett saying, 'John, there's a biker girl in that tent. Just so as you don't think it's me and scare the hell out of her.' 'What, by pouring gasoline over the tent, for example?' a voice, presumably John's, replied. Brett had clearly not been exaggerating when he'd said they might be mad at him. It didn't strike me as a particularly Christian attitude ... and nor did it when they were up shouting and slamming truck doors at six am, despite having been on the rowdy side until at least midnight and knowing there was someone asleep right next to them. Call yourselves Christians? Pah! I thought, groggily. Eventually they drove off and I slept on, waking hot, sweaty and stuck to the sleeping bag. As I packed, a coachload of people arrived in traditional dress – pants and checked shirts and cowboy hats, long skirts and shirts and bonnets, all rather bizarrely juxtaposed with Oakley sunglasses and plastic water bottles.

In the museum, I was greeted by Sister Saheli. Short, white curly hair, glasses, big blue eyes and very bad breath. Something about her brought an uprush of emotion and, inexplicably, I found myself fighting back tears. She looked me straight in the eye with the kind of sympathy that makes you feel unutterably sad for no apparent reason. I had no idea what the emotion was. Perhaps the reality of climate change, of what it will mean if we don't wake up and tackle it in time, had, even for me, remained largely abstract and was only now shifting into something real, frightening, tragic, worthy of tears. Perhaps it was my growing awareness of my own implication in it, my own flights, my own forms of consumerism, my own life as a microcosm of wider denial.

Or perhaps the history of the place had simply seeped its heartbreaking legacy into the grass and the stones. One group of Mormons, Sister Saheli told me, having safely crossed the Atlantic, had decided to carry on west despite how late in the season it was. They were caught in snowstorms right where I'd just slept – the sixth time they'd crossed the Sweetwater River. With no provisions, one of their party had gone for help. Some of those remaining froze; the rest were eventually rescued. The thought of those people pushing handcarts across the rocky Wyoming plains in howling winds and blizzards was almost unbearable. And more than a bit surreal in the current baking heat.

I left about ten. There was going to be no point singing to the wind today. It had got up in the night and was now thoroughly established. I pushed off into the vast plain. Pale khaki scrub grew out of bleached sand, and a silver half-moon hung in the endless, washed-out sky. On the distant horizon I could just see snow-patched mountains, shadowy, hazy, insubstantial and very far away. There was a huge wind. I had to cycle really hard to get *downhill*. Uphills, even slight, were an absolute battle. 'Love the wind!' I told myself, a little forlornly. A huge sign by the roadside helped. 'Wyoming Winds', it informed passers by, kept that unimaginable snow off the grass in the winter, which meant year-round grazing for bighorn sheep, elk and mule-deer, as well as cattle. In a heavily agricultural state, grazing was always an issue. Now it was fast becoming more so. The predicted impacts of climate change for Wyoming included further spread of the non-native, highly flammable, 'cheat-grass'. Cheat-grass was less nutritious than the native grasses. Cheat-grass was already on the rise, causing concern to ranchers and conservationists alike. In Wyoming, climate change was already affecting local ecosystems. Not good news for farming and food security, or for wildlife, especially on land already suffering soil erosion and other impacts of increasingly industrialised agriculture.

~

'Wind is good!' I shouted out loud, straining to keep moving forwards. I broke it down in my head. Thirty miles to the next junction. Then only another nine to Lander. I was creeping along, just above walking pace. A flock of white birds circled above. A couple of bleached looking prairie dogs peered out at me. Then nothing.

I'd never really thought about the term 'Wild West' before. Here, its wildness was evident. Not in the sense of lawlessness, but in the parochial sense that few white westerners inhabited it. Of course, it wasn't wild in the sense that people had never lived here nor left their impact on the land. Numerous First Nation peoples had lived on these plains since the last ice age. One of Bill's less than politically correct opinions had been that the national parks should 'reintroduce Indians', because they'd co-evolved with the forests and had long used fire to manage the density of trees and undergrowth. I'd winced when he'd said it, but the more I thought about it, the more I ended up wondering why. Talk of 'reintroducing Indians' made these people sound like a species of bird that had been driven from the area. Or perhaps on a par with the wolves, driven out by hunters and then reintroduced into Yellowstone Park. But why, exactly, was that analogy problematic? The thought that one group of people were entitled to relocate another or that white, non-native Americans might deliberately use a group of indigenous people as a conservation strategy was clearly outrageous. But offence at implying they were animals in an ecological system was surely misplaced.

Maybe that's the root of it, I thought, straining into the hot wind. We are *all* animals in ecological systems. But we've become somehow

126

disconnected from the simple reality that, for all our technological brilliance, we are still earth-bound creatures living in habitats. Not just dependent on the environment, but *part* of it. So much closer to that on a bike, in the wind, and the heat. Maybe I was still reconnecting with this reality myself and the Sweetwater tears had been part relief, part grief for the absolute preciousness of what climate change threatens. And maybe this was also part of the solution. To reconnect. To challenge and change the modern western image of ourselves. To recast the implicit understanding of industrialised humans as somehow separate from the rest of the living world; separate from – and superior to – the ecosystems we use science to analyse, understand and try to manage. To reconnect with our place in ecology and our deep dependence on other living things. And if we don't? Then, surely, as fast as we deal with one environmental issue, another will arise. And another. And another; springing up, inevitably, like cheat grass from a profoundly misplaced world view.

The sound of an engine drew me back into the present. A long, long hill stretched away ahead of me as far as I could see and a maroon saloon car was pulling alongside. The window hummed down. 'You're one tough girl,' said the man inside. (Girl? I was clearly shedding years on this trip.) 'Would you like a cold Gatorade?'

'I'm fine, thanks,' I said, a touch testily. There was something I didn't quite like about this man; though maybe I was really irked at the hill and the hot headwind.

'How about some water?' he asked mildly. It must have been over a hundred degrees. I was low on water and what I had left had been heated in black plastic water-bottles to just short of boiling point.

'No, thanks,' I heard myself say. 'Thanks for asking, but I'M FINE.'

He pulled away and in seconds was a dot in the distance. How odd that people in the same physical space could be having such utterly different experiences. Maroon car man, music playing, cruised effortlessly up the hill in his cool car and was probably barely even aware of the wind. On the bike, I was downright battling just to move forward at all. Some considerable time later, I reached the top of that hill. In the middle of the hard shoulder, on my side of the road, stood a bottle of orange Gatorade. I got off and circled it, warily. The seal was intact. Then I laughed out loud. It had to be him. Drinking the hot, sweet, orange liquid in the hot wind on the hot hill, I reassessed maroon car man; and enjoyed a blast of optimism about humanity in general.

~

The Empty Quarter had probably only given me a mild taste of how harsh it could be. But, despite the wind, I loved it up there. I would have stayed for much, much longer, just to be alone in that immense landscape. There was something elemental about being in that wide, wild, hot space, just me and the bike, straining into the wind. Now I'd dropped a couple of thousand feet and still the hot wind hammered against me. I could feel it stretching my skin back across my face and searing into my eyes, even behind dark glasses. Farmland returned; grass, trees, barley. At last I reached the junction for Lander and felt the wind swing slightly more to the side as I turned. The top gear was gone again. I tightened the cable. It worked for a bit, and then stopped. I sprayed WD40 over the mech and adjusted the limit screws. It worked for a bit, and then stopped. I carried on without it.

By the time I crawled into Lander I was trashed. The thermometer on the bank read 101 degrees. I stopped at a bar advertising salads and ate a 'Hungry Hippy' pitta bread and salad, sitting in the cool, dark, quiet bar-room. I was dazed. In the toilets, the mirror reflected a woman with a spacey, wild look. I drank glass after glass of cold water until, gradually, I began to feel more or less normal.

As I left, a waiter pointed to the bar across the sidewalk. 'They're showing the Tour in there,' he said. 'If the front door is shut, just go round the side.'

The thought of spending the afternoon in a cool bar drinking cool beer and watching the Tour de France was cruelly attractive. At the very least, though, I had to see if I could get Rocky sorted first. The intermittent fault had thoroughly defeated even my much-improved understanding of front derailleurs. I needed help. Luckily, I was in the right place. Lander was home to the headquarters of NOLS – the National Outdoor Leadership School. It had a funky, lively, friendly feel, and a host of outdoor shops. I cycled down the attractive main street – shopfronts straight from a cowboy movie, cafés, bookstores, a cinema – to the big, and rather empty, bike shop. I explained the gear mech's erratic behaviour, and its erratic responses to my attempts to fix it. As usual, the mechanics, seeing the 'I'm on tour right now' panniers, stopped what they were doing and put Rocky on the stand.

They tried all the things I'd been trying – tightening the cable, adjusting the limit screws, spraying lubricant at random. No top gears. They put in a new cable. No top gears. Then, one of them tweaked the angle of the changing mech slightly and bingo; all my gears were suddenly smoothly accessible. It made no sense at all. They agreed it made no sense at all. I paid all of $8.42 for this wonderful service and asked them about the road ahead.

'It's eighty miles to Dubois,' they said. 'You can't really stop before then. It's an Indian Reservation. You need a special permit to camp.'

'What about Fort Washakie?' I asked. Fort Washakie was about half the distance.

'Don't think so. It's very small. You should stay here today.'

Eighty miles after lunch in a howling head-wind or... I rode back down the main street with my smoothly changing gears and straight to the bar. The bar turned out to be another microbrewery, called, for reasons I never discovered, Cowfish. I had a cold, malty, utterly delicious beer and sat with a row of guys on bar stools and watched Frank Schleck win the Alpe d'Huez stage. I'd cycled up Alpe d'Huez with friends and, in a crowd of millions, watched Armstrong overtake Basso, the year that the steep ten-mile climb had been a time-trial. It was awesome stuff. And it made my trip feel like a breezy holiday.

I spent the remains of the afternoon in the bookshop café, writing and chatting. The owner, a Vietnam vet, and the younger man who was serving, told me they thought it was all too late. 'Global warming doesn't even exist, according to Bush. The guys behind him know it does, though. But people won't deal with it voluntarily. Needs to be federal legislation. And control of Exxon. Fast. And that's not going to happen.' They asked me how many huge trucks and SUVs I'd seen between there and El Paso. They said the USA needed a decent rail system and that they thought SUVs were outrageous. Neither of them drove. 'There must only be two men in the whole of the USA without a car. And they are both in here!' the owner said. Then they told me what a good place Lander was. 'It's diverse. NOLS brings in lots of interesting folk. There's free camping down at the park. And people will look after you. If you're ever in trouble on your ride, come back to Lander.' It was an oasis of an afternoon.

~

19th July. A month into the trip! I rode out of lovely Lander feeling full of bounce and gratitude for the blue sky and a slight wind, and into the First Nations reservation. A sign read 'Mother Nature needs help. Please do not litter', followed by a row of trailer houses surrounded by dead cars and burnt-out machinery. A dispirited air seemed to hang over the whole reservation, and it was the only place so far that I'd met sustained unfriendliness – from whites and First Nations alike. It took me completely by surprise. The exception was a trading store just outside Fort Washakie, where I was greeted by two young girls who sold me a flavoured 'snow-cone' for a dollar. I told them I would send them a postcard from Anchorage, and chatted to the storeowner, and an artist called Daniel. Both said they were disgusted at the lack of action on climate change, and that they were looking into getting solar panels. 'It is talked about,' Daniel said, 'But mostly in private. This is an oil state...'

At Crowheart Butte, a flat-topped hill that seemed to rise from nowhere, I finally learned something of Chief Washakie. He had been a chief of the Eastern Shoshone, and the hill marked the site of a battle against the Crow Indians, over hunting-rights. Washakie's people had won; and the heart of a Crow Indian had graced the end of a spear in the celebratory war dances. It was not a particularly edifying story, though Washakie had been a diplomat as well as a warrior. He had forbidden his people to attack white settlers – even when they were wiping out the animals the Shoshoni hunted – and his good relations with the U.S. government eventually allowed him to secure the Wind River reservation.

The headwind returned. I bought some pink lemonade and a power bar in a gas station from a woman who refused to return my smile, and drank it outside on a bench in the shade. I'd just lost the top gear on the front changer, again. Fortunately I realised it must be the new cable stretching just before I took violent action, and tightened the barrel adjuster instead. 'Please,' I said out loud, 'let me have ONE DAY with no gear trouble!' As the day wore on the scenery gradually changed from immense to spectacular. Salmon and terracotta buttresses striped with cream rose from the banks of the Wind River – clearly named for good reason. Well into the evening and with twenty miles still to go before the first campsite outside the reservation, I had a flat tyre. The back wheel, of course. No problem, I thought: the slime will seal it. I pumped the tyre up. A mile or so later, it was almost flat again. Green slime had splattered all over the wheels, the panniers and my legs, but appeared to have achieved little else. Stupidly, I had no inner tubes left that hadn't already been punctured. The tyre was holding just about enough pressure to cycle on. Dusk was imminent. I could stop and mend an inner tube, or keep going. At that precise moment, the wind dropped, and hundreds of hungry mosquitoes immediately converged on my arms, legs and head. I kept going, the almost flat tyre making for a sludgy ride along the beautiful valley, whose striking stripy buttresses I failed to fully appreciate. I crawled into Dubois under a huge orange sunset well after nine, and squeaked into the KOA campsite just before the friendly receptionist left the already closed office. I put my tent up, and crawled straight into it. Even the shower could wait.

Next day, I woke late and still tired. The face in the mirror after a wonderful long shower still had a wild, drawn look, though there was something peaceful there too. I was ravenous. I walked into one-street, wooden-fronted Dubois and had breakfast in the Cowboy Café, as recommended by the Lander bike shop. Fried eggs, hash browns, toast, orange juice and a hot chocolate. The café was packed. I sat outside. A young man with a gaunt face, shaved head and a white T-shirt with 'US Army' on it was loudly holding forth. 'My dad and I, we're known by the sheriffs here for taking on an armed man who was cutting trees in the middle of a national forest campsite ... I designed the logo for the Vietnam Vets and they liked it so much they made me an honorary vet, the youngest ever...' And so on. Every topic of conversation was swiftly turned to his achievements. He'd raced bikes at champion level, shot firearms and had relatives in any country you cared to mention. It was fascinating – and irritating as hell. When everyone else on the table had left, he turned to me. 'Hi, I'm Dan. Good to meet you. I remember when I was cycling in the Nationals...' There was no staunching the flow. Even when I carried on writing my journal he carried on talking.

In the end, I gave up and listened. In between the list of achievements he did, in fact, have interesting things to say. He talked about the awfulness of war, and how outrageous it was that the presidents who declared them never actually had to fight themselves. Most interesting to me were his views on climate change. 'The United States could and should be a world leader in dealing with global warming,' he declared. Mayor Chavez had said pretty much the same thing. There was something in that, I thought. If the United States ever did take a constructive stance on climate change, it was unlikely to want to be seen following someone else's lead – Europe's, say, or China's. More likely that the USA would position itself as world leader in that context, like so many others. There was a potential source of real optimism in that thought.

Back at the campsite, I sat in the sun and fixed inner tubes. I was finding it hard to get the glue to take properly. Just when I thought one was done, the edges of the little patch would curl away from the tube, and I'd have to peel it off and start again. Before I knew it, it was lunchtime and the wind was up. I wanted to keep moving. Chris was now on the same continent, and we were hoping to coincide in Missoula, about seven days away – headwinds permitting. On the other hand, I was still feeling (and looking) pretty wind-blasted. It was six days since I'd had a full day off, and even the previous day's half day had been over forty miles of solid hot wind slog. And there was, I'd noticed, an internet café in town. I went to the campsite office, just to see if there would be space for me that night. 'No problem, honey. And there's live music here tonight.' Live music! Practically next to my tent! That settled it. I would have a day off, and then tackle Togwotee Pass in the morning.

I spent the whole afternoon in the internet café. By the end of it, the blog and I were – at last! – in the same place. Then I sat on a bench in the campsite in the early evening sunshine writing postcards. Various people came and visited. A mountain-biker from the Netherlands, who was riding the off-road continental divide route. Barb and Don from Florida, who had one of the campsite cabins. A woman in a turquoise tracksuit with bright red hair and a Pekinese dog. 'My ancestors lived in *tepees*,' she said, with a curious mixture of pride and disgust. A chuck wagon and food stall had been setting up all afternoon and barbecue smells drifted across the site. When food was announced, the sole vegetarian item was potatoes. Even the beans had meat in them. I stacked a plate with potatoes – which were delicious – and went back to my bench to listen to the music. It was classic country and western. 'Now here's a song about a wonderful cattle dawg...' Even I thought it was bad. I wrote my journal. People drifted by to chat. The light faded and I sat on, watching the musicians pack up and experiencing again that recurring sense of peace.

Not far from El Paso, New Mexico

A dairy farm in hot, dry New Mexico

The first, hot campsite in New Mexico – with
wilting cacti and concrete pitches

Yep, they did!

Kate, Rocky and flowering cacti, New Mexico

Flowering cacti, New Mexico

Ranch sign, New Mexico

Tempting to leave the beaten track....

Even downhills are hard work in hot headwinds

Crossing into Colorado

'Don't worry, I'll bring a small one' – Kate,
Rocky, and Tom's neighbour's plane

The ancient settlement of Mesa Verde, Colorado

Mule deer, often seen from the road

Spectacular evening light, on the far side of Poncha Pass, Colorado

After the shortcut

Wyoming pony

Split Rock, Wyoming

A great hill-dog when not on roadworks duty...

Peaceful cycling on quiet roads in Wyoming

Running out of energy in Yellowstone National Park

Jackson Lake, Wyoming

Beautiful Montana – where the roads only go downwards

Montana – a succession of hot dry summers

Northern Montana

Chris' introduction to long distance cycling ...
early days in Montana

The bikes getting reaquainted in Northern Montana

Leaving the USA for Canada

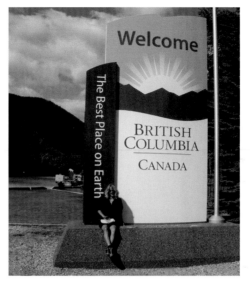

Into Canada – the greener, saner neighbour?

The best ice cream ever – 'tiger tiger' (orange and liquorice)
and butterscotch, at Grasmere, British Columbia

Chris, just north of Grasmere, BC

Chris dodging crickets in BC

Kate and the bikes just north of Grasmere, BC

Exposed river terraces, off the Columbia River

Whole mountainsides of dead trees

Glacier Highway, Alberta

Chris at the entrance to Mount Robson National Park

Chris on Highway 16, en route to Prince George

Kate contemplates an RV. Environmental bad
guys or downsized, modern nomads?

Chris with Miko, who'd acquired the habit of carrying ten extra litres of water

Round the world x4: Karl and his huskies

Coming into Smithers

Kate dwarfed by a truck at the Kitwanga Junction

Sea-level rise predicted as far as the Rockies?

Kate and the ultimately doomed attempt
to keep Chris' bike on the road

Chris near the beginning of the beautiful Cassiar Highway

Chris on the Cassiar Highway

Flowers on the Cassiar Highway

Duct tape – never leave home without it!

Chris on the Alaska Highway, looking toward Kluane National Park

There's a Great Divide between where we are and where
we need to get to..... Chris on the Alaska Highway

Decision time – heading North to Alaska

Autumn approaching fast

Aspen leaves

Autumn colour

Autumn on the Alaska Highway

Chris, not far from Sheep Mountain, Alaska –
about to be rescued by the Clooney-man

Chris on the Alaska Highway, back wheel only
just holding up. The Wrangell Mountains.

Chugach Mountains, Alaska

Arresting scenery near Sheep Mountain Lodge

Columbia Glacier, Alaska

One of the snouts of the Columbia Glacier, Alaska

~

I woke rested and ready to go. Barb and Don, swinging gently on the suspended wooden seat in front of their cabin, gave me a bag of walnuts. 'We couldn't think what else to give you,' they said. I was touched. They seemed to spend hours on the swing-seat, and they both emanated a deep sense of calm. I cycled out of Dubois via the food mall and the post office. Then I couldn't resist the Bighorn Sheep Centre. It was odd (from a British perspective) to think of sheep as wild animals. These particular sheep had evolved in Asia a few million years previously and crossed over to North America on snow bridges. When the bridges melted, they were stranded, and had remained ever since. Displays explained how drastically we had affected their habitats and reduced their numbers, but how we were now working to remedy the situation. The tone was optimistic. The message: we have entered an era of conscious conservation, after an era of unthinking environmental damage. What a wonderful vision! If only it were true. It might even *be* true, I thought, in relation to the local threats to bighorn sheep. How could it be made true in relation to global climate change? That was the question. An era of conscious climate conservation after several generations of unthinking environmental damage. How best to usher it in?

I finally got going for real just after ten. It was glorious easy riding. There was a big blue sky, and sunshine. My body was going through that wonderful transformation that happens on a long outdoor trip. I was tanned (in a stripy sort of way) and, despite all the bagels, steadily getting thinner. And fitter. That day, I felt great.

About an hour later, I ran into road works, and was brought to a halt by a man with a stop sign. A tiny dog in a fluorescent jacket stood on her hind legs at his feet. 'I'm really sorry,' he said, 'but we can't let cyclists through. I can give you a lift, though.' I heaved Rocky into the truck and sat in the front with the little dog – a poodle-Chihuahua cross, he said, and a great hill dog when she wasn't on roadwork duty. It was a gift of fourteen uphill miles. Accepting a lift after being told by roadwork people that I had to was definitely not cheating. Back on my two own wheels, I climbed steadily up the Togwatee Pass. I was just thinking that I could do with a café, when one materialised around a corner. Inside was a chef, wearing a huge, multicoloured chef's hat. He made me an enormous salad, and commented on the weather. Hotter than usual. A gift of an opening.

'Do you think it's global warming?' I asked.

'No,' he said, 'I think it's the sun.' He rapidly warmed to his theme. 'The sun is putting out more heat. They call it sunspots. Plus, anything we're adding to the atmosphere now came from the earth in the first place. Oil was always in the ground combusting and causing emissions. What do you think caused the end of the last ice age, cavemen smoking too much dope?' I struggled to muster a response, but fortunately he didn't seem to want one. I sat outside digesting this extraordinary point of view, watching the world go by and enjoying the sun and my salad. Cola, a brown collie-cross, lay under the table while a sandy coloured mutt watched my plate, intently, from a respectful distance.

The next ten or so miles climbed steadily upwards. There were flowers everywhere: lilac, lupin-like flowers, brilliant yellow daisy-like flowers and masses of tiny, violet stars. The road was flanked by huge meadows, swathed with colour. The flower meadows sloped up towards big stands of tall trees and, behind the trees, high mountains reared pale on the far horizon. A creamy yellow butterfly flew alongside me for a while, and then gently overtook. The only thing marring this idyll was the swarm of blackflies that accompanied me as I climbed. Too slow to get away from them, they landed with ease and took chunks out of me, with a clear preference for my left thigh. Cycling shorts were no barrier whatsoever. Bill had mentioned blackflies.

'Do they bite?' I'd asked.

'Bite?' he'd said, with a grin, 'They drill into you. By the time you realise they're doing it, it's too late. The itch afterwards makes a mozzi bite seem like a pleasant sensation.'

It was not a bad description.

At the summit of Togwatee Pass (pronounced 'Togatee', a park ranger told me later) a tiny lake was set against the mountains. I wandered about taking photographs of flowers. The road stayed high for miles, mountains and meadows alongside. I sat at a vista point and gazed and gazed. It would have been so good to stay up there. More and more I wanted just to *be* in those wild places, rather than endlessly move on. Like life. To be really in it rather than just passing through. Eventually, I pulled myself away and started the long, intermittent

,descent toward Moran Junction. The road rose and fell. Suddenly, around a corner, a spectacular line of jagged, spiky mountains were silhouetted pale grey across the horizon. The Tetons. It was one of the most stunning mountain skylines I'd ever seen. For miles I cycled towards them, dipping in and out of the trees.

~

Just before the junction, I stopped at a service station. The woman inside gave me a hard look. 'Yes? What can I help you find?' she asked, in a tone suggesting she harboured a strong suspicion I didn't really want anything other than to bring my undesirable presence in out of the heat. The gas station sold real ice cream. I had a double scoop of almond-fudge and huckleberry and stood outside, against a wall in the shade, exchanging greetings with motor-bikers coming in for gas. One of those brief times when the snagging and clutching of ordinary life suddenly lets go and there you are, out of the mainstream, free from any 'next we must do this, this and this', present and at peace in that moment.

At Moran Junction, a beautiful ox-bow in the river curved in front of the Teton Mountain range, rising vast and silent on the skyline. The place had a deeply serene feel. Definitely a place to come back to. For now, I turned north, heading for Yellowstone. It was not long before I crossed into the Teton National Park. The next camping, a ranger told me as I paid my entrance fee on the park boundary, was at Colter Bay Village, ten miles ahead. I was suddenly tired and a touch sun-dazed. The young man at the campsite entrance reduced the rate from $5.80 to $2.00 on the grounds that I was the first cyclist that summer going from south to north. He gave me a map, which seemed a bit excessive until I realised that Colter Bay Village was an enormous complex sprawled over several miles and complete with RV pitches, tent campsite, gift shop, food mall, launderette and showers (all a good mile or so from the tent sites). It was very commercial, very large, and very busy. I lost my way to my designated tent spot and by the time I'd found it and put the tent up, and then cycled back for a shower, they'd closed for the night. I took my smelly self back to tent city, ate a tortilla wrap with nothing in it, put my stuff in a bear box and retreated. On the brink of arriving at Yellowstone, my camera card was full. I scrolled through hundreds of snaps, looking for deletable ones. The pictures of the Tetons were all foreground. The mountains themselves had vanished, like ghost mountains or grey rainbows in the sun.

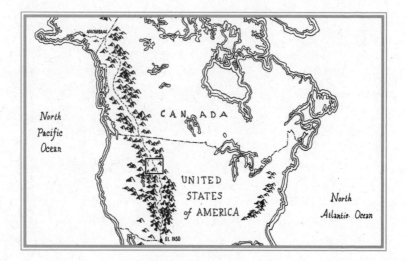

CHAPTER SEVEN
Calling Chris

'If the people lead, the leaders will follow.'
Gandhi

I woke tired. I looked tired, and I felt tired. I remembered from previous trips the fantastic feeling of hitting a rhythm on a big hill; the exultation at realising that my body could do this and at feeling I could keep going indefinitely. On this trip I had scarcely felt that at all. I was doing the miles, but they almost always seemed a hard slog. And I shouldn't have been so weary after such a great ride the day before. I didn't understand it. Neither hills nor heat were new to me. The thought that age might have something to do with it still lurked at the back of my mind. It was not a thought I wanted to entertain.

Rocky's pannier rack had worked loose, and needed the one Allen key I wasn't carrying. I stopped at the service station on my way out of Colter Bay Village to borrow one. The mechanics came out to watch me wield it. They were friendly and incredulous. 'You started where? You're headed WHERE? Are you on medication or what?'

The northwest corner of Wyoming essentially consists of two huge parks. I was cycling through Grand Teton National Park, headed for Yellowstone National Park – which I realised when I arrived I'd confused in my head with Yosemite. I kept wondering when Half-Dome was going to appear on the horizon. It was an odd day. I spent most of it cycling through pine trees I couldn't see beyond, on a road with no hard shoulder and lots of traffic. It was hard not to come to hate the traffic, and not just because of the occasional idiots. One of these blasted his horn and shouted 'Get a f*****g car' as he revved past. It was the first time I'd had any hassle at all from motorists, somehow ironic that it was in a park dedicated to conserving and celebrating nature. I wished him (and some of the RVs that routinely shaved my legs as they roared past) a recurring flat tyre. Mostly, though, the traffic was benign but relentless. It was surely a positive thing that people valued mountain environments and were coming to spend time in them. But what kind of crazy culture are we that we put fences around 'special' bits of nature and then travel to view them in cars in such huge numbers that we end up threatening to harm the very places we've chosen to treasure? Disconnection gone mad! It wasn't just Yellowstone, of course. The intensity of traffic in a beautiful mountain park reminded me of nowhere so much as where I'd not long left – the English Lake District.

Occasional views broke through the trees. One was of the Tetons across Jackson Lake. The mountains looked more solid in the morning light and patches of snow shone on the high tops. (Grand Teton is a little under 14,000 feet.) Then a spectacular canyon with Snake River hurtling along the bottom of it and a forest of dead trees – just trunks, grey and without branches – on either side. A sign explained this to be the legacy of a 1988 forest fire that had leapt the 500ft canyon, putting human-made 'fire barriers' thoroughly into perspective. I sat on a wall looking down into the canyon watching the swallows. These ones had emerald green backs, buff heads, white tummies and tails that were flat rather than forked. Watching those birds, I felt a powerful emotion. It was familiar, but I struggled to analyse it. The swallows – the wildlife in general – lifted my spirits, and left me a sense of peace. But there was also a twisting sadness at the ways we threaten their worlds and lives; an anger, a desire to protect, a sort of fierce compassion. As I sat, a raven landed on top of a dead tree next to me, flew over my head and landed again. He stopped croaking and made a noise I hadn't heard before, a bit like wood knocking gently on hollow wood. The bird lowered his head each time he made the sound. Knock. Knock. Knock.

I was expecting a long downhill into Grant Village. The downhill never came. It was flat or uphill all day. Beyond Grant Village, two passes were marked on the map. By mid-afternoon, there was no way I felt like climbing over two passes. The derailleur was playing up again. I'd only cycled forty-two miles, and I was already dead beat. For the first time, I wondered, seriously, whether I could make it to Alaska. Two thirds of the ride was still ahead of me.

Wild camping is not permitted in National Parks. The official – and not at all wild – campsite at Grant Village was almost as big as Colter Bay, and had a highly formalised allocation system. I was assigned C91. C91, when I reached it, turned out to be entirely on an incline. There was no flat ground whatsoever, not even enough for my diminutive tent. I cast about for an alternative, spotted an empty one and cycled back to reception, explaining my lack of enthusiasm for a night on a slope.

'Could I have C101 instead, please?' I asked.

'Sorry,' came the firm reply, 'C101 is not a "hiker/biker" site. It is for RVs only.'

'What if I pay the same as an RV would?' I suggested.

'Ma'am, we are not allowed to sell RV sites to hiker/bikers. End of story.'

The Yellowstone campsites had a totally different feel from the Kampsite of Americas or KOAs. The KOAs always left me feeling they would find *somewhere* to fit in a late cyclist, even if it was the laundry room. In the parks, there would be a rule about it, and no one would bend an inch. The cyclist – clearly a form of low-life – would be tolerated within the rules but would, if necessary, be expelled back out on the road with no compunction at all.

~

Next morning I was woken at 6.00am by that most hated of morning alarm calls, 'Rise and Shine!' hollered across the ten identical yellow tents housing a Christian Bible Class/Scout Group that clustered on the site next to mine (which I'd been told was empty!) A couple of helper/parents, Mike and Barb, had come over the previous evening. 'The Scouts are back at eight. We're not supposed to drink in front of them. Quick, have a beer!' Mike had handed me a delicious cold Cromo – oh boy – and then a shot of lemon vodka that, remembering the vodka hangovers of my distant youth, I'd resisted. Now I gave in to the racket – Christians again! – and got up, thinking that an early start would not be such a bad idea anyway. I re-re-re-adjusted the tension on the gear cable and was away about eight, heading for the two passes and, beyond that, Old Faithful.

It was cloudy. Little outbursts of rain scattered across the morning. The two passes – both traversing the Continental Divide – were, to my surprise, barely climbs at all. Sometimes it is a great psychological advantage to be cycling with a small-scale map from which you can glean only the barest hints about the road ahead. Suddenly I was there. Old Faithful. The small town consisted almost entirely of an enormous, disorienting tourist site with bad signposts. Signs for 'Food', for example, appeared and then disappeared before you'd actually encountered anything edible at all. I found my way to the main geyser. There was a steaming mound in the ground, surrounded by a huge crowd in a viewing amphitheatre. Nothing happened. I waited, camera at the ready. Nothing.

Giving in, I tracked down some food and decided to get out of there as fast as I could. There was something constraining and depressing about the huge commercialised area that completely surrounded Old Faithful. And I never did see it erupt. Back on the road, though, the landscape was powerful. Steam rose all around in wisps and billows from the pale ground. It must have looked astonishing in winter, steam emerging from snow. A single buffalo stood still, framed by trees. A little after Madison Junction I stopped by the river and ate a bagel. A sign told me that the Madison Elk Herd favoured this valley. I could see no elk, but fish were jumping in the river and large red dragonflies dipped and hovered above it.

I was just about to cross the park boundary when a maroon car pulled along side. The window hummed down. 'Did you drink the Gatorade?' enquired the male occupant, with a broad grin. It was maroon-saloon man! We both pulled off the road. He introduced himself as Mike. I apologised for my less than gracious response to his Gatorade offer. Mike said he'd realised exactly what sort of headspace I'd been in – and that I had in fact needed a drink. 'I've put you in my book. It's about people I meet when I'm on the road,' he said. And then that global warming was 'a pile of crock. For every scientist that says it's happening there's one that says it isn't.'

'I'll put you in *my* book,' I said, deciding that, under the circumstances, a lecture on the degree of scientific consensus would be badly misplaced. We parted after I'd accepted a bottle of icy cold water.

Not long afterwards I saw elk grazing in the distance and then, just beyond a sign saying 'Bald Eagle Management Area. No Stopping', an enormous bird that was unmistakably bald, sitting in a dead tree right by the road. I stopped. The eagle didn't seem remotely bothered. Cyclists deserved *some* perks in this park, I thought.

I reached the town of West Yellowstone about three-thirty and refuelled in a great bike shop/café. I drank coffee, ate cookies, bought new inner tubes and a patch kit, used their high-pressure pump, and chatted about the road ahead. 'Big Sky, the next town, is about fifty miles away. There's not much between here and there. But you've got light until nearly nine...' I decided to go for it. I'd been having mixed feelings about Chris joining me. I wanted to see him, of course. But I was enjoying travelling solo; enjoying the ready connection with people I met, enjoying my independence. Travelling alone is in some ways very easy. No negotiation about when to stop or how far to go. No dealing with someone else's emotions or energy levels. But I had dreamt about Chris the previous night and woken, for the first time, feeling straightforwardly impatient to see him, as if I had resolved something. I left, aiming for Big Sky with a sense of relief at being out of the National Park (which I was sure I hadn't done justice to) and headed out with hard tyres and high spirits into Montana.

~

It was about four in the afternoon. Fifty miles down, fifty to go. The landscape opened up. A lush river, distant hills. It was beautiful, and the first fifteen miles were a fast downhill exhilarating scoot. Then a steady climb. Thunder. Clouds were gathering, though the sky looked less ominous when I took off my sunglasses. At one point I glanced left and saw lightning framed between the mountain skyline and dark trees. Occasional blasts of rain and the smell of water on hot tarmac.

At the top of the climb the landscape opened still further into a really gorgeous valley, wide and green, wooded hills on each side. Best of all, the Gallatin River was running the same way as me. For miles and miles the road was either flat, or sloped gently downhill. Once, in the distance, I saw a dark, huge-antlered moose, and then a flashing 'moose-warning' sign, powered by solar. I stopped to photograph it and a mosquito bit my underarm. Montana mosquitoes seemed to have mastered the art of flying in the wind though this, admittedly, was a mere breeze by Wyoming standards. When I stopped, the crickets sounded like static electricity in the grass. Standing there with Rocky in the beautiful evening I thought about Mike's throwaway comment. For every scientist that says it's happening there's one that says it isn't. It was such a widespread view. And hardly surprising given how climate change was reported. Even in the non-Fox media, some notion of 'balance' often gave the climate change sceptics almost equal air-time, leaving the impression that there was a 50:50 split in the scientific community. In fact, the number of genuine scientists genuinely uncertain whether human-caused climate change is underway is minute. The actual ratio is more like 99:1.

Not long after, I passed a tempting row of small wooden cabins for rent, right by the river and bathed in evening sunshine, vivid between dark clouds. Then the Corral Hotel that Mike had mentioned – a proper motel with cars and trucks outside and a café/restaurant that looked lively and fun. But for some reason I had it in my head that I was going to make it to Big Sky or bust – and that I didn't need to spend $60 on a motel when camping would do. So I blasted on, reaching Big Sky just as the light was beginning to fade. Big Sky was almost entirely a building site, full of future ski resort developments. There was no campsite, and nowhere obvious to wild camp. A truck pulled over and a friendly local inside warned me against continuing. 'The road ahead is really dangerous,' he said. 'It gets narrow and the trucks are bad. Not somewhere to be at dusk.'

I went to the only hotel – The Comfort Inn – and paid much more than I would have at the Corral for a characterless, overpriced room by the road, way beyond my budget. What the heck. It was nine in the evening, I'd just done 104 miles and the shower was awesome. I ate a tortilla, and tackled the mini-mountain of jobs that always veered into focus as soon as I spent a night inside. I wrote my journal, recharged the phone and camera, washed socks, tried to find a computer for blog-writing and made various phone calls. Motel nights were busy – it was much more relaxing in the tent. Finally, I rang Chris. In the middle of talking to him I had such a powerful premonition that I was going to be hit from behind by a truck the next day that it completely derailed me from what I was saying.

Leaving Big Sky in the morning, the next thirty miles were horrendous. Death valley! It was narrow, had virtually no hard shoulder and was infested with hundreds of heavy trucks (as in lorries) many towing truck-length flatbed trailers and all driving as if on drugs or working piece-rates or both. It reminded me of the bus-drivers on the road into Bogotá, Colombia, all going totally flat-out and leaning at crazy angles. Only this was worse. A sign at the beginning of the narrowest, busiest section proclaimed that 'Accident Reduction Measures' were in effect – but what these were or whether they were having any positive impact was not clear. White metal crosses at the road's edge marked where they'd failed. I didn't feel fear, exactly – just a keen awareness that this was dangerous. And a fierce determination to stay in one piece. I concentrated on trying to hear what was coming up behind, difficult given the noise of traffic coming the other way. The truck that nearly got me was on the approach to a bridge. The bridge was narrower than the road and had no shoulder at all. Metal barriers all along it penned the traffic into a slender space. Some instinct prompted me to stop just before it and immediately a double-length truck blasted past, not slowing at all, missing me by inches even though I'd pulled over. It would have smashed me into the metal had I been on the bridge. I stood still for a bit, absorbing what had just not happened, and then cycled on, totally focused on staying alive.

The road widened out at Gallatin Gateway. A sign said 'Pottery and Award Winning Cinnamon Rolls, 5 miles.' I cycled straight to it, a small shop set back from the road, and sat outside in a suspended chair drinking coffee from a beautiful red and brown handmade mug, swinging gently in one of those set-aside moments of peace while the highway traffic blasted onwards just across the lawn.

~

I swear that Montana, if you're travelling south to north, is all downhill. There was always a river running alongside me, and it was always going my way. Montana began to restore my confidence, which was seriously flagging after days of feeling too tired too soon. Perhaps the conditions really had been quite hard and it wasn't that I was aging and past it after all. I sent Chris an exuberant text. 'If it's not 110 degrees, or a 5000ft climb or 90mph headwind, I can still do the miles!'

Then, on a small, quiet road in the outskirts of Belgrade, something extraordinary happened. A black Subaru slowed alongside. A woman inside shouted, 'Kate, Kate!' I looked into the car. It was Marcia, my friend and housemate from Fort Collins days. I hadn't seen her for eighteen years. She, her husband Chris, and son Andreas – neither of whom I'd met before – now lived on the east coast. They'd just flown into Bozeman and were heading for a Yellowstone holiday in a hire car. They'd taken a wrong turning when they'd passed me. 'Look!' said Marcia (who had no idea I was even in the country) 'a woman, cycling alone. How unusual.' And then, 'Good heavens, she looks awfully like Kate.' 'Yeah, right,' Chris had replied, but had turned the car to humour her... We sat on the grass under a tree and spent

145

an hour or so trying to catch up on nearly two decades. And then I cycled on. A totally weird and wonderful encounter.

At Three Forks I stopped at the tourist information, which was housed in a converted caboose. Extracts from the story of Lewis and Clark, key characters in the extraordinary tale of European expansion across the 'New World', were recounted in large posters on the walls. In 1804, Captains Lewis and Clark had been charged by Thomas Jefferson to trace the Missouri to its source and to find a way of connecting the east and west by river – a sort of southerly Northwest Passage for trading purposes. Lewis and Clark led the 'Corps of Discovery' (also tasked with making contact with native tribes, finding suitable sites for forts and trading posts, and drawing up scientific accounts of plants and animals) 8,000 miles from St Louis, Missouri to the mouth of the Columbia River. Amongst other adventures, Clark and a companion had been caught, somewhere nearby, by members of a First Nations tribe. The companion was killed, but Clark was stripped and given a head start on a six-mile run across prickly pears. He outran all his hunters save one (whom he killed bare-handed) made it into forest cover, dived into a river and came up under a log pile where he hid until dark. He then trekked naked for seven days back to a base camp. Whether or not the native people had reason to be hostile to these incomers was not recorded.

I climbed down the steps of the caboose feeling vague. Was it the awesome accounts of derring-do? I cycled passed a row of cafés somehow unable to decide which one to go into. Not derring-do; blood sugar. I managed to make myself stop at a supermarket just before the town ended, and then, eating fruit in the air-conditioned doorway, wrestled with the now familiar dilemma. Stop and catch up with things, or carry on? A hot headwind, also familiar, had picked up over the last few miles, and I had plenty to do if I stopped a bit early. On the other hand, I wanted to get to Missoula the same day as Chris, if possible. And the road for Townsend – a little over thirty miles ahead – was about to turn north, which should leave me with more of a sidewind than a headwind – at least in theory. Once the food hit home, I still had some bounce. I decided to keep going.

Two miles later I ran into roadworks at the foot of a hill. Gravel all across the road. A friendly, trustworthy man in a blue pick-up truck asked me if I wanted a lift to the top. 'Thanks, I'm fine,' I said. This was even more stupid than my response to Maroon Saloon Man. As he drove away the almost cyclable section immediately transformed into ankle-deep gravel. I got off and pushed, slogging my way up the rough surface in the heat until, as the gravel got thicker and thicker, I finally admitted defeat and accepted a lift from a man in a red truck who I judged to be slightly less safe, but on the boundaries of safe enough. He told me he'd just been fired from a platinum mine and said that he was relieved. Then he told me the road ahead was dangerous even beyond the traffic works and offered to take me on at least to Townsend if not Helena. But he stopped and let me out without protest when I declined and even held Rocky while I reloaded the panniers.

It was a wonderful ride after that. I kept thinking the road was going downhill. The whole state seemed to be downhill, though it might have been just that it wasn't uphill. Wide plains stretched ahead, some golden with barley, some green with grass. The plains were rimmed with hills and there was a sweet smell of hay. Swallows rose over the river and the evening sunshine played golden and deep blue shadows across the land.

I came into Townsend. A ninety-eight-mile day. There was a post office and a huge grain processor. A couple of cafés, a bar and the Mustang Hotel, bearing a horse with light-bulb legs lit to look as if they were galloping above the 'Vacancies' sign. At the far end of town was a tiny self-service RV site. I pitched my tent on a grassy spot at the end of the RVs next to a friendly couple with two dogs, and had a shower in a startlingly immaculate shower room. Back at the tent, the couple introduced themselves as Mike and Dee. A storm was brewing, and the high-wind forerunners were already blowing through. The site owner appeared from nowhere. 'Reckon you should move your tent to a more sheltered spot, and away from that tree. Lightning,' he explained cheerfully. Large raindrops began to spatter down as he spoke. Mike came over. Unasked, they both helped me move the tent and all the stuff in it onto a scrappy patch of ground behind the shelter of a row of metal containers in the suddenly torrential rain. When I was safely rehoused, Mike and Dee (who'd offered to let me sleep in the horse compartment of their trailer) invited me over. They were from Pennsylvania, but wanted to move to Montana, buy some land, bring their horses. Quarter horses.

· 'The East is mad,' Mike said. 'Too busy. You can't drive at all at rush-hour. It's violent. And it rains the whole time.'

Dee smoked. She was slim, tall, long dark-blonde hair. Mike had huge smiling brown eyes. They were attractive, and I liked them both.

'Is global warming happening?' (This was Mike.) 'For sure. But people aren't going to change. We need a new source of energy.'

'And maybe a new president?' I asked.

'The president is irrelevant,' Dee said. 'It's the oil companies who are in control. As soon as anyone comes up with a way of using oil more efficiently, they buy the patent and bury it. At the end of the day, it's up to us to sort it out anyway. We are the government.'

They invited me for coffee in the morning. I went back to my tent, deeply happy. I felt alive. I wondered about what Dee had said and how 'we the government' could overcome obstacles to meaningful action. Then I read about the Yellowstone wolves until the storm subsided and slept like a log on my scruffy patch behind the truck containers.

~

25th July, 2006. A blue, blue-sky day. I left the wet tent drying in the sun and had coffee with Mike and Dee. They were off to look at a house with twenty-eight acres. At $289,000, properties with land were a heck of a lot cheaper in Montana than in Cumbria, UK. I hoped they would find what they were looking for. And yet, Jared Diamond in Collapse[32] describes the way in which incomers to Montana, willing and able to pay more than the agricultural value of land for somewhere beautiful to keep horses, somewhere to ride, fish, hike, and retire in peace, have pushed up land prices way beyond the reach of local long-term farmers. Agribusiness elsewhere has not helped either, of course. It made me think of Berry again, and his argument that modern market forces were displacing both sustainable (or relatively sustainable) farming practices – and people. 'What we have called agricultural progress has,' Berry writes, 'in fact involved the forcible displacement of millions of people ... the force used by the communists was military; with us, it has been economic – a "free

---

[32] Jared Diamond (2005) Collapse Penguin Books

market" in which the freest were the richest.'[33]

And Montana, while beautiful, is undoubtedly damaged. Diamond details the cumulative impacts of the sorry history of ecologically ill-informed ways of making money in Montana. Toxic wastes from mining for metal ores, still affecting water, land, wildlife and livestock. Poor logging practices that had often turned 'a forest into something approximating a huge pile of kindling', leaving a legacy of out-of-control forest fires that were fiercer, hotter and altogether more destructive than they would naturally be. Invasive species displacing local biodiversity. Soil erosion and salination. And of course, overuse of water in a state already dry. It did not make for cheerful reading. Hard, too, not to be stuck by the stark contrast between the surface beauty and the underlying destruction; the dark underbelly of our 'civilised' modern lives. Now add climate change to places already under such ecological stress. No wonder their resilience is expected to be low, the predicted impacts so severe.

A quick egg and cheese croissant in town – I could feel my body soaking up the egg in particular – and then back out past the grain plant and the Mustang Hotel. For all Montana's problems, I liked Townsend. A few miles later, at Canyon Ferry Lake, a sign told of gold so plentiful that the prospectors' pans had clogged up. A cyclist stopped and offered me some banana bread. It was delicious. He introduced himself as Elmer, and laughed when I told him I aimed to be in Missoula in two days time. 'You'll never make it in two days,' he said. 'There's a lot of climbing.' Not by Colorado standards, I thought, and couldn't help noticing that Elmer was eating his banana bread with his mouth wide open to reveal bad teeth.

By the time I rode into Helena, the capital city of Montana, it was definitely lunchtime. Helena – also the county seat of Lewis and Clark County – had been nicknamed 'The Queen City of the Rockies'. It was built on the proceeds of gold. In the nineteenth-century gold rush, about $3.6 billion dollars worth of gold was taken from Last Chance Gulch in about twenty years. The main road was still called 'Last Chance Gulch' and followed the meandering path of the original stream, making Helena one of the few US cities not mapped out on a square grid. I was hot, and a bit disorientated. After dithering

---

[33] Wendell Berry (1977) *The Unsettling of America* Avon Books

between a Pizza Hut that did salads but was on the wrong side of the road and a 'Grill' that was on my side of the road but looked overly posh I cycled past both, and found a Taco Bell instead.

Sitting outside I chatted with two of the staff while I ate my burrito. The temperature was in the high nineties. They told me that Montana had not witnessed summer temperatures above the eighties for decades. Now it regularly reached the nineties and hundreds. It was drier, too. And there was hardly any snow in the winter any more. They were convinced it was global warming, and that cars were a key culprit.

'The town is three times the size it used to be. And everyone who used to have one car per family now has three or four. Including us.'

'What would encourage people to drive less?' I asked.

They didn't know. Increases in fuel prices (still unbelievably cheap by European standards) weren't making any difference, they said. This didn't really surprise me. Many cities and towns in the States have been constructed so that people live miles from their nearest source of food, from schools, hospitals, the places they work. With no public transport to speak of, how would people survive *without* a car? Of course, whether they needed four per family and whether those four all needed to be trucks or SUVs was another question. But having multiple trucks was normal. Having a high impact life was normal...

Up ahead was MacDonald Pass. The road rose steadily out of Helena for about ten miles, climbing something over two thousand feet to 6320 feet. If this were Colorado, 6320 feet would be the bottom of the pass, not the top, I thought with, just possibly, a touch of smugness. There were open, all-round views at the summit; not super-dramatic but lovely. Wooded hills, wide valleys. Then a winding swoop down the other side. A sign said 'Water'. I stopped. My three bottles were all nearly empty. A small stone construction with a pipe emerging from it sat by the side of the road, and a constant stream of clear cold water ran from the pipe. Perfect!

At Elliston there was a gas station, and a saloon bar. I asked the young man serving in the gas station whether there was any camping. 'Yes,' he said, 'just before you get to the Interstate. About twenty miles down the road. But if you turn off and take Highway 141 instead it's a whole lot prettier. A bit hillier, and definitely longer. It'll be a much nicer ride, though.' Decision time. Chris would arrive in Missoula the next day. The fastest route I could take was definitely the interstate. But that would mean seventy-odd miles of interstate, which was less than appealing. The 141 swung north-west before it headed west to Missoula. There were no towns at all for the first fifty-odd miles. It would definitely be quieter, and much more beautiful. Remote even. But it would put me in Missoula very late the next evening. Chris wasn't exactly expecting me to make it early, or even necessarily the next day. We'd already agreed I would probably take the scenic route, and he was expecting me sometime over the next couple of days. But I'd been racking up the miles to try to get there as early as I could, so we could have a leisurely first evening together.

The junction was about ten miles ahead. 'Any camping on the 141?' I asked.

'Nothing official. But you can wild camp, no problem. Well, except for the grizzlies.'

I sat outside the gas station eating cherry ice cream. The gas station man, who was also the local fire chief, wandered back out to join me. 'You can camp here, behind the shop, if you like,' he said, with a friendly grin. This was definitely tempting. But I still had some more miles in my legs and I wanted to get my journal up to date before I joined Chris. I strongly suspected that, if I stayed where I was, I would not get much writing done at all, but would end up chatting in the saloon with the fireman. 'Thanks,' I said, 'that's really kind. Need to do some more miles, though.' I cycled slowly away. Shortly afterwards, one of Rocky's gear cables suddenly went slack and the gear shifter stopped working altogether, leaving me with only one gear. Fortunately, it was a good one. I kept going. I would sort it later.

We were in an utterly beautiful valley – sunshine, river, swallows, mountains on the skyline ahead – and I was torn. I badly wanted to be cycling into wilder areas and absolutely the last place I felt like spending my final day of solo cycling was the interstate. On the other hand, Chris had been so accommodating in so many ways, and was now making a huge effort to meet up with me, much further south than we'd originally anticipated. Before all those days off in Colorado, we'd thought we would meet up in Banff, Canada, and Chris had arranged a week's work in Vancouver. Now he was coming all the way from Vancouver to join me in Missoula, by Greyhound bus. The least I could do was get to into town at a civilised hour, ideally less than completely trashed. After six weeks or so apart, we deserved a romantic evening. In addition, Rocky's gears were currently not functioning at all, strongly suggesting that seventy-odd miles on the relatively flat interstate would be a smarter choice than ninety-odd miles on a hilly route. The opt-out would be to wild camp tonight just before the turnoff and make the decision in the morning. But my period was just ending, making me especially attractive, I'd been told, to grizzlies. It would be silly to be eaten just before our reunion. And so, with a pang, I cycled past the turnoff for Highway 141 and an off-the-beaten-track section of road that was to join the list of alluring options I hadn't chosen. It would remain wild and beautiful in my head.

I reached the campsite at Garrison well after eight. It was wonderful. I felt bizarrely rewarded for my decision. I was greeted by the owner whose mission in life seemed not just to make campers feel welcome but also like valued and trustworthy human beings. He showed me around. There were warm, clean bathrooms, open all night, and a large kitchen with a table – perfect for journaling. 'Please, use the coffee supplies, microwave, book swap, videos...' he said. 'Nothing is ever stolen here. You can trust all the campers. But,' he said, a harder expression fleeting across his kindly face, 'if vehicle lights come down the drive after eleven at night I'm there in thirty seconds. And I AM ARMED.'

I pitched my tent on grass by some tall trees. The couple next to me, sleeping in the open back of their truck, offered me a sandwich and told me that Kalispell and Glacier National Park up ahead were unbelievably beautiful. I had a gorgeous hot shower and sent a text to Chris, who was, according to *his* text, just about to cross the border from Canada into the USA. Then I sat at the kitchen table, catching up on the last few days. I wrote and wrote, until about midnight. And then I went to bed, at peace with the interstate decision and ready to blast to Missoula (gears permitting), rejoin Chris, and begin the part of the journey that would be shared.

~

I woke late. My neighbours had gone, taking with them the expensive super-strength Colorado Deet mosquito repellent I'd loaned them the night before. This was so out of keeping with the campsite's ethos

I decided they must just have forgotten. I worked on Rocky's gears, swatting mosquitoes and eating my morning bagel. Rocky's gears were absolutely fine upside down, and they remained immaculately well behaved while I rode unloaded around the campsite. It was ten by the time I got away. I gritted my teeth and joined Interstate 90. The gears stopped working completely about two miles later.

After twenty something miles I stopped in Drummond for a second breakfast or an early lunch. A man came over to chat. He and his wife and daughter had cycled across the States from coast to coast three years earlier, and seeing other touring cyclists made them nostalgic. His wife came to find me in the Wagon Wheel café and told me about their trip and how they'd not just remained on speaking terms (the daughter was a teenager) but got closer. As I was leaving, Mike offered to help with the gears. I was riding around the Wagon Wheel car park, trying to coax them back to life and, even as he spoke, they started to work again. Besides which, his main suggestion had been to pour a pint of WD40 into the grifters, a course of action the wisdom of which I was less than fully convinced. No sooner had I left than the gears jammed again, this time in top gear on the middle ring. F*** it! I thought, *I am not stopping again.* This particular gear was fine on the flat, anyway. Every time I came to anything remotely uphill, though, I had to take the panniers off, turn the bike upside down, change gear by hand to a lower one, re-right the bike, and put the panniers back on again. It was, to say the least, frustrating.

The whole day was frustrating. For much of the way, a quieter road ran parallel to the interstate. But this road had not been designed with the landing of fighter jets in mind and I constantly had to choose between largely uninterrupted cycling in heavy traffic or the frequent need to engage in upside-down manual gear changing on the quieter road. My loyal companion the hot headwind had picked up in strength and was with me all day. And there was no word at all from Chris, despite a stream of messages from me. 'Surprise! Am coming in on the I90, should be at Missoula early pm XXX'. 'Am fifty miles away! Where are you? XX'. 'Am twenty miles away! Where are you? X'. 'Am nearly here! WHERE ARE YOU?!' The last section was especially unpleasant, with trucks blasting past on the huge road, my single gear constantly too high or too low, and the unremitting headwind making every pedal-stroke more work than it needed to be. I was hot and definitely a touch bothered by the time I finally strained my way across the bridge over the Clark Fork River and into downtown Missoula.

There was still no word from Chris. I called his cellphone from a pay phone in case there was a problem with my cellphone. No response. Then I sat in a café, alone, until nearly nine, trying to figure it out. My best guess was that Chris' phone was flat. But if he was off the bus, why hadn't he used a landline? If the bus had been delayed, wouldn't he have borrowed a phone? I rang the Missoula Greyhound Office. Yes, the lunchtime Vancouver – Missoula bus had arrived on time and no, there was no one with an English accent lurking at the station with a bike box. But if Chris was in Missoula, why wasn't he making contact? Surely he couldn't have been kidnapped in broad daylight? It made no sense at all. Eventually, with the café closing, I decided to go to the Greyhound station. It was our only known shared point of contact. I would spend the night meeting all buses from Canada.' I paid and went outside where Rocky was chained to a lamppost – with a totally flat back tyre. 'Enough!' I thought, and hailed a taxi. The Greyhound station was very small. It would be hard not to notice a stray mouse there, let alone a tall man with a bike box. The office had shut. I checked into a motel opposite the station, feeling very despondent. Some romantic reunion! Then I rang Greyhound Head Office and explained the situation. 'I wouldn't worry,' said a female voice with a strong east coast accent. 'The local office could be wrong. Most likely the bus was delayed. Sometimes they are delayed for days!' Feeling somewhat reassured I had a shower and went to meet the 22.40 from Toronto. No Chris. I taped a message on the office door. 'Chris! I am in Brownies Motel opposite. RING ME!'

I'd just got back to my room when my phone finally rang. 'CHRIS!' I spluttered. 'What the hell...?' He'd arrived at noon as planned and, not having heard from me, had cycled out on the scenic route, sitting at a bench on a bend in the road with a beautiful view – and a carefully chosen picnic. He'd waited until dusk. And then he'd decided I must be in the hills out of range somewhere, and had come back to a motel on the other side of town. 'But I sent you hundreds of messages!' I squawked. It turned out that Chris' (Canadian) cellphone had stopped working as he crossed the border into the United States. But it had done this surreptitiously, and appeared still to be sending

154

messages, even though it wasn't. It hadn't received any since the border, either. A brief discussion ensued about whose motel room was the nicest. I lost. 'He's found!' I said, to the friendly Brownies' staff, on the brink of organising a man-hunt on my behalf. Rocky and I crossed town in a taxi, again, to Motel Eight, where Chris and I were finally reunited shortly before midnight. He'd cycled nearly twenty miles on the Ovando road to meet me while I'd come in on the interstate so we could have more time together. It was a very late night.

North
Pacific
Ocean

CANADA

UNITED
STATES
of AMERICA

North
Atlantic Ocean

EL PASO

ANCHORAGE

ST. MARY

GLACIER
NATIONAL
PARK

KALISPELL

83

MISSOULA

90

MONTANA

NORTH

GARDINER

Yellowstone
National
Park

DUNRAVEN PASS

CHAPTER EIGHT
Wolfsong

'The American attitude toward wilderness is far older and more complex than we usually assume. After the advent of herding and agriculture the main component of that attitude was impatience, fear and even hatred.'

Roderick Nash [34]

'The West of which I speak is but another name for the Wild, and what I have been preparing to say is, that in Wildness is the preservation of the World.'

Henry David Thoreau [35]

In the morning, we confronted another carbon dilemma. I'd made contact with a Yellowstone ecologist called Jim Halfpenny. I very much wanted to talk to him, but it wasn't that simple. While I was cycling through Yellowstone, he was out on a remote field trip. 'I'd be happy to visit with you next week, though,' he'd said on the phone. Should we give up the chance to meet someone immersed in the practical, on-the-ground reality of how climate change was affecting mountain ecosystems – or use a CO_2-emitting engine? We plumped for the engine and hired a car, leaving Chris' bike in the car hire office, and depositing Rocky firmly at the bike shop. Then we headed our small silver Sunfire towards Yellowstone, skimming back over the miles it had taken days to cycle. As we drove – or rather, as Chris drove – I was still minus my driving licence – we began catching up. I'd assumed I'd have the edge on adventures, but Chris' journey had included ricocheting bullets when a lad at the back of the Missoula to Vancouver Greyhound opened fire (for no apparent reason) on the driver. The driver was encased in bullet-proof glass but the bullet scraped across the cheek of the woman next to Chris before bouncing

---

[34] Roderick Nash (1982) *Wilderness and the American Mind* Third edition. Yale University Press

[35] Henry David Thoreau (1862) 'Walking' published posthumously in *Atlantic Monthly* May 6th

off the glass to the floor, whereupon the driver had calmly invited the marksman to disembark. Welcome to the USA!

Jim Halfpenny, bearded, in his early sixties, and clearly not a sufferer of fools gladly (we were late), took us to dinner in Gardiner and told us about his work. Not only was Jim a highly respected wolf and bear ecologist, he was also known for extraordinary tracking skills. He'd trained generations of students in the art of noticing: paw prints, a strand of fur, displaced twigs and leaves, the many slight traces a wolf leaves on the landscape as she pads through it. And he'd worked for years on one of the longest-running ecological climate studies in the world, on the slopes of the Colorado Rockies. 'Yes, there is clear evidence of climate change,' he told us. 'It's unquestionable, in my view.' During the thirty years he'd worked on the project, the climate, he said, had changed beyond any natural parameters known since the last ice age. As the climate shifted, so did the distribution of a wide range of species. Trees, for example, were gradually moving further up the slopes and the high-alpine flora and fauna had become increasingly marginalized on the summits.

'Of course, once you've retreated to the top of your mountain in search of cooler temperatures,' Jim said, 'if the temperature keeps rising, there is nowhere left to go...'

'Hence the "mountain species are the canaries of climate change" adage?' Chris suggested.

'Exactly,' Jim agreed. 'Their main, and often only, coping strategy leaves them even more vulnerable. But there are other changes too. Changes in timing and behaviour that are every bit as worrying.'

'Such as?' I asked.

'Many examples,' he said, and reeled off a list: the migration and nesting dates of birds; the emergence of butterflies and pollinating insects; when bears begin to hibernate and when they emerge from their dens; when plants start flowering and when they begin to produce berries.

'Okay, so these things are happening at different times,' I said, 'but is that necessarily a problem?'

'Well, it wouldn't be if the differences were the same across the board,' Jim agreed. 'But they aren't. The problem is that different species are responding to these changes at different rates. Bears, for example, are coming out of hibernation early, but the food they rely on isn't yet there. So they starve, or at least, their cubs do. Think of your own sea-bird populations as another example: thousands of terns, flying halfway around the world to get to Scotland and their summer breeding grounds, only to find that the fish species they depend on are simply no longer there. There may be other reasons in that case too, of course – industrial fishing of sand eels has probably had as much impact as climate change, at least until now – but basically, what we are looking at is the unravelling of the relationships between predators and prey that make up the food web.'

We sat for a moment, trying to absorb the implications of what Jim had said. 'But if food webs unravel...'

'Exactly,' Jim said, again. 'The implications are immense. Our own survival is completely bound up with the survival of food webs, and of the world's major ecosystems more generally. Let alone that of all the other millions of species we share the planet with.'

Despite Jim's appalling clarity in relation to the threats, he was more than a little pessimistic about the likelihood of anyone doing anything much about them. 'From the National Park's point of view, for example,' he said, 'climate change is seen as just one issue amongst many. It has no special priority. Climate change is lumped in with other special interests, such as brucellosis in the buffalo or the reduction of elk numbers.'

'But that doesn't make sense,' Chris said. 'These are local issues and, however serious, have limited impact. Climate change is affecting species across the entire world and could wipe us all out!'

'I agree,' said Jim, 'but you have to look at it from these local perspectives and in the timeframe of right now – then you can at least understand the logic, even if not agree with it. Fewer elk can make a difference between the kids of a hunter going to college or spending that semester working in the gas station.'

'And it's probably these local, short-term issues that most people vote on, not longer term concerns about climate change,' Chris added.

Jim agreed. 'Not that climate change is going to be a "longer-term" issue for much longer, of course.'

Just as this train of thought was moving us to order large quantities of whisky, Jim decided it was time to move on. He took us back to the headquarters of 'A Naturalist's World'. It was a treasure-trove of a place, with drawer after drawer of plaster of paris hoof, paw and foot print casts, photographs of animals, plants and amazing landscapes, and a wonderful series of stills from videos of bears and wolves on every wall space. Upstairs was a teaching area and two small dormitories. And a balcony, from which we watched a vivid sliver of moon and a single planet tracking slowly through the dark night sky. For a time, we stood still with our thoughts. Then, breaking the spell, Jim directed us towards the bedding cupboard.

'As for the rest,' he said, gesturing towards the wealth of books and specimens, 'read whatever you like. Look at whatever you like. Make yourselves at home.' With that he was gone. I already felt at home, and it seemed Chris felt the same. We sat on the balcony and fantasized about coming back for a winter wolf-ecology course, tracking wolves on skis, with steam rising over snow amongst the Yellowstone geysers.

Jim had been deeply involved with the wolf re-introduction in Yellowstone. I'd been carrying his book about it for days before reluctantly posting it home. The wolves had been brought to the park from Canada rather than the USA because they were more suited behaviourally – the Canadian wolves hunted similar prey species to the ones they would depend on in Yellowstone. Thirteen wolves, in two packs, had been released in 1975 and 1976. There were now about two hundred wolves, in a number of separate packs across the park. It was a wonderful success story – though the Bush administration was, tragically, to undermine it a few years later by taking wolves off the endangered species list, prompting an automatic lifting of the hunting ban.

Clearly, people were divided over wolves. For Jim, the wolf was the ultimate wild animal. He loved the fact they were back in Yellowstone because of their wildness, and because their wildness subtly but surely enhanced the wildness of the park. His views on wolves were aesthetic as much as anything, though he thought there were also strong ethical reasons for reinstating a creature that we humans had exterminated from the area. But others detested the wolves and would gladly see them exterminated a second time around. Sometimes the hatred had an evident rationale. Ranchers and hunters often blamed them – mistakenly in Jim's view – for reduction in elk numbers. And then there was the widely held, if also mistaken, view that wolves are the ultimate big, bad, fierce and thoroughly dangerous animal.

In fact, wolves are highly social, living in complex family groups.

The groups are hierarchical, but gratuitous aggression is rarely seen. With each other, they are quite gentle. As for aggression towards people, most reports agree that about seventeen people have been killed by wolves across the whole of Europe and Russia in the last fifty years, and none at all in North America. You are many millions of times more likely to be killed by a car in Yellowstone than by a wolf. All irrelevant if sufficient people have a vested interest in preserving the 'evil wolf' myth. Like committed wolf-hunters. There was a deeper divide too. Jim clearly connected to 'the wild' as something to be celebrated, something he loved, wanted to lose himself in, wanted to protect. I recognised Jim's position as my own. For others, though, the wild – and the animals in it – was something to be feared, conquered, even despised as godless; a mindset with roots at least as far back as the early settlers if not well beyond. The vast majority of our history as a species lies well before the advent of 'civilisation'. As for the European settlers, landing on a totally unknown continent, they had been confronted by a vast and genuinely threatening wilderness they literally had to tame to survive.

Chris and I were both keen to seize the chance of seeing wolves that driving back to Yellowstone might have made possible. We were also seriously tired, and had in mind a lie-in, a late start and a leisurely breakfast. Jim soon dealt with that particular daydream. 'If you want to see wolves,' he said, 'drive up towards Dunraven Pass. Look out for the wolf-watchers by the side of the road. They'll be there early. A 5am start would be good...'

~

We spent the night in bunk-beds in the dorm and crawled into action as the 5am alarm sounded, driving the little silver Sunfire into the park through unmanned gates. To be honest, we didn't really expect to see wolves. But the early start was worth it anyway. We saw a buffalo, utterly unperturbed by our presence, right by the road. Then a mule deer with velvet antlers picked out in the early sunshine. And a coyote, who came out into the road behind us and sat down, nose high, trying to pick up our scent. We cut the engine and watched him – his whole body inquisitive, a little tentative and only a few feet away. For me, it was like a second chance. Cycling through Yellowstone, my experience had been dominated by the traffic and crowds and I

161

hadn't really got beyond that. Now we were there on almost empty roads, in the beautiful, hillier, northern part of the park, with wildlife strolling onto our path.

We found the wolf-watchers on the road to Dunravin pass. A group of people with binoculars and enormous telescopes, just as Jim had said. We joined them, keen to see what they were looking at. At first we could see nothing save the open hillside and a distant forest. Then, 'Look! Over there! Just by the creek-line!' With our naked eyes, we could just pick out several tiny moving shapes. With binoculars, the indistinct miniature figures leapt into clear-cut wolves, playing and roaming in the Lamar Valley. Five or six adults, and about the same number of pups. Most of the adults were silver-grey, though some were a dark charcoal, and the pups almost black. They loped leisurely across the hillside then stopped for a play-fight, pups and adults in a tangle of fur, ears, legs, tails. An adult picked up an old antelope haunch and trotted off, a string of pups bounding behind her. It was mesmerising. And the atmosphere amongst the humans was lovely, too. Those with telescopes seemed as keen for other people to use them as they were to use them themselves. Generosity welled up from the shared sense of entrancement. Only one small girl had lost interest and wandered off. Her sudden shout of, 'Look at this amazing caterpillar!' reduced everyone to gales of laughter, followed by a hasty round of, 'Yes you're right, it is amazing, of course it is ...'

As we watched, switching between distant figurettes and wolves in high resolution depending on telescope access, we were treated to a wonderful commentary from the gentle-mannered and highly informative warden, Rick. 'Folks, we've got two black pups in the telescope, anyone not seen these pups through a scope yet?' 'Folks we've got a female in the scope, probably 141, the sister of the alpha-female.' The rationale behind the researchers giving the wolves numbers rather than names was, we learned, that names would be too anthropomorphic; and the schoolchildren involved in the project would get too attached to animals with names, and be overly upset should anything happen to them. Names or numbers, Rick clearly knew each animal, and not just by their appearance but by their status in the pack, their personalities and particular characteristics. The alpha male in this particular group was, in his opinion, particularly smart. 'He keeps his lead well-established,' Rick said, 'but he's also

162

good at avoiding confrontations. Very clever. On the other hand, quite a few of the females fancy the number two dog. If you're going to have an affair as a wolf, going for number two is not a bad strategy. He's still an attractive beast, but the consequences of being caught with him are nothing like as severe…' Suddenly, a group of pups and a young adult some distance from the rest of the group started to howl. The entire wolf pack responded. We humans fell silent. Wolf cries echoed across the valley. It was an incredible sound, not at all fearsome, but wild and evocative and full of subtlety. Beautiful, powerful and deeply moving, in the way that the sudden arching of dolphins around a bow-wave can unleash an unexpected uprush of emotion hard to name.

We watched the wolves – and a distant grizzly – for about three hours while the valley slowly warmed up and the delicate morning sunshine hardened into bands of heat. Eventually the wolves were lost to sight and people began to leave. We talked with Rick a little longer, appreciating his combination of deep knowledge and utter lack of arrogance. A friend with the job of controlling deer numbers on a Scottish nature reserve once said that sometimes, when he was out with his gun in the hills, ravens would circle above the deer, helping him to find them. Chris asked Rick if he had ever seen ravens working with wolves in this way. 'Oh yes,' he said, 'I've definitely seen that. The ravens circle above the deer. That helps the wolves locate them. Then, if the wolves make a kill, the ravens get some of the pickings.'

~

Back in Gardiner we'd arranged to meet a friend and neighbour of Jim's. Sandy was a lecturer in anthropology, photography and wildlife – what a wonderful combination! – and had recently finished a thesis on people's perceptions of wilderness in Yellowstone Park. As part of the research, she'd spent a summer interviewing Yellowstone visitors. 'The park,' she told us, 'has iconic status for people. Most people who come here have a strong sense of being on a pilgrimage rather than a holiday.'

'A pilgrimage to wild nature?' I asked.

'That's what I expected,' Sandy said, 'but it wasn't the case. It's more often a pilgrimage to what you might call national pride and the wonders of the USA, on the same circuit as Mount Rushmore and the Statue of Liberty. Often it's the dramatic physical features people most want to see, rather than the wildlife.'

'Wasn't it set up to protect wildlife originally, though?' I suggested.

'Well, yes and no,' said Sandy. 'You have to keep in mind that back then – we're talking 1870s – the West was viewed as a vast, wild, empty space, despite the fact that indigenous Americans had lived here for at least eleven thousand years. The newcomers valued the area for its resources, not for its wilderness; the whole point was to mine it or farm it or settle it or log it.' Even in that context, Sandy explained, the Yellowstone area was recognised as uniquely magnificent and Congress had moved to protect it by declaring it 'a public park or pleasuring ground for the benefit and enjoyment of the people.' For the benefit of people, notice, not for wildlife or nature.

Searching for destinations people would pay to travel to, the North Pacific Railroad, Sandy continued, financed several expeditions to Yellowstone, and even paid for a famous artist, Thomas Moran, to paint it. His best-known picture helped inspire Congress to pass the Yellowstone National Park bill. Sandy showed us a reproduction of Moran's 'The Grand Canyon of Yellowstone'. It was fantastically dramatic, a classic romantic masterpiece with two tiny humans completely dwarfed in the face of a vast canyon, full of startling contrasts. Ethereal light blazed at the craggy canyon tops and ominous darkness shrouded the depths below. Even the geysers, sketched in the far distance, were rendered tiny by the canyon's massive presence. 'So the park was always about people,' Sandy concluded. 'Officially, it was about preserving it for people, from those who wanted to exploit the resources. The rail companies were smart enough to realise it could be exploited in a different way.' And now? I asked. 'Well, as I said, now it is primarily a place of pilgrimage, for honouring the wonders of the USA. It's about national pride, rather than pride in nature as such.'

We were both keen to unravel this further, but Sandy wanted to hear about the bike ride. I tried to summarise what I thought I'd found so far. People who seemed genuinely not to have heard of global warming at all. Sandy just nodded when I suggested Fox News might be a key culprit. People who knew about it in a distant sort of way, but for whom it was simply not on their radar in relation to more pressing day to day concerns. People who thought it was real and important but – either genuinely or tendentiously – believed it to be a natural phenomenon about which nobody could do very much. And people who thought it was happening, that it mattered and that human activity was contributing to it, but who didn't seem to be making connections with their everyday lives, lifestyles, choices about trucks, flights, food, and so on. 'It's just *normal* to live in ways that have a massive carbon footprint,' I concluded. 'And even when people want to reduce their impacts, it's not always clear how best to do it. It's hard.'

'In other words,' Chris suggested, 'there's a whole range of different reasons that add up to it making perfect sense for any given person to do very little about it?'

I nodded. 'And actually, I've realised I'm not exactly angelic myself, when it comes to burning carbon. Not that it's *only* down to us as individuals to do something,' I said, thinking of the Montana women, and their spread-out, car-dependent community. 'We need changes in infrastructure and laws and so on that only governments, really, can bring about. We need a new normal, in all sorts of ways. And of course we need some way of reigning in the massive power of oil corporations and other vested, pro-carbon-burning interests. But I still think individual actions and changes have to be part of the picture. And to be honest, I haven't encountered a huge amount of commitment to that. Not so far, at least.'

Sandy said she thought that was about right. And then she said something that took me by surprise: that our reluctance to accept the reality of climate change, let alone act on it, was strongly connected to the myth of the Wild West.

'How so?' I asked, not seeing the link.

'Well,' Sandy began, 'this myth didn't die in the 19th century. It's very much alive and strong. It's a core part of the American Dream, that we can all head west, conquer the wild and exploit boundless nature. And this is one of the things Yellowstone still stands for in people's imagination – the boundless natural resources of the world, waiting to be tamed and harnessed by superior sections of humanity. And it's not just that we *can* do this – we *should*: this is considered to be the manifest destiny of the American people.'

'Not a view readily compatible with getting a smaller car and cutting back on carbon emissions,' I suggested.

'No indeed,' Sandy agreed. 'Nor with the concept of sustainable development more generally. The whole idea that the natural world might have limits we need to respect completely clashes with the Wild West mythology, the value of freedom and the idea that it's our positive duty to go out and exploit the natural world. You need to tackle that, to tackle climate change. You need to tackle the story we Americans are telling ourselves about who we are.'

We mulled over the conversation with Sandy for most of the long drive back to Missoula, in between debating the relative merits of my driving uninsured versus Chris falling asleep at the wheel. What Sandy had said seemed to ring deeply true. And, while the Wild West might be an extreme version of the story of superior humans taming and exploiting boundless nature, it seemed just as telling in relation to modern industrialised societies in general. Wasn't the story of the natural world as a place with unlimited resources we were destined to exploit, precisely the same story that the whole of the 'developed' world, with its commitment to endless growth, unbridled consumerism and material progress, was still recounting? Despite decades of information about how our 'growth' is changing the climate, decimating other species and generally undermining our own life support systems. Despite libraries-worth of information about natural limits – limits to resources, limits to the earth's ability to absorb pollution – about the impossibility of sustaining five- or even three-planet living. Despite all this we were still trapped in the utterly unrealistic, ultimately destructive myth of boundless, unlimited, five-planet 'progress'.

'It's not just North Americans who need a new story about who they are and how they fit in,' Chris agreed. 'We all do. Or, almost all.' The American writer Thomas Berry had come to a similar conclusion, arguing that the only way of moving towards sustainable and equitable societies involves a profound re-telling of our deep connectedness to the earth and a profound rethinking of the way, as he puts it, we 'think of the universe as a collection of objects rather than a communion of subjects.'[36]

I agreed with Berry's sentiments but wasn't entirely at ease with his language. 'We've got 2500 miles to write our version,' I said, with a grin. '*Humans on earth, the sequel!* Or maybe, *How to live well and*

---

[36] Thomas Berry (1999) *The Great Work* Bell Tower

be happy while acknowledging natural limits. Not the snappiest title...'

'Mmmm,' said Chris, 'and then breakfast.' His attention was clearly beginning to stray. At last, a bit before midnight, we found a distinctly sleazy-looking hotel near the centre of town and checked straight into sleep.

~

The next day was declared a day off. We slept late and spent the morning sorting kit and parcelling piles of stuff to post home. Then we walked into town to rescue Rocky from the bike shop. Rocky was continuing to mystify.

'Yours is the smart little touring bike?' the woman behind the till asked.

'Yep,' I said, 'it is. Smart, but weird!'

She agreed. The mechanic, the chief mechanic and the shop owner had all worked on him, she said. And *they* all agreed – Rocky was weird. The front derailleur was near impossible to set up. It would be happy on the top ring but decline to reach to the bottom. And then it would switch to the opposite, for no apparent reason. This was reassuring in relation to my dented esteem as a bike mechanic, but much less reassuring in relation to the two and a half thousand mountainous miles still ahead.

'Don't despair, ma'am,' the woman said, 'we think your bottom bracket was too small. We've put a larger one in, and it seems to have helped.' I couldn't imagine that Charlie, after building bikes for a couple of decades, would suddenly make such a basic error. But we departed the shop changing smoothly into all known gears. Logic or luck, I was happy either way.

That evening, we met up with Michael Deme at the Iron Horse in downtown Missoula, just across from the café where I'd waited so forlornly for Chris only two days before. We sat outside, working our way through a selection of local beers and a vast plate of nachos, salads and quesadillas. Mike worked for 'Adventure Cycling', an organisation that helped people plan long-distance cycling trips. [37] They researched routes up, down and across the country, publishing the best routes in a series of special maps. They offered advice about cycle-touring, and generally encouraged people to get on their bikes and go.

---

[37] Their website: http://www.adventurecycling.org/

'Our aim,' said Mike, 'is to put adventure back into people's lives. We have forty-three thousand members.' Fort-three thousand! I'd encountered a goodly number of them as my route had turned out to cross one of theirs. In truth, I hadn't really understood why anyone would need an organisation dedicated to designating bike routes on existing roads. Surely you just figured it out from existing maps? But many cyclists I'd met were astonished that I wasn't on any 'official' route and had simply made up my own. Such rash, independent behaviour was practically unheard of.

'Most people we deal with just wouldn't do that,' Mike said. 'They're only cycling because our routes have made them feel it's possible.' Forty-three thousand people having low-energy, low-impact bike adventures! It was a hell of an achievement. Good for route maps, I thought, if that's what it took; though the rationale behind all this was not intentionally climate change-related. With the help of a further round of beers – Moose Drool, Trout Slayer, Summer Sunshine – we moved the discussion in this direction. 'You could *mention* it, if you wrote an article for us,' Mike said, 'but only in passing. Not as the main story. It's far too political.' And with that, we were onto the next election and Hilary Clinton's chances of becoming president of the USA.

After Mike had gone, Chris and I sat on in the evening sunshine. We were still catching up on stories but emotionally we were reunited. Despite my doubts about how I would feel when Chris joined me, right then, I was at peace. Happy, even. Happy with having done the first two thousand miles alone. And happy to have a partner who was willing to join in on 'my' trip; who shared my values; who was unfailingly supportive of what I was trying to do.

~

There was a minor flaw in our planning that had rather an adverse effect on Chris' first cycling day. It was Sunday. The post office was closed. On top of the already heavily loaded panniers, we added the parcels of stuff we'd meant to post home. My one-person tent. Unneeded clothes. Books. The huge pedal-removing spanner that had already crossed the Atlantic with me, been dispatched home, returned with Chris and was now going ahead of us to Alaska. Not only was it Chris' first day of cycling on the trip, it was his first

168

time cycling with loaded panniers, ever. I cycled behind him out of Missoula, watching his back wheel sway and remembering my own waverings round the hotel car park in El Paso. Bizarrely, given that Chris was not a fan of heat, the precise day we set off together the temperature dropped twenty degrees. This was great for Chris, but left me, now well acclimatised to a hundred degrees, feeling chilled and searching for fleece.

We spent most of the first day not quite in synch. I was not accustomed to adjusting my food breaks around anyone else's hunger pangs and kept sailing past potential sources of sustenance just when Chris was thinking it high time to stop. And Chris, who had already ridden some way out of Missoula on the road we were now taking, made the grave error of issuing me instructions. 'It's left here!' he would say, with an exasperating smile, even though I was carrying the map. I bit my lip and smiled back until it happened a time or two more than I could take. My positive musings on partnership were temporarily suspended as I heard myself snarl, 'I've managed two thousand miles alone and I don't need directions now!'

For the next few days we rode north on Highway 83, heading for Kalispell and, beyond that, the Canadian border. Disharmony was rapidly dispelled. I persuaded Chris to experiment with slipstreaming and soon we were both feeling the benefit. Many years before I'd ridden, occasionally, on some of the Fort Collins cycling squad's early season training rides (before they'd speeded up well out of my range) and learned the necessary art of sitting an inch or so behind someone else's back wheel, while hurtling along in a big pack. I loved it: the focus, the extra speed, the absolute concentration on that narrow shred of tyre in front of you and the need for trust as you spun across a road-surface whose approaching pot-holes and pitfalls you could no longer see. Now, after all those solo headwinds it was a joy to be able to sit on Chris' wheel, sheltered from the wind until it was time to pull past and take a turn at the front. It was not taking us long to figure out how to cycle together. Chris, despite his relative lack of cycling experience, was strong. And I couldn't help notice a certain determination to figure out how to co-exist on these long, headwindy roads. He put up with my snarls. And he fast figured out that I functioned best without spoken words from when I first crawled into consciousness until about, well, noon.

Highway 83 was generously bestowed with national park campsites, ranging from 'unimproved' – i.e. you'll be lucky to get water here – to fully equipped with toilets, electricity hook-ups and camp hosts. One evening, on a site in the latter category, the hosts came over to chat. They'd retired from the Air Force and now spent every summer in a different part of the USA, living and working in the parks.

'It's a great deal,' they said. 'Free RV parking all summer and two days off every week to explore the neighbourhood.' I could see Chris doing the same mental calculations I was. If we abandoned work and became camp hosts instead, could we afford to eat in the winter? This particular campsite was beautiful, and serenely peaceful, until a group camped close by returned from their evening walk. We were on the brink of going to bed despite the racket when a young emissary from this neighbouring party came to invite us to join them for 'smores'. The party were a local family – father, three sons and a granddaughter – out for the weekend, and 'smores' turned out to be marshmallow, Graham's crackers and chocolate, melted in the campfire.

'So delicious you'll want s'more,' explained Justin, the middle son, who also told us he was keen to join the army and see the world, as an advocate for the Mormons. Just as we were trying to figure out if there really were some kind of contradiction in any of that, he added, 'Though really, I'm a history geek,' and spent the evening feeding us piles of sickeningly sweet gloop while grilling us for information about Europe and The Rest of the World.

Next morning, a chestnut-coloured prairie dog came over to check for scraps. She accepted the almond I offered her, and sat with it held between delicate paws before moving on. Later, we saw an osprey and two chicks sitting on a high post among the pine trees. Occasional glimpses of mountains where the trees thinned were often marked as viewpoints. At one of these, we got chatting to a group of bikers. They had beautiful black Harleys with seats like armchairs and tail-ends stacked up with camping gear. 'These bikes are fantastically economical,' one of the men told us. 'They do thirty to the gallon.' Thirty to the gallon! That was worse than your average clapped-out UK estate car. 'With gas prices so high, it's the only way to travel,' he continued. Since gas prices were at the time about $1.50 a gallon, this was evidently a relative statement. The bikers were from Alaska, and trucked their bikes south every summer in order to then ride home, each year taking a different route. 'We love it; it's how we recharge,' they said, and insisted we take their phone numbers in case we should meet any difficulty up north on their home territory. I had the distinct sense we were being treated as some sort of honorary Harley riders.

~

The road got busier as we got closer to Kalispell. I had a sudden intuition to look at the 'total miles' function on my computer, set at zero at the beginning of the trip. It read 2000.01 miles. Chris took a photo of Rocky and me at that milestone, leaning against a road-sign that read 'Elvis Presley Boulevard.' Coming into the town, I fantasised out loud about a café that would have an outside seat, be set back from the road, and have tons of vegetarian food. Just past the All-American Food Joint, which singularly failed to meet that description, Chris spotted it. A small deli on the other side of the road, with amazing veggie sandwiches stuffed with avocados and sprouts, and gorgeous broccoli and courgette soup. We sat outside with mounds of food. We had already stopped to buy a large bag of red 'flathead' cherries from a stall by the roadside, most of which we'd eaten on the spot. On top of a two-bagel first breakfast. We usually stopped for an eggy second breakfast meal somewhere on the road, too, and then had tortillas stuffed with cheese and veg in the evening. This had all become normal for me but Chris was amazed at how much more I was eating. I recalled my brother saying, in the days when he'd done a thirty-five-mile bicycle commute as a student, that he'd spent more on doughnuts than he would have done on car fuel.

'I wonder how the energy embedded in, say, 4000 calories would compare with a day's worth of Harley Davidson diesel,' I mused as I munched. It would depend what the calories were, of course. Where they'd come from, and how they'd been produced, packaged and transported. There would be big differences between, say, locally produced in-season cherries and out-of-season tomatoes flown in from far-off heated glasshouses. One thing I'd learned for sure, though, was that vegetarian food almost always had a much lower energy cost than meat. Meat production has a disproportionate carbon footprint: the livestock industry alone accounts for about a fifth of the world's climate change emissions. That's more than every plane, train, car and skidoo on earth. Or, as Jonathon Porritt once put it, better to be a vegetarian in a Hummer than a meat-eater on a bicycle.

While we ate, we agonized – though not, I confess, about the embedded energy of our avocados. The turn-off to Glacier National Park was just ahead. We'd planned to head north-east, crossing the Continental Divide on the famous 'Going to the Sun' road, and then camping at St Mary, a small town on the far side. But we kept hearing rumours of forest fires and road closures. 'Yup, it's true,' the café owner said. Not only was the road closed but St Mary was being evacuated. A photograph from St Mary's webcam showed only dense smoke and flames. Going over the divide was clearly not an option. But we could ride in that direction, far enough to see the magical Glacier Park mountains, camp, and come back the next day. Everyone we'd spoken to said that the park was absolutely unmissable, and there was a compelling aura of mystery about the place. Until then I'd seen no actual pictures of it, but in my mind it had a wilder kind of beauty, with turquoise lakes and huge mountains sculpted into vast, rearing, craggy buttresses.

We sat on, tormenting ourselves with brochures. The Blackfeet First Nations, we read, had considered these mountains to be the 'Backbone of the World' and the 19th-century explorer, anthropologist and naturalist George Bird Grinnel – an amazing character who'd worked alongside native peoples, fighting to preserve the buffalo from the onslaught of white hunters and poachers – was so inspired by the scenery he'd called it the Crown of the Continent and spent two decades working to establish it as a national park. The rocks in the park – this appealed to Chris particularly – were apparently the best-preserved Proterozoic sedimentary rocks in the world, with astonishing records of early life-forms and details echoing back from the ancient oceanic environment, clear down to ripple marks, mud cracks and raindrop impressions. As for the current life forms, the four thousand square kilometres of 'pristine ecosystem' were said to include virtually all the plants and animals that existed when white explorers first entered the region. Grizzly bears and Canadian Lynx, possibly wolverines; the mountain goat – the park's symbol – moun-tain lion, bighorn sheep, moose, elk, mule deer, coyote, badger, river otter ... as well as hundreds of bird species and thousands of plants. Wolves had never been extinguished from the area. And then of course, there were the two hundred waterfalls, in excess of a hundred and thirty named lakes, a couple of mountain ranges and the glaciers.

'But we can't go, can we,' said Chris. It was more of a statement than a question. The reality of the time I'd 'lost' in Colorado was really kicking in and it seemed particularly unfair that Chris should miss out because of my days off, though he never complained. And of course, it raised the question of Anchorage. Did we want to blast on past 'unmissable' places in order to get there, or revise our goal? It was to be a recurring question. For now, we turned away from the park, back into the wind.

'It is kind of symbolic, isn't it,' said Chris, searching for a positive take. 'Turned back from Glacier National Park by fire, on a global warming trip...' The links between global warming and forest fires were actually somewhat tenuous, though some researchers thought the reduction in glacial meltwater led to smaller rivers and streams and a generally drier environment – increasing the risk of fires. Others argued that climate change was causing the longer, drier summers that in turn left vegetation drier and fires more likely – and less controllable. What was not tenuous at all, however, was the link between global warming and the glaciers themselves. The park's most spectacular features had been carved by the huge glaciers of the last ice age. A hundred and fifty glaciers had been recorded by naturalists in the nineteenth century. In 2006, only twenty-seven were left, all receding. By the time the park celebrated its hundredth anniversary in 2010, the remaining glaciers would be a fragment of what they were when the park was established. And, at the current rate, the predictions were unanimous. By 2050, Glacier National Park would have no glaciers at all.

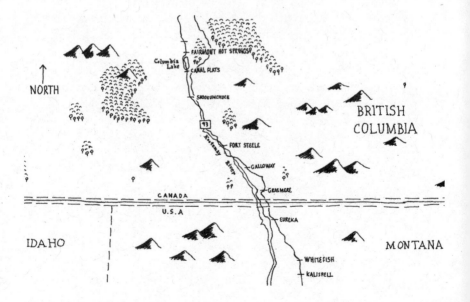

CHAPTER NINE
Folks Round Here Drink Bud

'Today, the average European uses 43 kilograms of resources
daily, and the average American uses 88 kilograms. All in all,
the world extracts the equivalent of 112 Empire State Buildings
from the earth every single day.'

'If everyone lived like [North] Americans, Earth could sustain
only 1.4 billion people.'

State of the World, 2010 [38]

We went west. North-west. Back out into the traffic, heading for
Whitefish, Montana. I'd imagined northern Montana to be vast,
wild and quiet but we seemed to be cycling through an endless housing development. Immense plains with Montana mountains in the
background but, in the foreground, miles and miles of box-like houses,
piles of torn up soil and ranks and ranks of diggers steadily transforming the plains into acres of suburbia.

Venturing into a gigantic shopping mall, we sought bagels and
directions to the bike shop. Glacier Cycles, at the edge of what would
have been old Whitefish – a street of flat-fronted shops and wooden
buildings – was a friendly oasis. 'Nah, nothing to see in Glacier,'
teased an assistant. 'Just a bunch of goats and mountains. You're
lucky to miss it!' We bought various bike bits, tried not to look at
the 'Going to the sun' posters – all featuring hairpin bends winding
up towards towering buttresses past icy turquoise glacial lakes into
a blue sky full of swallows – and got directions for a back road that
would by-pass the busiest ten miles out of Whitefish.

We were both tired. It was a relief – almost physical – to get onto
the quieter road. The traffic noise and stench fell away and we rode
side by side for the first time in many miles. Not far from the road,
a family rounded up a herd of cattle – kids running, adults on quad-

---

[38] Worldwatch Institute (2010) *State of the World 2010; Transforming
Cultures from Consumerism to Sustainability* Earthscan

bikes and dogs racing gleefully across acres of grass. Occasional vast, newly built houses looked out across the meadows, but despite these minor mansions, distant mountains and forests quietly reasserted their presence in the landscape. We stopped just before rejoining the main highway and sat by the edge of the road, finishing off some cherries in the evening sunshine. As we were leaving, a huge bird rose up from a stand of trees close by. Vivid white tail, pale head. A bald eagle! We watched it soar and disappear, unhurried, in its own world.

Back on the main road, twenty miles from the next campsite, a blustery head wind dragged out the distance. We were low on water. The cool temperature had been making me blasé about drinking and I'd forgotten to fill up our bottles at lunchtime. On even the smallest inclines our muscles just ached, declining to give any power at all. We shouldn't have been that tired. But we were. At last, Lake Dickey campsite crept into view. We cycled slowly through it. It was ominously full. A giant RV was already ensconced in every pitch and the only tents on the whole site appeared to be RV extensions. Chris looked dazed. 'It's not looking good,' he mumbled. I could tell he was envisaging being forced to cycle back out onto an endless road, devoid of campsites but rigorously patrolled by park rangers on the lookout for stray wild-campers who had somehow managed to circumvent the dirt tracks and barbed wire. I went in search of the human attached to the RV with two tents pitched below it. She was large and blonde and initially defensive.

'Yep. That's our site,' she said, and walked away. Then she came back. 'Are you guys just staying one night?' I nodded. 'Use the site. In fact, use the tent. It's only there for the kids to play in. There's an air mattress in it...'

With that, our evening was transformed. From exhausting slog to luxury in one stroke, without even the need to put up a tent! Our ready-made abode was a pink and blue palace with a foot-thick king-size air mattress taking up barely half of it. We sat on a bench nearby and ate tortillas stuffed with cheese, tomato and coriander leaves and then took mugs of tea down to the lake. The lake had that cool, flat, blue inviting look and I almost went for a swim but couldn't quite get it together. Finding the right stuff, even just a towel, seemed simply too daunting. Instead, we watched the sunset streak the eggshell blue with pale pink and listened to the eerie, wild sound of loons; a cry with the same sort of emotional qualities as the call of curlews, evoking the love and aloneness of wild places. Then a troupe of Girl Guides began to sing too, drowning out the loons with great exuberance. We retired to our thick, bouncy mattress, waking briefly in the night as the Guides fell silent and the cry of the loons echoed across the lake, answered by the wonderful, high howling of distant coyotes.

~

I woke ravenous, and so well-slept and rejuvenated I felt like doing cartwheels. Our hostess (we never did exchange names) came and joined me while I ate two bagels and half a muffin. Her two rescue dogs, Buddy and Cleo, watched intently for crumbs. The campsite was cool and shaded with trees but we cycled out into warmth. The sun was shining, the traffic was quieter, the bikes were purring and we were headed for the Canadian border.

Just before Eureka, the road opened out into a wide valley. An information sign told us we were in Tobacco Valley and that First Nations people had grown a form of tobacco in the area for many years – until the white settlers forced them out. Also that there had been various gold rushes, followed by fur-trading booms. I could see why Gwen Maka had called her book *Riding with Ghosts*. [39] Sometimes I could almost see horses alongside, and wagons, and men in beaver-hats and, more faintly, the hundreds and hundreds of years of First Nations peoples that had preceded them. They all accompanied us for the easy, swishy sixteen miles to Eureka which, I said jokingly to Chris, would be an old-fashioned cowboy-fronted town centre, plus at least one café with a state-of-the-art expresso machine. Slightly unnervingly, it was. We sat outside Jax café on the single main street, hung with banners for the forthcoming annual Eureka quilt festival, feeling in holiday mode and eating a huge brunch of eggs and hash browns, orange juice and expresso coffee.

True to form, Montana ended with a typical downhill swoop. Now we were about to leave the USA altogether, and cross into Canada. We were looking forward to spending time in a country often characterised as the States' greener, saner, more environmentally aware neighbour. It felt, in fact, like a fairly major transition, though the

[39] Gwen Maka (2000) *Riding with Ghosts* Eye Books

border crossing itself was hardly substantial. One 'First and Last' duty free shop; a Canadian flag; a checkpoint; a few questions about where we were going and how much money we carried and we were through, in Canada, and taking photographs of each other by a sign that proclaimed British Columbia to be 'The Best Place on Earth'.

The first town across the border was marked on the map as Grasmere. Given that we worked just down the road from Grasmere, England, we were keen to get there. How would Grasmere, BC compare with Grasmere, UK? But there was an unexpected impediment. Crickets. From the moment we entered Canada, the number of crickets had exploded. There were so many on the hard shoulder that trying to avoid them meant dodging and swerving so much as to barely make progress. If you just rode, a horrible crunching sound filled the air. There seemed to be hundreds more butterflies too, huge dark creatures with wings edged in bright yellow, and the verges were packed with flowers. It was an extraordinary explosion of wildlife, though you would probably have to be on a bike rather than in a car to fully appreciate it. The 'green neighbour' was, we thought, living up to its reputation already.

We'd cycled through Grasmere and out the other end almost before realising we'd arrived. One petrol pump and a store in a wooden shack that sold ice cream. I had a immense double scoop of butterscotch and 'tiger tiger' – orange striped with liquorice – utterly delicious and completely over the top. And more or less the only foodstuff in Grasmere. In the space of a few miles we'd gone from Montana, groaning with traffic, the remnants of wildness pushed ever backwards by wave after wave of housing developments and shopping malls, to this scattered edge of British Columbia where towns on the map barely existed on the ground and the landscape was still vast, and largely shaped by other species. We cycled off, on the brink of exploding with ice cream, into a beautiful wide valley. A wonderful, long descent to a stunning spot; a bridge over a wide slow river with turquoise colours pooling in the water. Huge flats leading out to a vast lake in one direction and distant mountains in the other. Wildlife spilled out onto the highway. The traffic was light. We grinned and grinned.

Ahead was another junction, and another decision. We were aiming for Canmore, just south of Banff, to meet up with a friend of Chris'. There were two ways to get there. We could cross over the Rockies and then ride north along their flat (and perhaps even more windy) east flank, with the mountains to our left, then bypass Calgary over a mountain road proclaimed to be gorgeous. Or we could continue to the west of the Rockies, keeping the mountains on our right. There were pros and cons either way. We stopped at the junction, anticipating some sort of tourist information but finding only pink lemonade sold from a tiny hut. The lemonade was delicious. We consulted various lemonade drinkers, who all disagreed. 'Go east! The mountain road is unmissable!' 'Stay west! It's just as beautiful, and definitely shorter!' Whichever route we chose, we would close down a set of experiences and possible adventures forever. There wasn't really any rational way to decide between them. Life in miniature! Our intuitions were silent, too. In the end, we stayed west, probably the faster route. Keep focused on Alaska ... A raven called as we cycled away and, not long after, two golden eagles flew almost across us. The road was wide and beautiful. Little furry caterpillars, a pale straw colour, arched across the warm tarmac like short fat barley heads on the move.

We stopped early at a tiny RV site just beyond Galloway: a railway junction, a woodyard and an osprey platform, complete with resident osprey. The campsite lay between the road and a wild river and we sat enjoying the last of the sun, watching robins hunting the lawn and night hawks hunting the sky. Soon we were falling asleep to the sound of bonfire flames, lit by campers returned late from fishing. The smell of roasting fish wafted into our dreams with the roar of the river and the roar of trucks, and the occasional distant, mournful train.

~

The next few days were full of contrasts, and one distinctly unnerving near-miss. Wildlife was always strongly present. Each time we stopped at the side of the road, crickets and butterflies rose in a cloud around us. At times, the crickets were so loud they drowned out the traffic, singing, whining, whirring. But the dead pine trees I'd encountered since Colorado were also becoming more and more numerous. The usual beetle culprit was endemic to this region, too. And there seemed to be the same debate about the root cause of the pine beetle's explosion as there had been further south. It had got out of control because the trees were stressed by various factors, such as the practice of growing them packed tight together to increase logging profits. It was climate change. It was because winters were warmer and the beetles could survive the cold season where once they would have been largely killed off. It was all the above. No two people agreed but, either way, we were beginning to see whole mountainsides covered in brown, like a deciduous forest in the autumn. Except that these weren't deciduous forests. And it wasn't autumn. The juxtaposition of vibrant, buzzing, multifarious life and acre upon acre of dead brown trees was deeply unsettling.

In a lesser way, so was the occasional reconnection to our intuitions or to some strange sort of foresight. It was affecting me in particular and it appeared to operate in a manner both intermittent and mundane. Approaching Fort Steele, for example, after miles of 'empty' road I said to Chris, 'What we could really do with now is a fresh fruit stall by the road, selling cherries, plums and nectarines. Just round the corner.' Just round the corner was exactly that. The friendly man who served us, his shirt covered in melon designs, was highly amused at the suggestion that we'd imagined him into existence. We bought bags of fruit and sat eating on a bench.

'Hey you!' he shouted as we cycled away. 'Don't stop thinking of me!'

The road came and went from the shores of the Kootenay River. Over the years, the river had had a number of names, reflecting the fortunes and interests of its human neighbours. 'Kootenay' was the anglicised version of Kootenai or Ktunaxa, meaning 'people from beyond the hills'. The People Beyond the Hills had also been known as the Flatbows, and some records in fact referred to the Kootenay as the Flatbow River. Others ignored the indigenous names altogether, and called it McGillivray's River, in honour of two not at all indigenous North West Trading Company partners. That name had, apparently, been chosen by the explorer, fur-trader and mapmaker David Thompson. Thompson, an extraordinary character, had set sail from England in 1784 at the age of fourteen as an apprentice of the Hudson Bay Company. Known to some native peoples as 'Koo-Koo-Sint' or 'the Stargazer' (and by white historians as the 'greatest land geographer that ever lived') Thompson had, in the course of his career, mapped over 3.9 million square kilometres of North

America. Including the area through which we were currently inching, into a hot and blustery head wind. We'd overshot the tiny town of Skookumchuk some time back, and were searching for somewhere to stop. Our options were limited. We turned off the main road and headed for Canal Flats, right on the river's edge.

The only buildings we could see ahead of us were logging mills and the state of the road disinclined us to believe we were headed for a town at all. We were. It was tiny. There was no obvious campsite or motel. The Colombia Inn at the end of the road was our main hope of avoiding a mosquito-filled evening perched on the edge of the river waiting eviction from hostile property owners. We went in.

'Are you an inn with rooms? Or just a pub?' we asked the young man on crutches behind the bar.

He asked if we were the cyclists he'd passed on the road earlier. Where had we come from? Where were we headed? 'El Paso? No shit! Alaska? NO SHIT!!' And then, 'Yep, we have hostel rooms. One free. But I doubt you'd want it.'

We went to look. It was large, with a double bed *and* a sofa. Fake wooden panels covered one wall, fake shingles another. Cream wall-paper featuring a bamboo leaf pattern adorned the far end. The wallpaper peeled back from the ceiling and hung in shreds at each corner. Red and white check curtains partly concealed torn sheets of plastic in front of the window and a large blue drape hung in the middle where the curtains declined to meet. On a low table by the sofa, a glazed white china swan cradled a bunch of pink plastic flowers in its wings. I could feel Chris recoiling. 'It's great,' I said, drawn to the air of edgy sleaze and intrigued to be in this place for a while. Besides, the alternatives involved effort. We put our bikes in the yard and lugged our stuff upstairs through a back room marked 'Employees Only', where the barman's father lay on a sofa stroking a chihuahua sprawled across his chest, while a small lhasa apso curled like a tiny furry terrier at his feet.

We were three miles short of two thousand, two hundred and fifty miles which, with a bit of luck, meant we were halfway there. We went down to the bar to celebrate.

'What do folks drink around here?' Chris asked. He meant, is there a locally brewed beer, but the question somehow came out a touch pretentiously.

The barman smirked. 'Folks round here drink *Bud*,' he drawled and sold us two at double the local prices. We took our beers and sat down in a discreet corner. Fake wood wallpaper adorned these walls too, but had been plastered on in diagonal stripes. Numerous stuffed elk-heads, mostly sporting sunglasses, adorned the stripes, and a mountain lion skin took pride of place, stretched out flat like a huge cat newly run over in a 'Tom and Jerry' cartoon. Between the elk-heads, two televisions beamed silent images across the room, one constantly reviewing the weather and the other a boxing match.

Centre of attention were two women in jeans, tight black tops and black and white bandanas. One was strikingly good looking, tall and slim with shoulder-length dark blonde hair curling out from under the biker-style headgear. Her cropped top revealed a pierced belly button and a single tattoo that read 'Jade' across the small of her back. Her friend's arms and back, visible through a lattice of thin black stripes, were more tattoo than skin. Various men orbited around them. Occasionally, one would come across to us to ask if we minded if they turned the jukebox up a bit. Soon the music was blasting and the group moved across to play pool and/or dance around the pool table. The barman's father, who had migrated to a leather-bound sofa in the corner, sat at a far edge of this by now full-swinging party, the chihuahua on his lap. He said not one word all evening. We sat at the other edge.

A solitary man in his fifties, not included in the pool party, briefly joined us. He wore jeans, a checked shirt and cowboy boots and looked like a lumberjack. He was a lumberjack. 'Moved west twenty years ago,' he said. 'I ain't never going back. More space here. Men grow straighter where there's more space. Like trees.' And with that he moved away. We bought more beer and became distinctly maudlin about the miles behind us, the miles ahead, the wonders of Canada in general and of Canal Flats in particular. It seemed just right, somehow, to be there, on our halfway mark, in that tiny Canadian town, most definitely off the beaten track, drinking bad beer on the far periphery of charismatic biker-women.

~

Canal Flats had also, like the river, been named in honour of the North West Trading Company partners – and was known as McGillivray's

Portage. The current name referred, we'd read, to a low strip of land a little over a mile wide as well as to the town; 'a curiosity of geology' that separated the lake headwaters of the immense Columbia River from the south-flowing Kootenay. A canal had, briefly, joined the two in the 19th century though only two ships had ever successfully navigated it. The intention had been for the canal to be part of an ambitious scheme to divert water from the upper Kootenay into the Columbia, opening up a north-south passage from Golden to Montana as well as reclaiming thousands of acres of rich alluvial plain. But farmers around Golden and the Canadian Pacific Railways united in opposing it and it was abandoned. A similar proposal in the 1970s to divert the Kootenay into the Columbia in order to generate hydro electric power met the same fate – strongly opposed by environmentalists and locals alike – and the Kootenay remains independent of the Columbia until, after flowing south into the USA, it heads north and joins the Columbia of its own freewill at Castlegar in Canada.

It was cool and windy as we climbed up out of Canal Flats to Columbia Lake and pulled into Fairmont Hot Springs for lunch. Fairmont Hot Springs could hardly have been more different from Canal Flats. It came as a positive shock. A vast golf resort unfolded before us, right at the edge of the mountains. We rode through a purpose-built estate of large twee houses, and into the resort in search of food. There were numerous options. We plumped for a restaurant that advertised pasta, sitting outside until the wind blew our un-needed sun-umbrella into the bushes. Retreating indoors, we perched in a smoked-glass conservatory, watching little white golf-carts glide around like vehicles in a sci-fi movie – one of those where the planet has become contaminated and everything is now under a vast glass dome.

Working our way through large quantities of nachos, quesadillas and pizza the conversation shifted from the mysterious attraction of golf – not one either of us had ever felt, but clearly compelling for many – to freedom. Even as a non-golfer, I could see the attraction of being outside, practising a skill, socialising on the greens and in the bars. But there was no getting past it: the plush golf-course, with its acres and acres of grass in an environment not at all conducive to grass-growing, and its acres and acres of centrally heated/air-conditioned luxury buildings was, beneath the glitz, an environmental monster.

It would need multiple mega-watts of energy to run and maintain. Many of its customers would have flown there. 'Basically, we are eating lunch in a resource-ravenous, climate-threatening, biodiversity black hole,' I said.

'Steady on,' said Chris, always more temperate. 'But yes. I guess we are.'

I wondered whether the reality of climate change would, sooner or later, force us to question our freedom to build and enjoy this kind of resource and energy-hungry recreational facility. There must be other ways, I thought, of enjoying the outdoors, developing a skill, socialising, keeping fit, and all the other positive aspects of a place like Fairmont golf club – without racking up quite such a high environmental cost in the process. There must be a way we could keep the positives and lose the negatives. For now, though, we were free to do whatever we chose, if only we could pay for it.

We left Fairmont into a big headwind: a real, head-down, full-on wind, with blustery blasts that occasionally brought us to a complete stop in our tracks. It felt good to be back in the real, wild world, blowing away the phoney pretension and shallow glitz of the golf-course hotels. At Windermere, we took shelter on the lee side of a fruit-stall/café, drinking hot chocolate in the temporary sun and buying cherries, enormous blackberries, a mango and a handful of apricots.

'In rites of passage stories,' Chris said, 'the threshold guardian is often the wind.'

'And the role of the threshold guardian?' I asked.

'To see whether you have the necessary resolve to cross over. To test whether you really *want* to cross over,' said Chris, with a grin.

We were at a literal threshold, a watershed, close to the source of the Columbia River. 1243 miles from here the river would reach the Pacific Ocean in Oregon. In our own small world, the halfway mark was a threshold of sorts, too. Another 2250 miles and we would, with luck, reach the Gulf of Alaska at Anchorage. Hunched away from the wind we were not sure how to feel. Daunted or exhilarated? Perhaps both. There was real uncertainty in the emotional mix too. It was August 4th. 2250 miles would, I worked out on a cherry-stained paper bag, take us thirty days – assuming we sustained the seventy-five mile a day average. Thirty days took us well into September. And that was without any days off. We were booked onto the last southbound ferry from Anchorage, on September 14th. There would not be another ferry until spring. There was not a lot of leeway.

Not long after we'd strained back out into the wind a truck towing a trailer of tree-trunks pulled out just ahead of us and overturned – blown over, presumably, by the wind on the corner. It was about thirty seconds in front of us. We raced to the truck. The driver was unharmed, in his cab, on the radio. Two women slowed the traffic behind. The tree-length logs and the metal trailer were slewed right across the hard shoulder. It was impossible not to imagine what could have happened. If we'd left the fruit shop a few seconds earlier. If we'd been cycling just a bit faster. Not long after, an ambulance went by, and Chris had an uprush of emotion. We stood with the bikes on the hard shoulder ahead of the crash in the sun and the wind and held each other, half-shocked, half-relieved, shaken by that glimpsed reminder of the sudden, random, meaningless way in which a life can be squashed out.

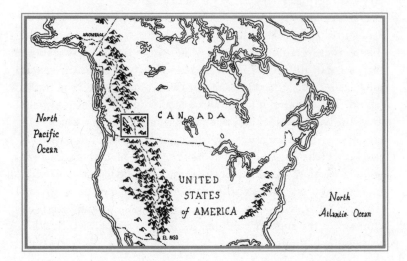

CHAPTER TEN
The Good, the Bad and the Ugly

'We are all environmentalists now. Yet we stand at no less a distance from the more-than-human-world: from 'nature,' from other animals and natural places. We are no more inclined to acknowledge – certainly not to really feel – that we ourselves are at stake with 'nature,' with the rest of the world: entwined, enveloped, submerged in it. Vanishing species, to take just one example, are only regretted in the way that we might regret the loss of a television series.'

Anthony Weston [40]

Arriving there from the States, Canada is an enigma. Similar in so many ways, and yet very different. Both countries encompass, if you include their lakes and rivers, a little under four million square miles. But in Canada there are fewer people. Far fewer people: the ratio is roughly one to ten. We soon experienced this geographical reality in the form of longer distances between food-purchasing opportunities. Chris caught onto this well before I did and would stock up with piles of bagels, fruit, pasta; even olives in tins. I failed to keep the scorn I was feeling from tainting my voice as I shared my views on what did and did not qualify as Touring Bike Food. Chris, in return, summed up my 'We've got a bagel, we'll be fine, there's bound to be somewhere on the road' attitude as verging on the irresponsible. In Canada, heading north through British Columbia, he was usually right. The distances between towns suddenly leaped upwards, and the few towns we did encounter tended to be one of two extremes. Tiny, no-frills logging towns in which the most likely source of vegetarian calories was beer. Or massively overdeveloped golf/hot springs/ski resorts with everything packaged and signed – 'Tourist Attraction'! 'Viewpoint'! 'Lodging'! – as if in response to these huge distances, seeking to control them, to render them manageable and safe. And the people we met, in or

---

[40] Anthony Weston (1994) *Back to Earth: Tomorrow's Environmentalism* Temple University Press

out of town, were in general much more reserved.

This was not the case with Ian. But Ian turned out to be British. We were at the top of the first of a series of passes, having turned off into Kootenay National Park and were, thanks to Chris' advance thinking food system, sitting eating raisin cookies, when a young man on a mountain bike towing a trailer appeared over the horizon. He was out of the saddle and sprinting for the summit. Skidding neatly to a halt alongside he dismounted and joined us, all long thin legs and muscle. Like us, Ian was heading for Alaska. But he had started his trip in Argentina, some four and a half thousand miles further south. His stops en route had included Butte, Montana for the Evel Knievel festival, an annual celebration of the extraordinary stunt-rider whose career had been kick-started by a sacking. Permanently relieved of his duties by the Anaconda Mining Company after he'd had the misfortune to take out the main Butte powerlines while doing a wheelie with an earth mover, Evel first jumped a twenty-foot-long box of rattlesnakes and two mountain lions as a way of making money. He went on, of course, to create and defend numerous records for jumping stacks of cars, mustangs, buses and the Snake River Canyon, notching up a grand total of thirty-seven broken bones in the process.

Ian himself clearly had a touch of Evel about him; a lesser Evel with a wicked, understated humour. In Arizona he'd paused to take in a twenty-four-hour mountain bike race. Exchanging his touring tyres for a sportier variety he'd won the race – to the disbelief, not to say disgust, of the local mountain bike fraternity – thereby qualifying for the world championships. Then he'd switched his tyres back, reconnected his trailer, and cycled on. For a while we raced down the far side together. I could only just hold him on the evenly tarmacked descent even though I had skinny tyres against his knobbly wide ones. The ride through the park was unbelievably beautiful; almost a caricature of a sublime mountain landscape. Mountains edged closer and closer on both sides of the road, their bald heads and dark green flanks sweeping down to the turquoise river, its vivid colour coming from rock flour in the glacial melt. The river often raced alongside the road or came suddenly into view from above, curling into a series of dramatic and gracious turquoise-glinting bends and curves. And yet, not all was well here. A section marked with glaciers on the map revealed only tiny, high remnants of ice. And we often saw the familiar patchwork of brown trees amongst the green. At one viewpoint, a sign pointing to a particularly striking swathe of fake autumn colours attributed the beetle damage to the changing fashions in fire management. Various First Nations people had used fire to shape and thin the forests, leaving them easier to travel through and to live among, with grass meadows in frequent clearings among the trees. But white forest managers had, for many generations, both fought the fires and done all they could to prevent them. Not surprisingly, the forests became much denser but – and this *was* unexpected – rather than relish this more 'natural' state of affairs, a whole range of species had promptly disappeared. Now, these stands of older, tightly packed trees had inadvertently created an ideal environment for our friend the pine beetle. A policy of allowing forest fires and restoring grass undergrowth was underway, but of course it wasn't that simple. The tightly packed old dry trees meant that forest fires were not the relatively contained affairs of the past, but infernos that left thousands upon thousands of acres of dead trees and tended to show scant regard for any human settlements or transport systems in their path – as we'd experienced at a safe distance with the closure of the Glacier Highway road to St Mary's.

Shortly after Vermilion Crossing we began the final climb up to the Continental Divide, long and steady until Chris had a back wheel puncture. We battled to remove his 'Armadillo' tyre, breaking a tyre lever in the process. The frustration was more than offset by the view. All things considered, a quiet mountain road with spectacular ridge views in the warm evening sunshine was a pretty marvellous place to have a puncture. Below us, the river was a tiny, distant strand of blue. Stands of grey branchless tree trunks etched bristly gaps in the tree cover and one vast mountain face was completely pink with rosebay willow herb – often the first plant to return after a disturbance – high up among the dead trees, a stunning wash of rose behind the grey. 'Fireweed', the Canadians called it. We took photographs at the Divide, a little under 6000 feet, and Chris' first crossing. And then rode for miles among the pink and grey mountains until the long, fast descent towards the main road in the fading light.

~

The next day took us to Banff, after a night camped illicitly in a packed-out site behind the RV of a sympathetic French-Canadian. We passed an elk with gigantic velvety antlers grazing by the side of the road, apparently oblivious to the cars screeching to a halt around him, drivers and passengers all leaping out to take photographs. And two cyclists whose only comment was, 'Those helmets won't do you any good on the panniers. Put them on your heads!' Hardly the friendly greeting we'd become accustomed to but, we already sensed, somehow very Canadian.

We cruised into Banff around lunchtime. After cycling around the busy Alpine-like town centre at least twice, my blood sugar was crashing, leaving me as usual with the entirely unhelpful inability to make any decisions – including where to stop and what to eat. In the nick of time we stumbled upon the Mountain Bistro, complete with upstairs patio in glorious sunshine and fantastic mountain skylines all around. Chris ordered beer while I was discovering that the toilets worked on a composting system and by the time I returned we were suddenly in holiday mode. Not only was the beer amongst the best ever, but the Mountain Bistro had fabulous organic food with loads of veggie options. We sat in the sunshine, eating, drinking, basking and grinning. And chatting to the waiter, who told us the Bistro was one of a suite of buildings owned by a man who'd insisted they all be built in accordance with the 'Hannover Principles', complete with specially designed gutters that caught and used the roof-water runoff, compost loos and recycled materials throughout. The Hannover principles, it transpired, were no lightweight hippy daydream but had been created for the 2000 'EXPO' World Fair in Germany. They were intended to guide not just architectural design but *all* design, and were essentially a manifesto for altering the entire trajectory of industrial society.

'World history,' the Principles' introduction succinctly points out, 'offers many examples of societies with environmentally sustainable structures and communities which have endured for thousands of years. However, we have also pursued other paths which have led to ecologically unsustainable practices. For the development and improvement of humankind, it is imperative to renew a commitment to living as part of the earth...' [41]

Living as part of the earth! In our modern societies, where detachment from nature is normal and it is so easy to kid ourselves that we are *not* part of the earth, this was a radical suggestion: as was the recommendation to 'design for the needs of all species ... never just for people's needs.' What this meant in practice was, our waiter explained, all around us. 'In sum,' he said, 'it's about designing buildings in which people can, amongst other things, eat delicious food while other species are left in peace to pursue their own lives.' Okay, it was still an upmarket café in a posh ski town, but at least it was a step in the right direction. It seemed only right to support the venture with another beer. And dessert.

Eventually, wondering at our luck in having stumbled into this particular café and with our idealistic view of Greener Finer Canada thoroughly confirmed, we dragged ourselves away to meet Chris' friend Julian at a prearranged rendezvous outside the Tourist Office. Julian had long dark hair in a ponytail, a beard and an open, welcoming manner. I liked him immediately. We loaded the bikes into the back of his truck and sat relishing the amazing effortless speed, while Julian drove with his hands crossed on the top of the wheel. The truck, he told us, had just turned up – a gift dispatched after a rich client who'd taken part in one of his outdoor courses had a dream in which he'd been told to give Julian a truck. So he did, conveniently in time to help with the move that he and his partner Saundy and young son Jago had just made from a remote mountain cabin to the outskirts of Canmore. 'Nowhere near as beautiful, but way more practical,' said Julian, with a grin, 'and ironically much gentler on the environment. Tons less driving.' We put our bikes in the garage and our stuff in a tree house in the garden – 'the only place you're gonna get to sleep more than two hours at a time.' And then we headed into town for the Canmore Folk Music Festival.

The festival was in a huge playing field. Impromptu walkways were lined with stands selling everything from food to flutes. Hundreds of people strolled along the walkways and sat in clearings listening

[41] Hannover principles available at http://www.mcdonough.com/principles.pdf

to music that swept in waves across the whole site and up towards the mountains. The atmosphere was wonderful and we were still in holiday mode. Then, having resolved not even to think about climate change for the rest of the day, we came upon the most inspiring climate-change conservation initiative of the whole trip. A stand marked 'Y2Y' in huge letters featured intriguing photographs of bears crossing bridges. We went to look. 'Er – bears on bridges?' we asked.

The attendant grinned. 'A huge part of modern nature conservation strategy,' he explained, 'is based on the idea that we can protect nature by putting a fence around it and creating, say, a national park, or some other conservation area.' We nodded. Yellowstone, of course, was the first ever national park, created in 1872, and the idea of parks and conservation areas is now common across the UK and Europe and beyond. Conservation areas have been hugely valuable. But they do nothing to make normal, mainstream human activities, such as farming and building cities and extracting resources – the activities that have the most negative impacts on natural systems, habitats and species across the world – any less damaging. Which, of course, is where something like the Hannover Principles comes in. 'Exactly,' agreed our Y2Y champion. 'But now, on top of the immense impact we're already having, throw in climate change. In a warming climate, what many species need to do is head higher or head north. But all too often, their movement is blocked by a city or a large road, or by the lack of suitable habitat. That's where Y2Y comes in. It's a coalition of conservation organisations and other groups, linking parks, nature conservation areas and chunks of half-decent habitat together, all the way from Yellowstone to Yukon.' [42]

'Yellowstone to Yukon!' Chris spluttered on his spinach and feta wrap. 'That's over two thousand miles!'

'Exactly. The idea is to form a vast conservation corridor, along which all kinds of species can move. It's a real shift in conservation thinking, from protected areas to protected corridors or networks. We think it's critical if as many species as possible are to have a chance of survival.' Sometimes, he explained, linking two areas up involved providing a bridge over a road, or a tunnel beneath it.

'But aren't most animals suspicious of these bridges?' I asked.

---

[42] Their site is definitely worth visiting: http://www.y2y.net/

'Yep, they are, to start with. But then they start to explore them and, eventually, they're accepted as normal. What's fascinating is that different animals come to terms with them at different rates. Elk, for example, learn to use the bridges much faster than bears. Why? Because elk are a herd animal. Once one animal has figured it out, she'll pass the information on to the others. Bears are solitary, so each animal has to work it out for themselves.'

We exchanged email addresses and wandered away towards the main music area. I was a little stunned. What a difference between this and the conservation displays in New Mexico and Wyoming that hadn't even *mentioned* climate change! In the context of the tragic implications of climate change for other species – especially mountain species – this was probably about the most positive, solution-focused response that either of us could have imagined. Y2Y offered a new vision of the way we could help protect other species from our own horrendous impacts on them. It was a supreme case of joined-up thinking. It was another example of leadership from the middle. And it was the second inspiring encounter of the day.

What was perhaps most powerful about the Hannover Principles and the Y2Y was that wonderful words – living as if we were part of ecological systems and respecting other species – had been translated into visible, practical reality. And both shared a deeper aim. 'Ultimately,' our interpreter had said, 'we aim to help shift the modern world view. At the moment, we tend to see ourselves as separate from nature, rather than part of it. So long as we see things that way, we'll never really be able to deal with climate change, or any of our environmental problems. Shifting worldviews is the hardest but, in the end, the most practical thing of all.'

Exactly my thoughts as I'd battled with the wind in Wyoming, thinking about cheat-grass. It was as if he had picked up my hazy thoughts and turned them into something tangible.

~

For the next few days we soaked up conversations. Julian was a wilderness guide of sorts, seeking, as we were in our different ways, to find ways of working outdoors that explored ideas as well as landscapes, that challenged values and, above all, that might bring about change. He worked with business leaders on an MBA that had an outdoor component. 'It's officially about sustainability but really it's about getting people back in touch with nature. Their own as much as any other kind. Always powerful,' Julian said. And he'd worked for many years with First Nations people on a project called Rediscovery. Rediscovery was about trying reconnect young people to traditional rites of passage – in a way that made sense in a modern world and that helped them find their feet. [43] He told compelling stories of the impact of some of these experiences and the often transformative power of encounters between people and wild animals like bears. 'But eventually,' said Julian, 'after you've worked with hundreds of these young people, typically angry, messed up, you think, this is endless. I'm just catching these kids as they float down a chaotic, turbulent river. We need to go upstream and stop them falling in in the first place ...' He often asked what was meant by 'deeper' experiences. 'That's what we need,' he would say, 'outdoor experiences that go deeper, that go to the source, that don't just seek to heal symptoms.'

Saundy had worked with grizzly bears for many years, riding alone into the mountains to track them and study their habits. She'd spent months of the summer living in mountain huts in the years before she'd had Jago. 'Grizzlies live alone, too,' she said, over a late breakfast. 'Mum brings up the cubs, and they stay with her for three or four years. After that, they're largely solitary.' She was about to embark on research on the impact that climate change might have on these animals. We mentioned Jim's research. 'Yep, that's what we're expecting to find here too. Changes in the time bears go into their dens and when they come out. Changes in what food is available to them. That's one of the things we think could badly affect them.'

'So, will the Y2Y help with the impact of climate change on these bears?' I asked.

'Well actually,' Saundy said, 'the Y2Y concept came into being before climate change was really on the agenda. It already had a significant role to play.'

'How so?' I asked. Saundy poured more coffee.

'Well,' she said, 'our national parks were created before the science of ecology was fully established. What we now know is that many of our natural ecosystems extend far beyond park boundaries. Kootenay,

---

[43] Their website is http://rediscovery.org/

for example, is only a small part of the Central Rockies Ecosystem. The whole ecosystem is about the size of Switzerland. And the range of many animals is much, much greater than we realised then. Have you heard of a wolf called Pluie?' I shook my head. 'She was captured and radio-collared in the 1990s, and then she was set free. Scientists followed where she went, expecting her to travel, say, a hundred kilometres at most. In two years she criss-crossed an area of more than 100,000 square kilometres! What these studies told us is that there is a fundamental flaw in our approach to wildlife conservation. Our conventional system of protected areas is just too small and too disjointed to meet the needs of wide-ranging species like wolves, wolverine, cougars, lynx and grizzly bear. These animals need more land than anyone previously imagined. One study concluded that at least 80,000 square kilometres of grizzly bear habitat are needed in the Rockies to buffer the bears against the negative effects of inbreeding, disease and forest fire. That's nine times the size of Yellowstone National Park! In other words, you can't look after these animals just by protecting the park. You have to protect the wider ecosystem too. And it's not just these animals of course, but many other species as well. Though it was the large animals that Karsten and Leanne focussed on when they did their Y2Y walk.'

We'd met Karsten and Leanne at the musical festival. 'Karsten and Leanne walked the Y2Y? When?' I asked.

'Well, Karsten did the first thousand-odd miles with his dog. Leanne joined him later. It was back in 1988/89. He was trying to travel the route a grizzly or a wolf or an elk might take as it moved from park to park, to see what obstacles these animals would meet. And then to bring the issue alive for local audiences and the media. Karsten wrote a book about it. *Walking the Big Wild.* You should get hold of it.'[44]

'It must be a relief to be living in Canada rather than the States,' I said later. 'The Greener, Saner Neighbour.'

Julian and Saundy exchanged glances. 'Canada likes to think it is way more advanced, more civilised, than the States,' said Saundy. 'Probably true in relation to, I don't know, gun crime – we have much

---

[44] I did, and it's a really great read: Karsten Heuer (2004) *Walking the Big Wild: from Yellowstone to the Yukon on the Grizzly Bear's Trail* Mountaineers' Books

less – but in relation to climate change? I'd say we're just as bad. There are some good things. There are tax breaks if you insulate your house to factor twenty and *all* houses are insulated to factor twelve. Winters are cold here and gas prices high, so people are good at insulating. But they do it for economic reasons, not environmental ones.'

Julian nodded. 'And at the same time as we're saving a chunk of energy through insulation,' he said, 'there's a boom in oil prices that's reached the point where it's economic to extract oil from the tar sands in Alberta. Extracting oil in this way uses up unbelievable amounts of energy, before you even start to use it. Completely outweighs any gains from energy efficiency everywhere else. The process is appalling in other ways, too. Areas of pristine boreal forest about the size of the UK are simply removed. The way they extract the oil then leaves the land absolutely devastated. It has all sorts of negative impacts on people, too – usually First Nations people, living downstream. Take a look at some pictures of tar sands. It's about the most depressing thing you'll ever see. It's the Bad and the Very, Very Ugly exemplified and rolled into one. And it's one of the main reasons why Canada has a carbon footprint per capita that is almost as high as that in the States. Even though we have ten times fewer people.'

'So the big green neighbour image is a bit of a myth?' I asked, reluctantly.

'Fraid so,' said Julian with a grin.

'But isn't there any opposition to this tar sands extraction?' I asked, reluctant to let go of this myth all at once, 'or climate change activism?'

'Well, some,' said Saundy, 'for sure. But many of our environmentalists and activists are working at a local level. They are typically focused on single issues, like land rights, land use, dams, access and so on. Important stuff of course, but big-picture environmentalism of the kind you're interested in is much less common here.'

'And at government level?' Chris asked.

Julian sighed. 'The Canadian government is very right-wing. Our prime minister, Stephen Harper – just elected in January – is a conservative, and very pro-market. He wouldn't countenance interfering to stop the tar sands oil extraction if there's a market for oil at that price. And certainly not for environmental reasons. He thinks that economic growth always takes priority over environmental issues, any environmental issues. And don't underestimate the sheer

amount of money we are talking about here. It's immense. As for
climate change, he's not even sure it exists. Convenient, given his
desire to see the tar sands go ahead.'

Too soon, it was time to move on. Julian took us back to Banff, on
his way to go canoeing, the bikes in the back and the boat strapped to
the roof of the truck. We'd intended to leave after a brief chat with
Colin Funk, who worked at the Banff Centre. But Colin persuaded
us to stay. Each day we lingered, the miles we'd have to ride to get to
Anchorage in the time we had left leapt a little higher. The chance
to find out more about the Banff Centre was, however, irresistible. [45]
It was our third inspiring discovery in as many days and a welcome
antidote to the depressing demolition job that Julian and Saundy had
performed, however reluctantly, on our naïve view of 'Green Canada'.

The Banff Centre, housed in a beautiful suite of buildings on a
lovely, wooded site in view of the mountains, was run as a not-for-profit
organisation, dedicated to creativity and leadership – indigenous
leadership, corporate leadership, environmental leadership – and
committed to creating a space where artists, scientists, writers, and
business people could all meet and exchange ideas. It seemed almost
purpose-built to develop the kind of joined-up, link-making leadership
needed to tackle climate change. Colin was Director of Creative
Development and interested in the power of drama. He had travelled
in the Philippines with a small troupe of Canadian actors, working
with local groups across the country to write and perform plays about
how various villages had been affected by the sugar plantations. And
then they'd brought the plays back to Canada, performing them as
a way of raising awareness of the impacts of certain kinds of trade –
products, like sugar, that we take for granted.

'The human costs of plantation sugar are usually completely
invisible.' Colin said. 'We buy sugar and never even think about it.
We tried to reveal these costs through the plays. Much more effective
than writing a report,' he continued, as we walked across the site to
the mountain culture centre. 'Really powerful, in fact. And certainly
transferable to topics like climate change.'

The mountain culture centre was showing an exhibition – previous
winners of their annual mountain photograph competition. They

---

[45] http://www.banffcentre.ca/

were stunning. What a difference between really good photographs and my snaps from the roadside! We were introduced to Lesley who, we learned later, had been the first Mayor of Banff. Lesley, clearly a force to be reckoned with, told us about some of their other projects. A conference on the impact of climate change on mountain cultures; bursaries for people working on projects that communicated mountain issues; a competition for artists in residence working on writing projects. More than a small part of was me tempted to resign my UK job on the spot, and beg to be signed up.

~

It was late the next morning before we dragged ourselves away, cycling out of Banff after a second breakfast of bread pudding and cranberry-chocolate muffins in the organic bakery, back out across the railway lines and onto Highway 1A heading for Lake Louise. The temperature had dropped dramatically, and the sky had clouded over. The cold spurred us on and we made good time until, after a brief lunch stop at a tourist complex just off the highway, we made the mistake of going into an Inuit Art Gallery.

By the time we left it was mid-afternoon. It had started to rain. Shadowy mountains reared up, dramatic and evocative in the cloud and mist, the Continental Divide flanking the road on one side; the Rocky Mountain 'Foothills' – with peaks at nine or ten thousand feet – on the other. Turquoise lakes shone amongst the pine forests. A sign announced 'Highest Point in the Park Region' (which presumably meant, highest point on a road) at about 6,800 feet. We camped at Waterfowl Lakes after a seventy-five-mile day, on a site near the astonishing turquoise river, rushing endlessly down from the stripy mountains among the pine trees. The Crowfoot Glacier was a dull glint in the far distance; the toes, formerly long and graceful, now barely in existence, shrunken back into stubby foot-ends.

For the next few days, it rained. We were cycling along the Icefields Parkway towards the Athabasca Glacier, rumoured to be another of the most beautiful roads in the world. The huge buff and grey mountains towered up on both sides, clouds rolling down them like steam. Thousands of umbrella-shaped seed-heads turned from cream to coffee in the rain on the verges, a gorgeous backdrop for the scarlet splashes of Indian Paintbrush. Clouds of small brown birds grazed on the seed heads, flying up like butterflies as we passed and resettling behind us. We were using a map that Chris had been given for free on the plane. It lacked certain details, like contours. That, in addition to the 'Highest Point in the Park' sign, meant that the sudden emergence of an ominously long uphill stretch rearing up ahead took us by surprise. We climbed at little over walking pace for about three hours, passing a 'Mountain Adventures' bus in the ditch, and slowly, painstakingly gaining height. At the summit, tantalising glimpses of snow-streaked mountains, one shaped like the Matterhorn, another with clouds streaming off it as if on fire, came and went in the mist. We stopped early at a roadside campsite after a cold descent. The climb and the weather had left us a little worse for wear and anyway, we wanted to actually see the glaciers ahead. Better weather was rumoured for the morrow.

Finding a relatively peaceful spot amongst the RVs in a small site by a water tank, we fussed with our fly-sheet and poles. A woman walking past sighed and said, 'Aah, tents. You know what we call them? Ziploc bags for bears.' And with that reassuring comment, she walked on. There was not much we could do about the possibility of a bear who had learned the benefits of searching tents for food, other than the usual precautions of not cooking in the tent and storing our food elsewhere. It would have been more useful if she'd warned us about the squirrels. 'Look, Chris!' I said, thrilled to watch a tiny scrap of red fur taking the tips off a pine tree nearby. I threw her a piece of fig roll. Tentatively, the squirrel inched over, took the crumb, raced off. I threw another. Many crumbs later, we were congratulating ourselves on our squirrel taming talents and general animal empathy as the little creature cautiously took fragments of biscuit right from our fingers. Then, without warning, the squirrel ran up my calves and over my body to the table behind, seized an entire fig roll and legged it to safety. It was hard not to conclude that this had been her plan all along. We had been well and truly duped by the Shy Squirrel Act. We put the biscuits back in the packet but the squirrel returned and, putting the shy squirrel act firmly behind her, climbed my leg to the table and proceeded to do battle with the wrappings. At one point, the entwined squirrel and biscuit packet both fell to the ground where the squirrel, clearly furious, continued to shake and rip at the plastic. By this time, Chris had the video camera out and the whole 'Shy Squirrel Dupes Stupid Tent Campers' routine was caught for posterity.

~

The next day delivered something of a wake-up call. It was still raining. We went back to sleep. We woke again after soaking up sleep for a whole twelve hours while the rain hammered on the tent. The huge sleep left us both feeling absolutely fantastic. Rain was still falling heavily. There was nothing we could do. Packing our wet gear, the tent dripping and leaden, we cycled off into the downpour. It was only a couple of miles to the Athabasca Glacier Centre but, out of the shelter of the campsite, it was seriously cold. The snowline was no longer all that far above us. Our feet and hands were in shoes and gloves still wet from the day before and within minutes mine were painful with cold – the kind of sensation that delivers a clear message. *Oi! You need to do something about this, preferably quickly!* By the time we got to the centre it hurt to get off the bike. I could barely put weight on my feet and had no feeling at all in my hands. 'Much longer and I'd've been part of the glacier,' I said, the dregs of humour creeping back with the warmth as I drank hot chocolate on a stool rammed up against a café radiator.

More or less defrosted we went, a touch reluctantly, to the glacier exhibition. There, in a pleasantly non-glacial temperature, we learned about watermelon snow, pink from algae that live by absorbing infrared light from the sun. We learned about glacier worms that live in the ice and that can grow up to two centimetres long. We learned that the Athabasca Glacier had lost over half its volume in the last hundred and twenty-five years and was still shrinking at a rate of two to three metres a year.

But we learned very little about climate change. Only one panel discussed global warming which, it said, 'may or may not be the result of human activity'. It said nothing at all about what we might be doing to try to avert it. Despite the clear and increasingly urgent information issuing from scientists around the world warning of disaster and calling for action; despite the overwhelming international scientific consensus about both the reality of global warming and its human causes; despite the visible and thoroughly documented evidence of the shrinking ice all around us – despite all this the exhibition mounted on the edge of the archetypal disappearing glacier was still in denial, apparently stuck in a bizarre notion of objectivity. 'Objectivity' seemed to mean, stay away from discussing anything to do with taking helpful, preventative action and restrict yourself to presenting the science of global warming – from both sides. Never mind that one side barely exists, or that the aim of achieving 'balance' ends up being downright misleading. And what a bizarre sense of priority. In my mind's eye I could almost see a contemporary museum curator reassuring his children in a decade's time. 'Well, it's true that we did nowhere near enough to avert dangerous levels of climate change and that you're having to deal with the consequences. Floods, draughts, shortage of food, conflict, disease, that sort of thing. But never mind, we may be going to hell in a handbasket, but at least my generation didn't say anything that wasn't *balanced*.'

It was still raining when we left. I dug out a balaclava and a neck warmer from the bottom of a now empty 'bad weather' bag. The battery was flat on the camera and Chris tried to take a photograph of me standing in front of the retreated glacier with the video. Had it come out, it would have shown me hunched and wet in front of a sign that marked the furthest reach of the glacier's toes in the 1840s. The nearest edge of the glacier was now about a mile away. It was streaked muddy grey and scattered with glacier buses that crawled up its icy flanks on caterpillar tyres and gathered in small herds on the skyline. The whole atmosphere was of something diminished and a bit shabby, like a once magnificent wild animal now in a zoo.

This was the third of the 'most beautiful mountain scenery in the world' roads that I'd either not really seen because of low cloud and rain – Trail Ridge – or not been able to ride at all, because of fire – the Road to the Sun. Judging by the number of minibuses towing trailers with 'Bike Adventures' written across them, it was a popular cycling destination. The buses hooted and waved every time they passed us. But we saw very few cyclists. Almost all of them appeared to be in the buses rather than on the road. Given the rain and the absence of views, this was hardly surprising. Despite the downpour, despite knowing we were surrounded by stunning scenery we could not see, not to mention the thoroughly depressing glacier, I was in a very good mood. The rain was relentless but we had lost a little height,

201

and it was warmer. My feet and hands were cold, but in a normal, unthreatening sort of way, leaving me with the kind of cheerfulness you get after feeling sick, at simply not feeling sick.

At a café stop, a couple in their early sixties came tentatively over to join us. 'We saw you on the road earlier,' they said. They had been cycling, with one of the adventure companies, from Whitefish, Montana. Tomorrow was their last day. They would finish in Jasper, a distance of over six hundred miles with some big climbs, and these were clearly not your 'normal' hard core touring cyclists. 'That's fantastic!' we said. 'Has it been a good trip?'

'Incredible. But,' gesturing towards a trailer parked in view, 'compared to you, we're cheating!' Then, waving aside our protests, they gave us a polystyrene container. 'We wanted to give you this.' I opened it a touch cautiously, no idea what I might find in there. Two huge slabs of chocolate and raspberry brownie crouched inside on a plastic plate. 'Dessert,' they smiled shyly, 'you've earned it.' And with that they walked away, leaving me almost in tears.

We cycled into Jasper in the early evening, drenched and dripping. A motel night! But motel after motel was full. We upgraded to hotels, with rain-driven credit-card recklessness. They were full too. The campsite was another ten miles away. It was in the wrong direction and we really couldn't face it. Finally, I went into the Whistler Hotel, an imitation Alpine lodge of generous proportions right in the centre of town. I put on my most bedraggled air, a task not difficult to achieve. 'Yes ma'am,' said the attendant, kindly, 'we have one room left. It is quite small but it can be yours.' Small and expensive. And wonderfully warm. We took it with not a little gratitude, learning later that it was their 'in case something happens' room, always held back for emergencies. I had looked so cold and wet they'd decided I was the closest to an emergency they were likely to get that night.

It turned into two nights. Our small warm room, soon festooned with impromptu lines of drying clothes and tents, was extremely quiet and we slept astonishingly late. We needed to stock up on food and I was badly behind on the blog. Plus there was the small matter of better gloves. It was going to be well into the afternoon before we got away.

'Chris,' I said, 'what if we stay today? Catch up with everything?' We hadn't planned another day off so soon and we'd pay for it later. But for then, it was a decision that left both our spirits rising with a sense of relief. We celebrated with a huge breakfast in the Soft Rock café, followed by some appropriate retail therapy. The best cycling overshoes we could find and gloves you could wear in a freezer and still be toasty. Then I left Chris to the joys of the town and headed for an internet café. Three hours later he came to extract me.

'Enough! We're going for a walk! Let's go!'

I'd been writing solidly the whole time but had only just reached Missoula. Between the lack of time and the lack of internet cafés I seemed destined never to catch up with myself. We walked a mile or so along the railway line and sat on a bench to take in the view. The mountains were back in sight, and glorious in that mixed, high definition evening sun-and-shadow way. A classic, old, Canadian freight train stretched on in the foreground and then, just as I was searching for the camera, a flock of geese flew straight across the tracks. It would have been a stunning shot. But the camera, though recharged, was still in the hotel and that particular visual summary of the Canadian Rockies was lost forever.

North
Pacific
Ocean

ANCHORAGE

CANADA

UNITED
STATES
of AMERICA

EL PASO

North
Atlantic Ocean

BRITISH
COLUMBIA

FORT FRASER

PRINCE GEORGE

MCBRIDE

Fraser River

CARIBOO MOUNTAINS

Fraser River

MOUNT ROBSON

Mount
Robson

Yellowhead
Pass

JASPER
Provincial
Park

CHAPTER ELEVEN
Decision Time

'[The Kyoto Accord is] a socialist scheme to suck money out of wealth-producing nations... [The Accord is] based on tentative and contradictory scientific evidence about climate trends.'

Stephen Harper [46]

'By placing the economy above the natural world in importance, the global economy is destructive of local ecosystems and local communities. We have to examine some of the most deeply held and cherished assumptions about conventional economics...'

David Suzuki [47]

It was mid-August when we rode out of Jasper. For four days we headed constantly northwest towards Prince George, the Cariboo Mountains flanking us to the left and the long ridge of the continental divide on our right. A railway line and the Fraser River also ran alongside, switching from one side to the other before settling down as steady companions on our right. The longest river in British Columbia, the Fraser, was named after Simon Fraser who, in 1793, had become the first European to follow the river from its source in the Rockies to its mouth in the Pacific at Vancouver; though Spanish explorers had already 'found' it the year before. Fraser confirmed that this river was not connected to the Colombia, and that it was not fully navigable – though the Hudson Bay Company, keen to use it for transporting furs, sent George Simpson along a few decades later just to be sure. Simpson, initially certain he could find a way to transport furs by boat, rapidly changed his mind. 'I should consider the passage down to be certain Death, in nine attempts out of ten,' he wrote. The river's main flow has never been dammed and it had a wild, rich feel. When the road or a campsite took us close by, we often saw salmon on their

---

[46] Quoted, for example, on Climate Action Network Canada http:// climateactionnetwork.ca/archive/e/issues/harper-talks-kyoto.html

[47] David Suzuki (2003) *The David Suzuki Reader* Greystone Books

way upstream, twisting up out into the air and crashing back to the water at regular intervals. It looked like a hard way to travel.

The salmon might have thought the same about us. We were struggling to wake up at any reasonable hour and it was usually late morning by the time we got going, much to the amusement of anyone camping nearby who saw our bicycles and assumed, via some sort of association of cyclists with strenuous healthy living, that we'd be off at the crack of dawn. As we got underway at the crack of noon, we often met cyclists who had indeed been on the road since 6am. Their daily miles would be nearly completed, while we had a good ten hours ahead of us, typically culminating in a flat-out race to arrive somewhere habitable before dark. Sometimes we'd make a real effort to leave early and events would conspire against us – the alarm wouldn't go off or one of the bikes would develop a mysterious puncture just before take-off (though usually after the panniers were loaded). Once we'd pedaled several miles along the road before I realized I'd left all my spare underwear drying on a rock and had to go back. Usually, though, we'd simply give in to the urge to stay asleep. In the end I realized it was primarily a personality thing. To be fair, my personality. On top of being a sleep addict at the best of times – unable to function adequately in the world without a good nine hours – I have a 'muck about and prevaricate' mentality in the morning. This merges into a 'Heck, it's sunny and we're in a beautiful place, let's sit on this rock and have a picnic lunch' mentality. And then, if I were honest, I'd have to admit I sort of enjoy the 'It's 5pm and we still have forty miles to go!' end-of-day minor epic. Not something to own up to out loud on the days when the last minute race left us arriving somewhere beautiful and intriguing at nightfall, cursing the lack of time to explore.

We crossed the continental divide at Yellowhead Pass – a minor affair at a little under four thousand feet – taking us into the Mount Robson Provincial Park. A huge wooden mountain goat poised gracefully on top of the park entrance sign, its arching white body bigger than Chris and his bike together. Mount Robson itself towered behind, a massive bulk of grey rising up almost thirteen thousand feet out of the pine trees, the details of gulleys and buttress lines picked out in white and the summit icecap disappearing into high cloud. The Yellowhead Pass runs on into the Yellowhead Highway, which runs through the village of Tete Jaune Cache, named after an Iroquois with streaked blond hair who'd guided for the Hudson Bay company in the early 1800s. He'd also led a group to survey the Yellowhead Pass in 1825, with a view to opening it up. He was more than successful. 'By the 1830s,' the park information told us, 'the Yellowhead Highway was truly being used as a "trans-Canada highway". Red River carts rolled along it in 1841, miners used it for the Cariboo Gold Rush in 1856, the 1862 Overlanders followed it to Kamloops and Prince George, and settlers followed it to their new homesteads in the West.'

And, in the 21st century, a fair few cyclists followed it for fun, though most of the cyclists we met were, for some reason, heading south. Sal and Dave from New Zealand were amongst the most inspiring. Both in their sixties, they told us they spent two or three months cycling every year. This year they were pedalling from Anchorage to San Francisco. Beijing to Paris was next. They were a gold mine of information about what lay ahead. They told us that the station at McBride had a café that did very good lattes, and that forty kilometres beyond McBride there was a small and peaceful campsite on a beautiful piece of land just off the road at LaSalle Lake. Even more usefully, they said that the Cassiar Highway, about which we'd heard mixed reports – how much of it was still unpaved? Was it actually compatible with skinny wheeled touring bikes? – was perfectly bike-friendly. They'd just cycled it. 'It's beautiful,' they said, 'and only one or two sections, maybe twenty kilometres max, are gravel. Don't miss it!' They were full of stories about other cyclists, including their encounter with 'a very posh Welsh woman, running around the world, as thin as a twig,' whom they'd met resting at the side of the road under a reindeer skin. And it was from Sal and Dave that we first heard the rumours about a German cyclist not far ahead of us, cycling with three huskies and a trailer.

Sometime later, after riding through a couple of short but intense downpours, a mass of deep slate grey clouds ahead, flickering with lightning, promised another drenching. We pulled off the road to take shelter under a park information sign, conveniently fitted out with a small roof. Chris made tortillas and we sat on a pile of wood chips, munching while the storm broke around us, vivid whip-cracks of thunder and lightning flaring across the deep, dark sky and monsoon-like rain bouncing off the darkened road. A yellow 'Parks' truck pulled up alongside our sign. Two young women in British Columbia T-shirts hopped out and raced around the truck, picking up litter and clearing the drainage run-offs with a pick-axe, not stopping for the downpour but dancing in it. One of the women was especially exuberant, turning circles in the tumultuous rain with arms outstretched, her long ginger hair drenched under a baseball cap.

The station at McBride was still open when we reached it, and there was the café, with wonderful lattes as promised, a random mix of sofas and chairs and a bench in the sun outside on the platform, where we sat drinking our coffee, looking down the line, soaking up the immense mountains-all-around vista. Not far from McBride, another storm began to brew and the most glorious rainbow suddenly appeared right beside the road, arching out of the wet trees above two bay horses and back down to earth just beyond a white and brick cabin. As we watched, it echoed itself into a double rainbow, and the colours became more and more vivid. It was almost painfully beautiful: brilliant violet, blue, green, yellow, red against the deep grey sky.

Inspired with confidence in Dave and Sal's instructions after the magical lattes in tiny McBride, we cycled on in search of the La Salle campsite. At the top of a hill, they'd said, down a narrow track on the left-hand side. Hilltops came and went. Another rainstorm drenched us. Dusk set in. Of the campsite, there was no sign at all. A wide strip of grass between the road and the forest began to look increasingly attractive. 'We could just camp here,' Chris suggested. I nodded. We slowed down to survey the best spot. Then, 'Wow, look, a bear! A *small* bear!' It was indeed a small bear, otherwise known as a cub; black, shiny and picking berries on the verge we were assessing as our bed for the night. Our first reaction was glee. 'How wonderful!' we both exclaimed, 'to see a cub so close!' And then, as common sense slowly returned, 'Oh shit. A CUB!' Cubs of course, have mothers and, as stupid, dangerous behaviour around bears goes, the ultimate is to get between mother and cub – intentionally or otherwise. 'Where *is* mother?' we asked in unison, looking hastily around before cycling off at high speed. Recalling the advice that most tragic bear/human encounters occur simply because the bear has been taken by surprise, we began to sing as loud as we could, in the officially recommended manner, until it occurred to each of us in turn that we could not sing from here to Anchorage. We faded back into silence. It was soon dark. We stopped to turn lights on. We cycled some more. Many miles later,

208

the campsite entrance, barely marked, flicked into view in my front light and we freewheeled down through the trees to a beautiful site right by a lake, with one lone camper van already asleep. We pitched our tent as quietly as we could, and sat on the wooden lake walkway drinking soup and watching the stars come out. Chris got into the tent first and, as he was sorting himself out in the limited space inside, I saw three shooting stars, one huge and brilliant and two tiny, fiery darts, scooting across the sky and gone in an instant. I wished. And then I turned in.

~

We woke to sunshine. There was a diver on the lake, and shoals of tiny fish. How lovely it would be to stay for the day, soak up the sunshine, catch up with journals and just hang out with whatever wildlife might wander by. Reluctantly, we rode up the steep hill and back out onto the road. Deep blue-violet vetches and banks of lilac thistles stretched back to the trees. The forests were two-tone: dark conifers and pale aspen, some with brilliantly silver trunks and leaves that really did shimmer in the wind and sun. Whenever the river came closer, horsetails and bulrushes moved in amongst the vetches, dancing with yellow butterflies and enormous blue-green dragonflies. The sun was warm, but the air temperature cool. The road tracked steadily up, then down, then up, crossing tributary rivers and occasionally rising high above the valleys, gifting us a brief bird's-eye view of the trees and river below.

The road went on, and on. We veered between feeling daunted and feeling exultant at being beyond the tourist areas, somewhere bigger, wilder, more real, less traffic – though we did encounter another spate of cyclists. Miko from Japan was cycling the world, a continent each year. His most recent continent had been Africa. There he'd acquired the habit of carrying ten litres of water strapped to his bike in large plastic bottles; a habit he'd retained even in Northern Canada, where water was extremely plentiful. On top of this huge additional weight he sported, like some slightly mad caricature of a stereotypical hi-tech Japanese traveller, a small solar panel that recharged batteries for his phone, MP3 player and laptop, and a huge Nikon camera with assorted lenses. And a variety of spare tyres bungied on top of his large panniers, for reasons we never established.

We passed a dead moose in the ditch, only recently killed, antlers still furry. I was tired. And my knees were sore and stiff. That day I was feeling increasingly demotivated. I didn't seem to be getting any fitter, just a bit worn out. I'd started taking ibuprofen a few days earlier but the pain seemed to be seeping through. I kept thinking, everyone has limits. The question is how do you deal with reaching them. Not that I was *at* my limits; but I did sometimes feel they were making me aware of their existence. That night I sweated and tossed in the tent and woke feeling tired, emotional, vulnerable. As we were packing to leave I had a sudden, vicious attack of stomach cramps that left me writhing, trying not to hyperventilate and close to throwing up. I held onto Chris. It lasted about ten minutes. Afterwards, I said it: 'Chris, I'm tired.' Such a simple thing to say, but for me, after years of hiding any vulnerability behind a tough-guy loner act, it was a breakthrough. Not only did the world keep turning after this admission, but it didn't even feel all that dramatic. Just sensible; a pragmatic acknowledgement of a factor that could affect our plans.

Over second breakfast in a campsite café, we chatted to the café owner. Lindsay had spent most of her life in this part of Canada. 'I remember always having my cold snow clothes on at Halloween,' she said. 'Now it rarely snows before Christmas.' For many people in this area, the reality of global warming was, she told us, its impact on the skiing industry. 'People involved in the skiing business know only too well that global warming is real,' she said. 'The impacts are already with us. It'll be crippling if it gets worse. And then there's the pine beetle, too ...' And yet we'd also met people in northern Canada who loved the idea of warmer winters. 'Vineyards in the north! No more minus forty in January! Bring it on!' I never quite seemed to be on the ball enough to challenge the idea that we could simply pluck the positives from global warming; to deliver a coherent, impromptu explanation of why it might not just be a case of some will lose but others will win.

~

Not long after we finally left the campsite, we met a German couple brimming with the energetic glee of beings newly released from a cage. They had just taken eighteen months off work, had flown to Anchorage and, after a stretch relaxing on the ferry, were now heading

210

for Argentina by bike. It had been hard arranging to leave work, they said, but now they couldn't imagine why they hadn't done it years earlier. We swapped camping/café/coffee information, and compared notes about who else we'd met on the road. Like us, they had encountered the New Zealanders, Sal and Dave; and they claimed to have seen the mythical German cyclist, ever just ahead of us with his huskies. Almost all the cyclists we met seemed, despite whatever they were dealing with in terms of tiredness, weather or punctures, to be especially alive, especially happy. They usually radiated a relief at having finally made the space to leave work or other commitments to make this journey; to be out here on the hot/cold/wet/windy wonderful road. And they were always, always friendly. Here on these increasingly remote northern roads, we were beginning to develop the strange sense of being part of a biking community: loose, shifting and disparate, but a community nonetheless.

We rode into Prince George around 4pm and straight to an exceedingly helpful tourist information centre that warned us of thieves and brought us up to speed in relation to the best options for vegetarian food and cheap accommodation. The university halls of residence were a short ride away. We checked in, were given a full briefing on the dangers of leaving our windows unbarred, and rode off on unloaded, squirrely bikes to meet Annie.

Annie was in her early thirties, with short blonde hair and a pent-up energy that was hard to ignore. She taught environmental ethics at the university, was highly informed about all sorts of things we wanted to know about, and happy to talk. And she was angry. Annie was angry about Canada's environmental record. 'We're a small country in terms of our population,' she said, 'but we have a huge environmental footprint. The biggest in the world, in fact, in terms of water use. We import 60% of our food and are still selling good farmland for suburban development. We're even a net importer of grain, despite the vast monocultures of wheat in the heartlands. Canadians are just not environmentalists, for the most part. We resented the hell out of hydro-electric dams and got active resisting them – but only because we were selling most of the power to the USA. We're happy to trash the environment for our own purposes, though. And, despite our huge climate change impact, we're pulling out of the Kyoto conference – alone with the USA and Australia of all the so-called "developed" nations.' In case we had any vestiges of the Green Canada myth intact, Annie even disabused us of any delusions that the increase in flowers and insects we'd encountered crossing the border was anything to do with pro-environment policy. 'The United States spray their road-side verges, and we don't,' she said. 'It's that simple. But not because we value biodiversity. Because we can't afford the spray!'

Annie was also angry about modern Canada's treatment of the First Nations people. 'These are people who had been living sustainably for hundreds and hundreds of years. Now their cultures barely exist,' she said. 'Indians, of whichever tribe, are no more likely to be environmentalists than anyone else these days. But they *are* more likely to be in jail, in hospital, to be failing at school, or doing drugs. There is massive racism here. It seriously affects their opportunities for education, amongst other things. Out of thirty-three million Canadians, there are only twenty-two Indians with PhDs in the whole country. Twenty-two!' We asked her what it would take to get Canadians to act on climate change, and found she was angry about that too. 'They wouldn't,' Annie snorted. 'They'd expect the government to deal with it. It's one way in which the States has the edge. For all their flaws, US citizens are much less reliant on the government to sort things out for them than we are.'

For her part, Annie was working on ways of using land more sustainably by experimenting with plants that needed less water, and less herbicide, to flourish. 'Small scale,' she said, 'but could have a knock-on effect. Like growing different, hardier plants in public spaces, where people might notice them and think, hey, I could have some of those in my garden. It's not about what's "native" but about what's best adapted to be here now; and to be here as the climate changes. What grows best here is already different from thirty, even twenty years ago. It's bound to be. Temperatures are changing, there is less snow, very few really cold winters. Deer are moving into towns, followed by cougar. And yet people persist, for example, in growing grass that is utterly unsuited to this climate, that needs gallons and gallons of water throughout the summer, tons of herbicides and pesticides, and is a deer magnet – it's insane.'

I tried out the notion that vineyards and warmer winters might be a good thing, at least for some. The winners and losers analysis of climate change. Annie was scathing. 'Anyone who thinks we can pick and choose the good from the bad in relation to climate change just doesn't know enough,' she said. 'The key thing to understand is that, after a certain point, climate change will not happen in a nice, gradual, predictable, steady way. It will take sudden, dramatically large – *and irreversible* – leaps. The benign-sounding "positive feedback". It's the scariest aspect of the whole of climate change science.'

'What would be an example?' I asked, though I suspected I knew what she might say. I was right.

'Pine beetles,' said Annie. 'You know the story by now. Warmer climates on top of tightly packed trees. The beetles were normal and relatively harmless but now they're an epidemic. It's a complex relationship between beetles, fire, logging policies and climate change but the net result is that some parts of western Canada are predicted to lose ninety per cent of their forest cover. Ninety per cent! A massive habitat loss. And in relation to climate change, it's a double whammy. Decaying forests release CO_2 emissions. And then you also lose the forests as a CO_2 sink. The warmer it gets, the more forest ecosystems collapse. And the more they collapse, the more you get this double hit of increased emissions and lost sinks, leading to more CO_2 in the atmosphere, making it warmer... There are lots of these positive feedback loops. Like the melting permafrost you'll see as you get further north. Not positive at all from our perspective – or that of millions of other species. It means it could all change very, very rapidly. And that we will lose any chance of ever bringing it back under control. "Runaway" climate change is the result. Not a happy ending. If we reach runaway climate change we'll all be losers. Tell that to your prospective grape-growers.'

We left Annie, feeling distinctly battered, and retreated to our student room. Annie had deftly dispatched any remaining hope that in Canada we might find a state and a citizenry that could be emulated; an environmental role model. It was deeply demoralising. I wasn't sure whether I felt more like giving up in despair, or cycling ever harder. Lacking a stiff whisky, we perched on the small bed and surveyed the map of Alaska instead. From Prince George, the road headed either west or northwest for a little under five hundred miles to Kitwanga. There, we had the chance to shorten the journey. Kitwanga was the junction. We could turn north onto the Cassiar

Highway, as planned. Alternatively, we could continue west to the coast at Prince Rupert and hop on a northbound ferry for a couple of days. Plan B had two distinct advantages. It would buy us some time, cutting out about five days of cycling. And at the same time, it would be a rest. We could sit on the ferry, eat and sleep and watch the view glide effortlessly by. It sounded absolutely wonderful.

'But it's cheating.' I said.

Chris disagreed. 'No. You'll still have done a fantastic distance across wonderful landscapes. If you'd said your goal was to reach Canada, you'd have already achieved it.'

'But I didn't. The goal was to cycle from El Paso to Anchorage. Cycle. All of it. Not jump on a boat when it gets a bit tough.'

Chris sighed. 'It's not me that's feeling tired. If we take the ferry you can have a rest, catch up a bit, and still cycle into Anchorage. You'll still have done over four thousand miles. I don't get the cheating bit at all.'

He genuinely didn't. Not only that, but in his franker moments Chris would gently suggest I was caught up in some archaic residue of an old colonial mindset: the mindset that had spurred generations of Brits to vanquish mountains, open new trade routes and colonize resistant continents. 'Conquer! Achieve! Dominate! Push yourself to the limits! We don't have to do the trip that way at all. We could just be here, slow down, enjoy getting as far as we get and what we see on the way. You could just let go of Anchorage altogether.' But I couldn't. 'OK,' said Chris, ever imperturbable. 'It's your trip. So, what can we do to deal with this tiredness?' I couldn't respond. For days I'd felt that my fitness had not just plateaued out, but seemed positively in decline. I should be cruising the miles by now. I wasn't. But having admitted I was tired, I'd anticipated being judged as weak and found wanting, not this entirely nonjudgmental and eminently practical response. 'Vitamins? Better food? Or,' said Chris with a straight face, 'I could take some of the weight from your panniers ...' the rest of the sentence was muffled in feathers as I thwacked him as hard as possible with both pillows.

~

The next day I woke feeling much better. The sky was a glorious blue. We stopped at a shopping mall on the way out of town. Feeling a slight sense of unease about leaving the bikes, we locked them – a precaution we'd rarely ever taken so far. And then we dived in, intending to be as fast as possible. In positive action mode, I bought a ton of drugs: ibuprofen, aspirin, some other painkiller specially recommended for knees, and a bottle of enormous multivits. We bought some healthy food. And then, in an attempt to speed up breakfast by bypassing the need for a café stop, we ordered two egg bagels at a stand. They took forever.

'Someone is stealing our bikes,' I thought, while we finally ate. And then I dismissed the thought as daft. I was probably just picking up on how depressing the place was. Huge, entirely indoors, shut away from the sun and the sky and full of sterile chain shops glittering with stuff that was for the most part completely unnecessary but that people all around us had worked their lives away to earn money to buy. The pinnacle of civilisation!

At last we were done and finding our way back out through vast identical hallways to the entrance where we'd left the bikes. They were still there. Of course. But one of Chris' panniers was open, his shoes were sticking out and a bag with a toilet roll in it was lying on the ground. My back pannier was open too, with inner tube and chain lube half pulled out. But nothing had been taken. Odd. It dawned on us that someone had been rapidly searching all the obvious places where something of value might be. The speedometers were still there. The panniers were still there. Then, 'Oh no! My handlebar bag!' yowled Chris. It was open, and the video camera was gone. 'Bastards!' I heard myself spitting. First, the camera was not ours, but borrowed from a friend. Second, all that wonderful footage that Chris had been taking – some beautiful images of the stunning icefields scenery on a rare day when the clouds had been high. And the stills he'd taken when my camera battery was flat and I had no pictures at all. The footage of the sad, diminished glacier at Athabaska. And the entire 'red squirrel fighting fig roll' episode that had made us laugh aloud every time we replayed it. All gone. Chris hadn't used a video camera before but he clearly had a real flair for it, and we'd both realised how this footage would transform our slide show when we got home. There was no way we were going to get it back. How stupid to have left the camera on the bikes, when so many people had warned us; trusting in people may often be a good thing, but suspend it for Prince George.

Chris looked utterly downcast. 'It's Jo's camera,' he said.

'I know. But it's gone. Can we sort it?'

The last shop on the way out of the mall was a 'Digital Sight and Sound' shop. In fact, our bikes were leaning up against its windows. For a brief moment of hyper-suspicion I wondered if it had all been a sales ploy. Then I marched inside for a recce, leaving Chris on guard. 'I am so sorry,' said the assistant, when I told him what had happened. 'Apologies on behalf of the decent residents of Prince George. Why don't you bring your bikes into our shop? Would you like a coffee?' And with that, we were back in credit card mode, choosing between the ranks of sleek, grey, lightweight hand-held camcorders while our bikes leaned against a pillar of digital TVs, and a vast screen in the background played the Incredible Four behind us. After weeks on the road with a simplified existence we had no resistance to all this astonishing visual stimulation, and awesome fight scenes constantly pulled our attention away from the need to choose between Gismo X3 Mark 1 and Gismo X2 Mark 4 to supernatural heroes with elasticated arms flying at vertiginous speeds around skyscrapers in the excellent cause of catching villains.

Needless to say it was noonish by the time we were climbing the hill out of Prince George. The traffic was heavy and we were still berating ourselves for having been so stupid. 'Look on the positive side,' I said. 'All the things we didn't lose. Like the bikes!' And the pannier that had my journals in. I'd been keeping a journal for the whole trip, and had by now filled four notebooks. They would be the basis of the slide show and any writing and I couldn't bring myself to post them home in case they were lost. 'Now that *would* have been a disaster.'

Chris nodded. 'Want the other good news? We'll be out of here in minutes!'

Two punctures in quick succession immediately followed this statement, keeping us on the edges of Prince George for another maddening hour or more, pulled off the road in a small shopping complex. Having checked out the sports shop on the off-chance it sold inner tubes – it sold mostly guns, fish hooks and other ways of killing things – I sat on the tarmac outside a launderette mending my punctures while Chris went in search of coffee and fruit juice.

It was gone two by the time we were finally underway. But the sun was shining, the wind had dropped and I was feeling much, much stronger. And the road was easier. We were still crossing rivers, but the climbs on the far side were shorter and less steep than they had been. Heading west, we were moving further and further from the mountains and, for a while, our horizons became almost flat. Between the brown pine trees – at one point we looked back and the entire horizon appeared a dull chestnut colour – was intermittent farmland: barley, grass, cattle. For thirty miles we rode at a good fast pace and then stopped for lunch by a lake just as we were beginning to fade. Bread and cheese, zucchini, tomatoes, nectarines. I was having a sort of reverse food poisoning phenomenon – the way that, after being sick, you can usually identify the thing that poisoned you by reviewing everything you ate and noticing when your stomach cringes. I was thinking of all the things I'd eaten over the last couple of days and having a disproportionately positive response when I thought of the previous night's salad.

~

Our tiredness was conveniently taking turns. For the next few days I was strong, while Chris began to struggle with the long hours. Some afternoons I would lend him the tiny black music machine, knowing word for word, beat for beat the songs he was listening to and watching him too visibly pick up speed to the sound of Coldplay's 'Green Eyes' or the James Bond theme tune or They Might be Giants' wonderfully out of place lyrics. 'It's Istanbul, not Constantinople ...' Chris missed the mountains and found the countryside here monotonous. For me, it recalled the landscape north of Aberdeen: flat, rich farmland, fields with large round straw bales, occasional beef cattle, patches of woodland. Patches of deep purple-blue vetch and a tall-stemmed yellow coltsfoot-like flower grew in the verges, their heads turned not into the sun but away from the wind. In the distance were forests that looked like hills swathed in heather – the pine-beetled trees, almost purple in the sun. Farm buildings shaped like Dutch barns and a clutch of Dutch or German-sounding names – Vanderhoof, Engen – were scattered among the thoroughly un-European names. Ootsa Lake. Tchesinkut Lake. Sawchee Bay. Nechako River. We were in a land of peoples with utterly different cultures from the European: different values, different worldviews, a way of living as distinct from ours as any you'd find in any more 'exotic' destination. And it had all but been destroyed.

At Fort Fraser we bought fresh fruit and veg from a stall run by two women who told us that we'd see snowcapped mountains again when we reached Burns Lake. They told us that, since the pine beetle epidemic, the fish they caught in the lakes had gotten bigger through eating the bugs. And that the German with the huskies was about an hour ahead. Not long after, Chris crossed his thousand-mile mark opposite the Piper's Glen RV resort. We stopped to top up our water, and celebrated with lattes at a 'speciality' coffee shop. As I stood in the queue, Chris knocked on the window. 'He's here!' not sure who he was referring to I left the shop to find the German cyclist standing in the forecourt with his bike, a trailer and three dogs. He was a large man with a ponytail, wearing a vivid fluorescent jacket and cycling shorts. The dogs sat attentively, watching him, four dark brown eyes and two pale ice blue, gleaming from a depth of grey fur. I couldn't resist the dogs. They tolerated my attention without ever taking their eyes off their human pack-leader, whose name was Karl.

'When it's flat or uphill, they run alongside the bike and help pull it. Downhill, they jump in the trailer,' Karl explained, showing us how the three dog-leads attached to a metal spring on one side of the mountain bike. Then, standing there in the mall forecourt, he told us his story. It was extraordinary. For a start, he'd been cycling for eighteen years. 'I was diagnosed with a malignant form of skin cancer,' he said, 'and given a year to live. That was 1988. I thought, what have I always wanted to do but never done? Cycle in the Alps. I took off. Been cycling ever since.'

It had turned into a round-the-world trip. Wherever he went, he tried to spread a simple message. 'Cancer. Don't give up.' In Argentina, travelling with Shere Khan, the grandfather of the eldest dog, he'd been hit from behind by a truck that had left him for dead in a ditch – on a straight road in broad daylight. Shere Khan was killed and Karl was in a coma for two weeks. He came to in an Argentinean hospital with complete memory loss and half a leg missing. 'This one,' he said, pointing to a hitherto unnoticed prosthetic below his left knee. Confined to bed, he'd soon begun to feel restless. The hospital gave him his journals, recovered from the wreckage of his bike, from which he learned he'd been cycling round the world. He decided to repeat the journey in the hope that it might reawaken his memory. It did, in relation to those places; of the person he was before the ride began, he could recall nothing. He was now halfway through his fourth circumnavigation of the world, ceaselessly recovering old memories. And breaking world records. At that precise point, he was heading for the Yukon, hoping to break the record for cycling the longest number of days at sub-zero temperature which, at 153 days, he already held. 'It's getting harder to do,' he said, 'because the winters are getting shorter and warmer.' This unfortunate impact on sub-zero cycling was surely the most unexpected side effect of global warming we'd encountered on the entire trip. Except perhaps its effect on his other record attempt, the longest continuous bike ride on ice. 'We ride the Great Slave Lake and the Yukon River when they're frozen,' he said. 'The dogs love it. Suits their paws.'

We chatted with Karl for ages. His was an incredible story and he told it well. We would have loved to spend more time with him. Karl himself was stopping for the day – hotels and motels around the world gave him free accommodation and he carried a reference from several of them vouching for the dogs' good behaviour. We, on the other hand, still had a large chunk of that day's miles to ride. We left with some difficulty, having become part of a small crowd. The crowd included two women from Scotland who clearly felt a sort of distant clan-based allegiance with us, and a First Nations woman called Muriel who warned us about bears – particularly plentiful and particularly grumpy on the stretch ahead, she said. There did seem to be more bears around. We'd pulled into a rest stop earlier in the day and a man in a jeep shouted a warning: 'There's a bear cub up a tree over there. I don't know where the mother is. Be careful!' The cub was very high up a very slim aspen tree, its legs hanging down on each side of a very slim branch, looking like a stuck teddy bear and making an occasional mewing, cheeping noise.

We rode for hours in beautiful evening sunlight and had a spontaneous, luxurious night in a bed and breakfast run by a chiropractor – 'I work on horses or people. Prefer horses, though' – who looked us briefly up and down and handed over a bottle of Radox for the bath. PJ had played rugby for the United States and he and his wife Anne had lived in Hawaii for several years before settling in British Columbia. Over eggs, toast and blueberry pancakes next morning, they told us how the first year they'd arrived they'd met a moose and two calves on a walk and how the moose now came and ate hay with their horses in the winter. Various dogs and a very fat cat all came to see us off when we left. As we cycled back down their track to the road, I had an uprush of emotion: an old longing to do with wanting to live somewhere with animals. Dogs and cats and maybe even horses again, somewhere with wild animals in the vicinity, land to wander around and look after, wood to chop and a Landrover for which I'd have a legitimate need. For the first few miles we reran a familiar conversation about how to make all of that compatible, supposing some mythical future in which it would be affordable, with the equally strong desire to travel.

~

It turned into a long day. We rode hard for about eighty miles and stopped at Houston to buy more food. I wandered around the small supermarket failing to make decisions until Chris handed me a banana and some ibuprofen, claiming he could hear my knees creak two aisles away. We cycled on, past a campsite, intending to stop at Barrett Lake. Barrett Lake didn't materialise. We cycled on. Some friendly lads in a café had commented earlier that we were 'like the grizzlies. You can camp anywhere. You don't need a special spot.' But the countryside here was not readily compatible with wild camping. We cycled on. Chris had a back wheel flat. We fixed it. Dusk fell. We came to a tiny shed by the road signed 'Vic's Garage, OPEN'. Vic was just leaving.

'Is there anywhere to camp around here?' I asked, with my sweetest smile, hoping he would say, 'Heck, you're welcome to pitch your tent just here. No-one will bother you.'

He said, 'Telkwa. Another twenty kilometres. Lovely night to be cycling …' and walked away. We cycled on.

Then Chris had another back wheel flat. By now, it was dark. We positioned the bikes with their backlights pointing towards possible oncoming traffic in either direction and sat on the narrow hard shoulder. Neither of us had any fixed, let alone never-punctured, inner tubes. The one Chris was trying to patch turned out to have not one but three holes in it. After a while he gave up, and put in a tube with a single slow puncture instead. A police car with two armed officers drove past, slowed down, and continued without stopping. Then another car went by, stopped, turned round, came back. 'Are you guys okay?' the lone woman inside asked. She suggested we might find a closer place to camp at a sight with cabins at the top of the hill. With Chris' back tyre only just holding air and rapidly deflating we pelted off to the top of the road and then freewheeled down a dirt road in the pitch blackness, arriving at a small house with a madly barking dog at the bottom. A human emerged. The human was friendly!

'So sorry it's so late ... somewhere to camp?'

'No problem. Glad you found us! Too many bears for camping here. I'll go and check on the cabins, though.' He went into the house. 'I'm so sorry, our cabins are full.' And then, as our spirits sank in unison, 'But my wife's just making up the spare room.' We stood and chatted in the cool dark air.

A blonde woman in pyjamas came and joined us. 'Please, come in!' she said, as friendly as her husband and apparently completely unperturbed by this late and unexpected arrival of greasy, grimy cyclists. She showed us our room and the bathroom, gave us some water in tall, cool glasses and wished us good night. We sat on the stripy bedcover eating tortilla chips and musing about our luck.

Next morning, we were invited to join Wayne, Nina and their family for coffee and a DIY breakfast. A blonde child carefully advised us which of the various cereal options was the best. A gorgeous golden retriever played with a black and white cat. We sat in the warm kitchen and chatted. 'Round Lake Resort' was a relatively new endeavour. For three years they'd been building the business around their twenty-eight acres of beautiful forested lake-shore and five cabins.

'It's mostly word of mouth,' said Nina. 'What we offer is tranquillity. And nature. There are no speedboats on the lake, so it's peaceful, and safe for swimmers and sailors and kids in dinghies. The wildlife is really rich here, especially birds. We have lots of nature trails. And there's always a log fire alight when people arrive.'

'Is it working?' I asked, thinking about the furious debate around the banning of speedboats on Lake Windermere in England.

'Yes, it is. There are plenty of places for folk who want speed and noise. We offer something different. And it seems that there are people out there who are looking for that too. Looking for a sense of peace. Enough to keep us well provided for, at least.'

We asked them what they thought about climate change. 'You should go back and talk to the old woman at Vic's Garage,' Wayne said. 'She has lots of stories about how different life here is now. Hotter in summer. And nowhere near as cold in the winter. My main concern is air currents.' We looked at him quizzically, and he treated us to a short disquisition on the way planes cause turbulence, which mixes up the air, adversely affecting the local climate. The need to get going left us poorly positioned to pursue this intriguing hypothesis further. We offered heartfelt thanks for finding a space for us so late at night. 'Come any time,' said Wayne, flatly refusing to accept any money for the room. Nina gave us a hug as we left. 'Ride safely! Come again!' What lovely people.

I was tempted to go back to Vic's Garage but it didn't really make sense time-wise, despite the fact that our milometers were reading 'ninety-four' from the previous day. We headed for Telkwa instead. Making a living here was clearly not easy. We passed a closed-down motel, the roadfront row of blue and white rooms fringed with grass growing down from the roof. At Telkwa, the scattering of bars and restaurants were almost all shut, and building after building was for sale. Smithers, like a smaller and not-quite-so-cute version of Jasper was, however, alive and well. Flags flew above the malls and tourist shops and the mountains, definitely back on the scene, nudged up around the town. We found a bike shop and bought several inner tubes each. Chris bought some 'instant' sticky puncture repair patches that proclaimed glue and sandpaper a thing of the past. We sat in the sun and drank coffee. Another coffee-drinker called me over, gesturing to an opened magazine.

'Ramses the Second,' he said, pointing to a picture of a half-mummified skeleton. 'He was a red-head, you know.'

'Really!' I said, politely. 'No, I didn't know that,' and excused myself to use the internet. 'Half an hour, max,' I agreed with Chris, who headed off to mend inner tubes in the sunshine. I wrote about Jim Halfpenny, and Yellowstone, and the wolves, and Chris left me to it for nearly two hours while he worked away in the sun and listened patiently to a lecture on Redheads in History – Queen Elizabeth I, Napoleon, one of the Roman Emperors, and all of the Vikings.

Back on the road, a huge mountain topped with a glacier shone in the sunshine. We cycled on, talking about whether or not to take the short cut to the ferry at Prince Rupert. 'I'm up for carrying on north if that's what you want to do,' said Chris and, at that precise moment, the little peregrine mascot who'd been with me throughout jumped out of my handlebar bag and landed on the road. An affirmation or a bid for freedom to escape a stupid plan?! It wasn't entirely clear. I retrieved him and we carried on. At Moricetown, First Nations people were fishing in a canyon with nets. Smoked salmon was for sale at the side of the road. Beyond the canyon, the road was beautiful with big wide vistas and shadows. And, round the long corner at Hazelton, a huge line of mountains suddenly filled the horizon, their summits out of the trees and glowing pink and orange in the late evening sun.

Next morning we rode to Kitwanga and the junction, putting forty miles under our saddles before we stopped. At the junction was a gas station with two huge signs. One read 'North to Alaska' and the other, 'Petro-Canada', framed by a large red and white maple leaf. Chris took my photograph next to an enormous chrome plated shiny truck with white bull bars higher than my head. In the restaurant everything was meat, except for breakfast, which we'd missed. We talked them into making us fried egg and cheese toasties with chips, and a cherry pie chaser.

'Okay,' I said, as our pies arrived. 'Decision time. I can see the sense in heading straight on.' Straight on was the road to the coast, and the ferry short cut. 'But I really don't want to give in just yet.' With the map of Alaska spread over Nina and Wayne's stripy bedcover we'd worked out we could still make Anchorage in time – so long as we did a minimum of seventy-five to eighty miles a day and didn't take more than two days off in the next three weeks. I'd been feeling strong for the past few days but, as if the tiredness was a creature we passed back and forth between us, Chris had been feeling the miles – hardly surprising since he'd never done any sort of long-distance cycling before. Most of my stamina, I knew, came from my head; all those years of cycling adding up to the certain knowledge that when your body tells you it's absolutely done in you still have a good thirty miles left in your legs. 'It's your call,' I said. 'Whatever you want to do is fine.'

Chris grinned. 'Let's go,' he said. We paid for the food and went back outside to the waiting bikes. We were heading north. North for Alaska.

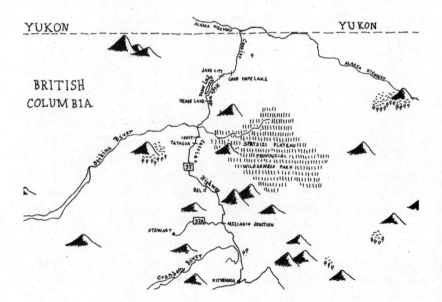

CHAPTER TWELVE
Riding to Alaska

'The "constantly expanding market" first opened in the New World by the fur traders is still expanding – no longer so much by expansions of territory or population, but by the calculated outdating, outmoding, and degradation of goods and by the hysterical self-dissatisfaction of consumers that is indigenous to an exploitative economy.'

Wendell Berry [48]

'Economists live in a land of make-believe. They aim at steady growth in consumption, material goods, wealth and profit as if it can be sustainable indefinitely.'

David Suzuki [49]

As soon as we'd made the decision it felt right. We crossed the bridge and stopped to watch the distant figure of a grizzly bear bathing in the river below. The air was full of silver rosebay willowherb seed and for almost ten minutes we had a tailwind. Then the wind noticed, and normal headwind services were resumed.

We'd been told we shouldn't miss the totem poles at the town of Kitwancool, twenty or so miles ahead. We cycled and cycled and saw no towns at all, let alone a town with totem poles. There was little traffic. We were now on the Cassiar Highway; beautiful, sparsely populated and heading north. We'd be on the Cassiar for a little over four hundred miles until we joined the Alaska Highway, otherwise known as the 'Alcan'. After that, it was only another thousand miles to Anchorage.

We cycled all day seeing barely a house. That evening, stopped for a rest on a bridge over the Cranberry River, Chris suddenly pointed downwards. There was something like a small log, floating – no, swimming in the water below us. A beaver! As the beaver swam under the bridge we scooted across to the other side. Out he came! And

---

[48] Wendell Berry (1977) *The Unsettling of America* Avon Books

[49] David Suzuki (2003) *The David Suzuki Reader* Greystone Books

then another. We watched the beavers for ages, swimming upstream and then gliding back down again and again, apparently just for fun, their brown grey fur streaked and tousled in the water, dark eyes and ears just above the surface.

We were a bit low on mileage, but not disastrously low. Sixty-eight. The light was fading and not only were the beavers entrancing but a tempting flat, grassy spot just off the road behind the crash barrier would make a perfect campsite. A bald eagle in a tree just beyond clinched it, and we put up the tent to the sound of energetic rustling in the branches. I went down to the river for water. *Three* beavers were cruising up and down. As I stood stock-still a beaver swam straight towards me, veering away only at the last minute. I was close enough to see her enormous feet plying the water like paddles. Occasionally one of the beavers would catch sight of me unexpectedly and slap a huge tail down onto the water as an alarm signal. Chris appeared, thinking I might have drowned. Apparently I'd been gone for a good hour. As we watched, a beaver followed by a juvenile emerged from under a low hanging branch and swam passed us, then turned and swam by again. The young beaver, outrageously cute, was clearly being encouraged to check us out. 'Go on, have a good look. That's a human! They used to turn us into hats but they're generally much friendlier now.'

Eventually we left them in peace and went back to the tent. The beavers had captivated us to the extent that we'd failed to notice the mosquitoes and we both had a row of bites like tiny red molehills across our foreheads. I fell asleep with beavers swimming across my mind's eye, feeling peaceful and at ease.

There was no sign of beavers in the morning. We cycled away through mixed woodland, rolling hills around us and black bears picking berries by the side of the road. Sometimes we would stop for a while and watch them from a respectful distance. One stood on his hind legs pulling berries and leaves towards him with his front paws, ducking his head down when a car went by. About fifty miles ahead was Meziadin Junction, where a side road – Highway 37A – left the Cassiar Highway and meandered through the Bear Glacier Provincial Park to the town of Stewart. Everyone we'd spoken to had said, you must go to Stewart. Stewart sits right on the border between the Kitimat-Stikine area of British Columbia, and Alaska. From Stewart, a narrow channel of water runs for a hundred miles to the Pacific. Huge glaciers crowd down to the ocean and you can watch grizzlies catching fish in the river, something I very much wanted to do. But Stewart was about forty miles off our route. We didn't have time for an additional eighty-mile detour, though we did toy with the idea that we might hire a car at the junction, just for a few hours.

As we got closer to the parting of the roads, our fantasies inclined more towards a big nosh-up in the café. At last we arrived. Two hitch-hikers stood forlornly at the roadside. The café was shut. Not shut for an hour, but shut for the winter. A small blue shed by the gas pump sold crisps and car oil, and the woman inside snarled ill-temperedly at Chris when he asked if she had any other food. We sat on the wooden steps of the closed café and ate our last tortillas and cheese – and a bag of crisps – laughing at ourselves for thinking we might have hired a car at this place. The hitchhikers waved sadly when we cycled away, leaving Stewart for another time.

I wondered again what on earth I was doing. Cycling endlessly past totem poles and wildlife hotspots and extraordinary scenery. Not stopping, because at some point in the warmth of my sitting room at home I had randomly decided that the end of the trip was Anchorage, and that I would get there by bike. Now, as Chris had pointed out, I was trapped in that narrative; and Chris too, in virtue of his support for 'my' trip. In my head, if we changed our plans now, if we detoured and didn't get to Anchorage, the whole trip would be in some sense a failure. On one level, I could see this was bonkers. On another level, I just couldn't change it.

By the end of that day the hills had become mountains again and we were cycling into huge views. Forested valleys stretched for hundreds of miles and the mountains surrounded us on every horizon. We swooped down to a metal bridge across a river we'd hoped to get water from. Through the metal grid we could see the water, rushing and boiling below. It was turquoise. Glacier melt. Undrinkable. We carried on, water bottles empty, the cool air masking our thirst until we reached the next river. That night we camped on irresistible flat grass at a rest stop, set back from the road and shielded from sight by the 'no-camping' signs. Chris cooked noodles and pesto sauce on a picnic bench while I walked down to the – non-glacial – river for water. A cloud of bats swooped from the trees, switching in the sky like a flock of starlings before they disappeared into the dusk.

~

The next day was to be, for me, one of the hardest. My tiredness, at
bay for the last week or so, came back out of nowhere with a venge-
ance and I hit a complete physical low. I'd slept for ten hours and
still couldn't wake up. Deep, sticky sleep kept pulling me back into
darkness. When I eventually came to we lay in the tent with the map.
There was an obvious stop at Bell II, about forty miles ahead. 'Let's
have a half-day,' Chris suggested, gently. We'd been doing seventy-
mile days, more or less – apart from the ninety-mile puncture in the
dark day – and needed to be doing a fair bit more, not considerably
less. But I knew it was not going to be a seventy-mile day for me, and
that was without even leaving my sleeping bag. 'Yep,' I agreed. I felt
exasperated but cornered. 'Okay. A half-day.' I dawdled over breakfast
and wrote my journal on the picnic bench. It was elevenish by the
time we got going. As soon as we were back on the road I realised I
really was tired. Each pedal stroke was an effort. I couldn't get any
speed up at all, and soon lagged miles behind Chris. My whole body
felt flat and unresponsive. 'Mind over matter!' I kept thinking, 'Just
do it! Speed up!' and absolutely nothing would happen.

There was no point thinking about the implications if I couldn't
work through this. I focused on the scenery, which my snail-like speed
allowed me to enjoy in some detail. The verges were full of flowers,
changing as the days passed. That day, dark burgundy and vivid yellow vetches were scattered amongst the familiar blues and violets.
White and pink clovers appeared amongst patches of mare's tail and
bullrush. From a distance, rosebay willowherb and tall, fox-coloured
grasses gave the verges a pinkish/orange glow. Tiredness aside, I was
falling in love with the Cassiar Highway. It felt very different from the
better-known Icefields Parkway. More remote, much less traffic. Wild
camping was suddenly easy. And on the Parkway it had felt almost as
if the mountains had been deliberately positioned along side of the
road for the benefit of passing traffic. We'd cycled by, looking out
at the mountains as spectators. Here, we were in the landscape. Less
melodramatic and less classically photogenic, but every bit as beautiful.
And of course, there were the bears: vivid black shapes standing out
for miles on the verges ahead, their fur lush and shiny in the sunshine.

It took me the whole of the rest of that day to cycle thirty-eight miles. Some half-day! I thought, as I crawled at last past the 'Bell II' road sign. 'It's going to be the complete opposite to Meziadin Junction,' joked Chris. 'A posh resort full of super-friendly people!' It was exactly that. There were log cabins, and a hotel with a restaurant.

'I'm so sorry,' said a charming woman on the desk, 'we have no cabins or rooms left. They're all full. But you can camp here, and our camping guests are welcome to use the hot tub.'

A hot tub! I could scarcely imagine anything I'd like more. We pitched the tent and had a shower, the first for some days. Then we had a 'nature lover's burger' in the restaurant. Then we did our laundry. And then we sat in the hot tub, watching the stars come out. It was a little hard to take in. Many miles from the nearest town, we were sitting in a hot tub, the gorgeously hot water bubbling around my stressed-out muscles just when I could most do with it. We soaked up the warmth and the bubbles and the stars for a good hour or so. And then we went back inside for a beer, in a bar whose walls were covered in geology maps and pictures of people skiing on pristine wild snow, their skis leaving gracious arks across the virgin white high mountain slopes.

The next morning, I felt almost fully revived. In keeping with the luxurious spirit of the place, we treated ourselves to breakfast in the restaurant, lingering over delicious omelettes and fresh fruit and toast. The restaurant was packed. 'It's because of the mining opening up,' our hostess explained. 'That's why the place is so full. The cabins have four or five men to a room. It's a contemporary gold-rush.'

'That explains the geology maps,' said Chris.

'Yes. It's great for business,' she continued, 'but to be honest, I'm worried what it'll do to the environment here. All those big trucks, and roads punched into the forest where there have never been roads before. Environmentally, it's bad news.' Conquering boundless nature. It was clearly still going on.

'And the heli-skiing?' I asked, cautiously. On the way to breakfast we'd seen a small red and white helicopter parked incongruously by some trees at the side of the road, and belatedly realised its connection with the skiing pictures.

'Oh the heli-skiing is fantastic!' she said. 'It's our main source of income. We take people up into the most wonderful snow where nobody else can get. So few people in such a huge mountain range – it leaves hardly a trace.' Her concern for the environment was surely genuine. There was just no connection in her mind between helicopters and any possible environmental ill-effects, like the global warming that, ironically, seemed increasingly set to wipe out most of their lovely snow.

The air was cool enough to be wearing leggings. We cycled away from Bell II and into a forest, a glorious chaos of multiple shades of green. The dark forest green of the conifers; a pale, grassy green on the mountain slopes; the silver of aspen leaves in the sun and wind and the grey green of aspen in shadow. I was thinking about heli-skiing. For around $10,000 you could spend a week living in this beautiful spot, eating delicious food and being transported daily by helicopter to the tops of mountains. Ski down the immaculate wild snow and then get picked up at the bottom for the next flight to another mountaintop. It must be absolutely amazing. But what an energy-expensive way to have fun. It seemed like a perfect example in microcosm of a much wider problem. Energy freedom. *Our* energy freedom. In modern industrialised countries we are free to consume energy, as much as we like, for whatever purpose we like, constrained only by our own personal wealth.

And we are incredibly profligate with energy. If you are rich enough, you can leave your house lit up like a Christmas tree, jump into your RV and tow your Hummer up north for a season's heli-skiing. Even those of us who do not quite fall into this category, but who live in Europe or North America or other industrialised nations, use vastly more energy per capita than citizens in developing countries. And vastly more than has been calculated as sustainable. We use it without thinking; without acknowledging that energy is precious stuff; that its mis-use has big costs and potentially catastrophic side-effects; that access to it globally is deeply inequitable. We use it this way because that, for us, is normal. But climate change surely brings with it the urgent requirement to sit down and figure out how to use energy wisely, fairly, efficiently, *and for things we really need.*

This train of thought butts right up against our fiercely defended freedom of choice. We are so quick to defend our entitlement, our 'right' to consume energy – and anything else – in any way we choose. It's the 'If I've earned it, nobody is going to tell me how to spend it' attitude; the conversation I'd imagined having with the stretch Hummer inhabitants. Big cars, cheap flights, unlimited heat and light, energy expensive forms of recreation, increasing quantities of 'stuff'. We want to be free to consume as we please. But should we champion this freedom at *any* cost? *Is* this the best way to allocate and use our precious and dwindling and costly energy supplies? What if the cost is a liveable planet? And do we need all this stuff for quality of life anyway?

The road climbed up to a fantastic plateau, coaxing my attention back to the landscape around us. We looked across a vast valley of trees to distant mountains streaked with snow and old glaciers; thick and chunky and creased with dust and rock in the gullies. A black bear grazing on the roadside ahead of us disappeared into the woods as a truck went past and then re-emerged as we arrived at her spot. She stood up on her hind legs and visibly contemplated charging. As we cycled a good deal faster, she dropped back down onto all fours. From a distance we could see her attention safely restored to the berries, not remotely camouflaged but starkly black against the gold and green verges. The truck was unusual: there was hardly any traffic. On the plateau we had an immense feeling of space. The clouds thinned and fell away. Barley-headed grasses glowed gold and whiskery in the sun and small black caterpillars marched determinedly across the road. And then, a tailwind! With the wind adding easy speed we swooped down an endless descent, one of those joyful, beautiful, effortless rides that makes the grungier days seem infinitely worth enduring.

~

The next day was puncture day. It was overcast and windy and Chris had a back wheel flat not long after we'd set off. It went down again, with a dramatic woosh, a few miles after he'd fixed it. There was a hole in his tyre from an earlier nail and I worried that this might be pinching the inner tube, though the holes in the tube didn't really line up that way. I patched Chris' tyre with duct tape anyway and we made it as far as a café at Tatoga with relatively hard tyres all round. Not only did the café do really quite edible veggi-burgers – we were rapidly becoming connoisseurs of Canadian veggi-burgers – but it was full of the worst of temptations in relation to back wheel problems and my personal consumption weaknesses. Books. Huge coffee table

231

books with fabulous photographs of the Spatsizi Plateau Wilderness area, just off to our right. Books about local environmental issues. And signed copies of most of the books of David Suzuki, a Canadian environmentalist who, the café owner told us, had a cabin nearby. 'One salad with blue cheese dressing, yuk, don't know how anyone could eat the stuff. And Suzuki, yes, he was here two weeks ago. You've only just missed him!' We sat with our piles of food – soup, burgers, salad, fries – and piles of Suzuki books next to a sign saying 'Please buy the books before you read them'. And then we bought three of them – just what our overloaded bikes needed. Having previously banned Chris from buying canned olives I felt honour-bound to add them all to my load.

A few miles later, I could see an ominous bulging in Chris' back tyre. It was still losing air. 'Let's change your tyres over,' I suggested, thinking that the tyre with the hole in would be fine on the front wheel, while the other relatively intact tyre could better take the weight on the back. We reached the tiny town of Iskut and pulled off the road by a large shop lined with half-empty shelves. Pushing the bikes to the side of the building out of the wind, we settled down to some serious puncture problem-solving beneath a poster that read, 'Hitch-hiking? Sister, it ain't worth the risk.' Four hours later we were still there. The tyre on Chris' front wheel was a brand new Armadillo and bloody hard to get off. We resorted to a metal spoon after breaking two tyre levers; and then it was bloody hard to get it back on again. Every time we fixed a flat and put the wheel back on, it would immediately go down again, each time for a different reason. The spoon pinched the inner tube. The inner tube had a leaking valve. Chris had already used his new inner tubes, and all were now mottled with 'instant' patches that were, we realised, systematically unsticking themselves after a few hours so that, having fixed one puncture, a prior patch would come loose. We began to feel we were cursed to spend days huddled behind this grim shop. Worst of all, the wind had been picking up and a force six *tailwind* was howling passed as we hunched for hours in the lee of a food mall surrounded by litter, endlessly fixing flats.

By the time we got going it was six in the evening and we were down to three tyre levers and two patches between us. We climbed out of Iskut and onto a gravel section. The gravel was packed down hard and oiled and, though it was slower to ride than the tarmac, it was by no means impossible. The glorious tailwind pushed us along. I was struggling to stay philosophical. Chris' back tyre still had a slow flat and we had to stop every few miles to pump it up. We needed to be doing bigger miles and today should have been a gift of a day. With this tailwind we could have flown along for an effortless ninety miles. Instead we'd spent it *sheltering* from the wind! I hung back until I'd more or less dealt with the upsurge of exasperation and forced myself to shift back into 'it is as it is' mode. Anger was pointless, and the situation was not exactly life-threatening. But I did need to figure out how to deal with the punctures.

A long descent took us down to the Stikine River. A couple of people were already camped there. We cycled down across grass and found a spot out of sight between trees – though still within earshot of two kids playing loud fighting games with sticks, in between bashing the hell out of the bushes. I made myself focus on the river, flowing past us only a few feet away. And on inner tubes. Chris' had patches on patches but one of my spares had only been fixed once, though with one of the duff 'instant' jobs. I peeled it off and reattached it with good old-fashioned glue. My inner tubes were thinner than Chris' but they might just be okay on his wheels. I held the patch tightly for ages until it was totally sealed and held my breath while I pumped it up inside Chris' tyre. So far so good. 'Fingers crossed it's still okay in the morning,' I said, as we sat on a log in the dusk eating noodles. Two squirrels chased each around a tree, chattering furiously, and some tiny mice with big eyes whizzed and darted at high speed, occasionally leaping into the air for reasons we couldn't discern. They were very funny to watch. One ran over Chris' foot and took a nip at his ankle. Later, we lay in the tent and – luxury! – read Suzuki books in the dim light of our head-torches.

I was only a few pages in before wishing I'd found these books earlier. Suzuki tackles head on the question that had been recurring half-formed and incoherent since my visits to the Mayor of Albuquerque and the Rocky Mountain Institute – and certainly since Aspen. Can we technofix climate change? *Is* this the solution: to take our modern, industrialised, polluting societies and render them environmentally benign through better efficiency and other technological wizardry?

Clearly, there was a question about whether it could actually be done. Somebody, somewhere, I thought, must be crunching the numbers on this; must be working out *how much* more efficient our lifestyles need to be if we are to make them climate-friendly, climate-safe. What factor efficiency do we need to take us from multiple to single-planet living? Factor ten? Factor twenty? Can we achieve it in the timescale we have?

Suzuki almost makes this question redundant. We *know* we can't simply take our current societies, make them super-efficient, and expect to emerge in a just and sustainable world. Not just because the technological challenge may be too great, but because industrialised societies are based on economic and political systems that are fatally flawed in principle. They are committed to indefinite growth on a finite planet: a planet that has ecological limits. They are committed to the impossible. It was my old demons, calling again for a rethink of basic unquestioned assumptions. How could modern societies not be based on growth? The assumption that growth is good and necessary underpins almost everything we do. It underpins our economic systems and our views about individual success. And yet Suzuki argues that we need to question this, the ultimate assumption of our age. Urgently. If we don't, we will bring ourselves down. Waves of growth, pushing out into the forests; endless extraction of ever more resources so we can have ever more stuff. Or is it the other way around? People like us, duped into thinking we need ever more stuff to be happy, so that the growth machine can keep growing. Either way, it is ecologically impossible to continue such a system indefinitely. Climate change is a symptom of this collision between our aspirations to growth and the planet's limits. The environmental costs of continuing on this trajectory are literally unbearable.

Next morning a park ranger dropped by as we were packing up. He was interviewing hunters, he said, to see what they'd caught. A certain amount of permits were given out each year for shooting bighorn sheep, moose and grizzlies. 'But there are plenty poachers for grizzly,' he said. 'They take the bile and the claws for the Asian market, and just leave the rest.' Aaargh, the horrible side-effects of the growth economy! 'Which way you headed?' he asked.

'North,' we said, in unison.

'Well, make sure you stop at Mama Z's at Dease Lake,' he said. 'Best food on the Cassiar.' And he wandered off, a gentle man, gently hunting poachers.

A steep, gravelly climb up and away from the main river took us virtually to the tree-line. We passed a beaver lodge on a tributary and came out onto a high, wild plateau. I was still thinking about Suzuki. Our flawed economic and political systems, he argues, are underpinned by flawed values and worldviews. We imagine ourselves to be outside of nature and in control of it, a profound disconnection from reality. Three months on a bike certainly begins to erode that fantasy, I thought. But this isn't the only flaw in our thinking. We value material wealth very much too highly and we devalue other species, holding them important solely in relation to their usefulness to ourselves, despite the fact that we are only one species amongst thirty million others. And we don't even realise how 'useful' – not to say critical – other species are; that those other species make up ecosystems on which all life depends. And then there is the question of whether we even *want* to keep industrialised lifestyles intact. Is the model of success, of progress, of development it offers us – the model of what it means to live a good life – really a wise, attractive, admirable one? Technological advances, then, are part of the solution but they are far indeed from being the whole answer. To deal with climate change and our other environmental crises we need to deal with these deeper issues.

Reading Suzuki was like suddenly seeing the big picture; seeing how a multitude of different strands connected; seeing why the technofix solution by itself could never be enough; seeing how our trajectory needed to change and catching glimpses of what a 'new normal' would actually entail. I would have loved to know how Amory Lovins and the Rocky Mountain Institute would respond to Suzuki's arguments. 'If only we had time to cycle back to Colorado!' I said, only half-joking. Chris, wisely, did not respond.

Several hours later we were sitting under a broken umbrella in the sunshine at Mama Z's, eating a huge pizza on a silver platter with wonderful crisp, fresh salad. Mama Z was from Yugoslavia. She was blonde, in her fifties, dressed completely in black and very charismatic. When she spoke you could feel her attention fully focused on you, as if your choice in pizza were the most important thing in the world. We were joined by a woman who told us about a music festival at Telegraph Creek, some seventy miles away on a side road. And that the Lord had told her to work with First Nations communities. 'I try to act as a voice for the Tahltan people here,' she said. Unlike many others, the Talhtans had never signed treaties with the government and so still owned their land. 'The government is putting pressure on them to concede their mineral rights,' she said. 'Would be a lot of money. The community is split over it.'

We left reluctantly and went into the town, in search of a hardware store. Dease Lake, which sits right on the Pacific/Arctic divide, had been established as a Hudson's Bay trading post in 1838. It became a major stopping point for streams of trappers and traders heading north and was at the heart of gold rushes on the Stikine River in the 1860s and 70s. The Dease River had been a much-frequented water highway for many decades, though it hadn't been used in this way since the construction of the Alaska Highway. It was currently being 'rediscovered' by paddlers and open boaters – a group of whom had been camped upriver from us the previous evening, prompting much speculation from Chris about how wonderful it would be to travel through this landscape away from the road. And on a craft without inner tubes.

The hardware store had fuel for our stove but no puncture repair kits. 'Try Julie's Variety,' the store owner suggested, pointing a couple of streets away. Loud music pulsated down the street towards us as we headed towards Julie's. Inside, a gang of girls were playing pool. Julie was helpful and apologetic. She had a tyre-repairing kit for a car, but not for bicycles.

'Try the garage?' she suggested. 'They might be able to help fix the flat.' We explained that we'd fixed the flat but needed some spare patches – just in case we had any more punctures. 'Patches! Oh. These little things?' said Julie, rummaging behind the counter and emerging with four of them. 'Take them!'

'Thank you. THANKYOU!' I said, the four tiny bits of rubber leaving me flooded with relief and gratitude and a disproportionate feeling of security.

Dease Lake stretched out alongside the road for miles, long and blue and inviting. At a rest stop, a woman from an RV came over to say hello. She and her husband had, she said, been on the road for six years. They had a postal address in Texas that they stopped by occasionally for mail. Otherwise they travelled. 'This year, we've been all over Alaska,' she said. 'We're just heading south now.' There were, she told us, just under two million full-time RV dwellers in the United States. 'After a while you start getting to know folk. People you get along with will end up pulling up next to you at a different site, just by coincidence. We're travelling with a couple we met that way right now. My daughter back in Tennessee calls them my fly-by-night friends but these days they're our closest friends. We stay in touch by cellphone and folk will often say, "You're only a hundred miles away, we'll come and visit." We have everything in common ...' She was slim and lively, in her early sixties, a regular hiker and clearly in good shape, as many of these modern-day nomads seemed to be.

We'd been thinking of the vast RVs as environmental bad guys but the full-timers almost made us think again. Most of them had sold up very large, centrally heated/air-conditioned homes and much of what was in them. The RVs were now all they owned. Bizarre as it seemed, they had effectively downsized! 'If you compared the environmental footprint of an RV on the road with a typical, large, professional American's home,' I said to Chris as we cycled on, aiming to reach the end of the latest gravel section before we camped, 'I wouldn't be surprised if the RV came out better. Not good, but better.' And they were in the mountains, or at the ocean, relishing the chance to explore their own country's beautiful, wilder places with no call for haste and no reason – aside from disapproving children – to hurry back to wherever they'd once come from. 'They're still gas-guzzlers and they still depend on electricity hook-ups and all that, but they do sort of have a different understanding of "quality of life" from the mainstream,' I mused. 'Quality of time and experience rather than quantity of stuff. Like the cyclists. Would Suzuki approve or disapprove?'

We spent that night in a large clover patch, out of sight of the road and surrounded by trees. Squirrels chattered but kept their distance and the hoof-prints of a large moose tracked through the soft ground at the edge of the woods. We ate soup and pasta while a brief and beautiful pink and grey sunset faded into dusk and the loons began their sad cries across the hidden lake.

~

The next day was, at last, a ninety-mile day. It was overcast when we woke and it started to rain not long after we set off. A moose and her calf were grazing in long grass on the far side of a small lake. I would have to live here for a long time before I took moose and bear for granted, I thought. For now, they were astonishing. It seemed somehow extraordinary to be so close to these creatures and seeing them always felt like a gift. At Jade City we dried out, temporarily, in a gift shop, drinking free coffee and hot chocolate and resisting jade jewellery (not hard) and more books with fabulous pictures of the Stikine Wilderness (much harder). Miles later, we stopped again at Good Hope Lake. The gas station had a small store with crisps, beer, magazines, a few tins of food, an odd assortment of baking trays, one pair of golden shoes, some DIY equipment and a bright purple shirt. The walls were decorated with framed jigsaws of pastoral scenes and two women at the back of the store sat at a table working on another. It had, they said, been unseasonably cold all summer and they'd just heard of snow at Seward, Alaska.

'There's a storm coming in from the west,' contributed a man perusing the beer selection. A large map hung on one wall. We went to consult it. About five days to Whitehorse and then another ten to Anchorage. We had two weeks left. Two weeks at seventy-five miles a day would just about do it. Assuming that the storm didn't arrive or, if it did, that it wasn't a snow storm and that we could cycle through it. But we had been cycling for fifteen days without a day off. We'd need to take a break at some point, and that would mean longer miles on the remaining days...

We sat outside on a bench under a porch and made sandwiches in the company of two young girls and two black and tan dogs with lovely tan eyebrows and tan feet with black toenails. The rain eased as we ate, and then stopped. 'It's getting to the point where we might have to rest for a bit,' Chris said. 'Not sure we can cycle a solid month with no breaks.'

'Hmmm,' I said, munching. 'What are you thinking?' '

Well, there's a Greyhound from Whitehorse to Anchorage,' Chris said, cautiously. It was a sensible suggestion. We could cycle to Whitehorse and catch a bus for the last seven hundred or so miles. Or some of them. Even as I worked it through in my mind I could feel a huge uprising of resistance and behind that, determination. I DON'T WANT TO GIVE IN AND TAKE A GREYHOUND! I yelled internally. I could feel myself drawing together and getting the bit firmly between my teeth. I wanted to get to Anchorage under my own steam, if at all possible, though I felt badly for Chris. He was picking up the costs of my days off in Colorado, and the bulk of his part of the trip was turning into an endurance marathon. But I still couldn't let go of wanting to get to Anchorage by bike. That was the story we were in; and a highly conventional one it was at that. A physical challenge; lots of mini-adventures; highs and lows; an uncertain ending. Will we make it or not? Given the plot, lots of miles, tiredness and a race for the finish were the almost inevitable final chapter. But, cliché or not, I was not about to change the ending unless I really, really had to.

Back on the road, the RVs were heading south in droves. They were all either white and grey, or black and grey, or very dark green – no yellow, red or blue ones – and they had names like 'Montana', 'Big Sky', 'Sleep Easy' or 'Slumber Queen' or, occasionally, 'Invader'. Chris and I rode along side by side, chatting in the slight tailwind. The mountains moved in and out from the highway in a slow dance and low cloud shifted our attention from the mountaintops to the verges and close-ups. Burgundy leaves at ground level, and brilliant red berries on tiny shrubs. Gentle yellows were appearing more and more often in the trees' leaves and the slender aspen trunks shone a brilliant white, their silver-green leaves shimmering in an endless quickstep against the darker greens. When the clouds lifted to give a longer view, the aspens were pale against the conifers. Occasionally a single tree, yellow, or pale orange, would stand out as a scatter of colour against the still dominant dark green and silver, an autumn forerunner.

We pulled off the road by a small creek after ninety miles and Chris said later he was sure that a raven led him to a clearing – a perfect tent spot. We ate soup and pasta in clouds of mosquitoes which, due to the quantities of Deet we had both plastered on our skin, largely declined to land on us; though hundreds had, Chris said, formed a well-mannered queue on the brim of my cap, patiently waiting for the Deet to wear off.

We were on the road again by ten the next morning which, for us, was pretty good. Chris had taken to bringing me tea and porridge in the tent so I could sit in the entrance of my burrow looking out at the world and slowly coming to. He was bouncy in the mornings whereas for me, however wonderful the context, mornings were always a slow and painful process of dragging myself back to consciousness. By the time Chris started to fade I would normally be reaching top strength; a convenient dove-tailing that meant we could typically take turns at supporting the struggling other.

With thirty miles to go before the end of the Cassiar the road was corrugated with short, steep ups and downs. The trees had moved in close and chipmunks regularly scooted decisively across in front of us; unlike the squirrels, who would rush into the road, stop, turn back, run halfway to the verge, stop and turn back again in an agony of indecision before finally racing off into the undergrowth. I had started composing a slightly maudlin Alaska song in my head and, when I shared it with Chris, he joined in, creating ever wackier lines about the nature of our destination. 'Where the muffins grow like toadstools and fresh omelettes sail the skies,' was one of the finest. It entertained us for hours and we even ended up with a relatively straight-faced version:

I'm riding to Alaska through an avenue of trees
I've got raw bits on my bottom and sore bits in my knees
But the bears are picking berries
And the sun is in the sky
So I'm riding to Alaska on a high.

I'm riding to Alaska through a landscape full of lakes
There are mozzies in the evenings
And a host of pains and aches
But the beavers glide the waters
And the stars are in the sky
So I'm riding to Alaska on a high.

I'm riding to Alaska through mountainous terrain
There are thunderclouds above us
And of course there is the rain
But the moose graze in the meadows
And our shoes are *nearly* dry
So I'm riding to Alaska on a high.

I'm riding to Alaska while the trees are turning gold
The days are getting shorter
And the nights a little cold
But the leaves glow red like fox-fire
And the geese call in the sky
So I'm riding to Alaska on a high.

We met one other cyclist. He had an accent which I thought was
South African and Chris thought was Australian. He was very thin,
with panniers and a bike that were definitely on the battered side,
and he planned to be in Los Angeles by October. He didn't linger.
Watching his thin frame disappear down the Cassiar the way we had
come, I thought I would be sad to leave it. But, as we drew closer to
the Alkan, I felt excited. It was the beginning of the next phase of
the trip, the last and possibly the wildest. Just before the junction we
crossed the boundary between British Columbia – which we'd been
cycling through for weeks and weeks – and the Yukon. 'Canada's True
North', proclaimed a large sign. And then a series of smaller signs:
'Use of Radar Detectors Prohibited'. 'No Overtaking School Buses
When Red Lights Flashing'. 'Seatbelts Required By Law' and, at the
junction itself, 'Permits Required for Camping'.

'Blimey! Welcome to the Yukon!' I said to Chris. There was a
café where the Cassiar and Alaska Highways met. It was closed. We
turned left, onto the Alkan, heading west for Whitehorse, a chunk
of the Yukon and a bakery rumoured to exist a mile along the road.
It did. Not only was it open, it was also a café. We sat outside in a
brief patch of sunshine, drinking lattes, eating veggi wraps, salad
and chips and listening to tinny versions of 'Don't worry, be happy'
and 'Take me to the river' sung by a large plastic fish that gave voice
every time anyone went into the toilets. 'Take me to Alaska!' I said
to Chris, as it clouded over.

'No worries, be happy!' he replied. We got back on our bikes.

North
Pacific
Ocean

ANCHORAGE

C A N A D A

UNITED
STATES
of AMERICA

North
Atlantic Ocean

EL PASO

NORTHWAY JUNCTION

BEAVER CREEK

Kluane River

BURWASH
LANDING

Kluane Lake

DESTRUCTION BAY

U.S.A.
CANADA

Saint Elias Mountains

HAINES JUNCTION

KLUANE
NATIONAL
PARK &
RESERVE

WHITE HORSE

Alaska Highway

RANCHERIA

BRITISH COLUMBIA

CHAPTER THIRTEEN
Two Wheels on my Wagon ...

If it doesn't move and it should, use WD 40.
If it does move and it shouldn't, use Duct Tape.

Essential bike mechanics, author unknown.

The Alcan was wider than the Cassiar. A generous hard shoulder, gentle gradients and little traffic made for good riding. For a while, there was little wind either. The trees had backed away from the road but they stretched into the distance for miles and miles. Rare glimpses over their tops revealed a line of hills far ahead of us. On the Cassiar, the trees had flickered only an occasional, discrete yellow amongst the silver greys and greens. Here, autumn was suddenly more advanced. Patches of glorious orange, fiery and alive, were vivid against the deep green of the conifers, and yellows and dark pinks splashed across the undergrowth.

We rode on and on under a gentle grey sky, pushing for a long day. A bear with lush black fur and a brown muzzle grazed on berries right by the roadside, completely unperturbed by the traffic. A glimpse of moose in the far distance, and beaver ripples on a darkening lake as the sky clouded over. Chris was tiring but dogged. Ninety miles on, we rolled downhill into Rancheria at nine in the evening, a huge rainstorm passing just to the south of us as we leaned the bikes against a still-open motel-café. A squall of wind battered a sudden downpour against us as we unloaded the bikes. It felt odd to be inside, shut off from the wind and rain. But the hot shower was undeniably wonderful. Back in the café, a group of men teased us good-humouredly about the distinctive shape of cyclists' legs as we downed soup, salad and beer beside an enormous glass tank, empty save for three meandering goldfish.

We woke to rain. The café was busy. Fabulous omelettes packed with peppers and mushrooms arrived at our table, with a side of hash browns, pancakes and toast. A woman from Miami, en route with her army husband to a new posting in Anchorage, was describing Highway 37 – the beautiful Cassiar – as empty and awful. 'I damn nearly starved,' she said. 'Is there any real food in Alaska? Subway, or Kentucky Fried Chicken?' She sent her omelette back to the kitchen. 'I asked for cheese. Not peppers and shit.'

The rain eased as we were leaving. Chris moved Rocky and discovered that one arm of his pannier rack had sheared, low down over the wheel. I made a splint from wood and duct tape and, when we finally got going, Rocky's mysterious creak, present for over five hundred miles, had vanished.

We crossed the Continental Divide a few hours later. At a couple of thousand feet at most, and barely a climb, it was a far cry from Trail Ridge Road and Cameron Pass. The rain came and went. We cycled past closed cafés, ate cinnamon rolls behind the shelter of gas stations shut for the winter, and stopped in the lee of boarded-up motels to pump up Chris' back tyre, which was going flat faster and faster. As if in sympathy with his bike, it was Chris' turn to slide into constant tiredness; hardly surprising since we hadn't had a day off for weeks. Now we were upping the miles, too. But I was loving the Alcan. It was easy cycling, we'd been lucky with the wind so far, and I was really falling for the huge spaces. When the road climbed above the trees an immense vista opened out across the forested valleys to the still-distant mountains, snaked with rivers and glinting with silent, dark lakes. I felt an enduring sense of relief and release, as if that part of me, the part we don't realise is constrained in human-dominated environments, had been let free and was drifting off out to the distant horizons.

A long skein of geese was calling overhead when we stopped to eat bread and cheese by the road. There were more conifers and fewer aspen and the deep pink of the undergrowth glowed through the straight, dark stands. Once a coyote trotted away from us, weaving back and forth across the road before turning to look briefly at us, and vanishing into the trees. We were taking turns to sketch out our life stories, but when we were cycling without talking it was almost meditative. I had a growing sense of peace. I could imagine falling in love with some place up here. The vast spaces, the wildlife, the strong sense of other living beings doing their own thing; all deeply attractive. But I'd want to engage, not just live off the radar; to try to do something about the many threats to this wildness. I fantasized about coming upon a group of folk living in a remote old ranch in

244

the mountains and beavering away on some critical environmental cause. They would say, 'Kate and Chris! Exactly the people we need. Please stay, and help us with this work...'

We stopped at a rare, still-open café and chatted to an English couple who'd lived in the Yukon for thirty years. 'Sure, people here are aware of global warming. And concerned,' the woman said. 'I have a whole wardrobe of "extreme winter" clothes I've not used in the last several years. But it's hard if you live in the north. Big distances and poor public transport. It's hard not to drive a truck.'

Her partner nodded. 'And Stephen Harper, our premier, is saying he's not going to make Canada meet its Kyoto commitments. Some say he'll pull Canada out of the Kyoto Protocol altogether. He argues Canada can find a better approach. But really, I think it's about showing allegiance to Bush. It's about keeping Canada in favour with its massive economic trading partner to the south. And what can ordinary people do about that?'

It was a good question. Ordinary people couldn't decide a whole country's approach to reducing greenhouse gas emissions, any more than they could create buses and trains. Or could we? We couldn't personally sign the treaties and create transport strategies, but we could be one hell of a lot demanding of our politicians that they do. Tell them loud and clear that we'll vote them out if they don't...

~

For three days we'd been cycling west or northwest, heading for Whitehorse. Whitehorse was the last big town before Anchorage and we badly needed to get there. The bikes were falling apart. Chris's back wheel had a definite wobble and all his inner tubes had slow – or not so slow – punctures that defied my best attempts to hunt them down and fix them. We were constantly stopping to pump up his tyres. The other arm of Rocky's pannier rack had sheered and my panniers, with all their weight, were now fixed to the bike with splints of duct tape and branches on both sides. They wobbled ominously and the splints came apart if I had to turn the bike upside down. As signs for Whitehorse became more and more frequent, Rocky had a back wheel flat. We were down to our last patch. I cut it in half. Fixing the flat, I found a spot on my tyre that was beyond bald. Brown strands showed through beneath the shreds of remaining rubber and the inner tube was beginning to bulge through. I retaped the pannier rack, and then taped the tyre too, leaving a circle of silver duct tape clear against the black rubber like an armband. It shredded the first time I used the back brake. I taped it again.

For twenty-five miles we rode with our fingers crossed and, in my case, without using the back brake; gently requesting of the cycling gods that we have no more punctures and that my tyre not split. And then, suddenly, we were there. A bald eagle flew high in the evening sky as we crossed the wide Yukon River and rode into Whitehorse. The town had a funky feel, with low colourful buildings and lots of kids out and about in clothes that suggested serious attitude. We made for what we guessed to be the cheaper end of town and a motel base camp. Within an hour we were transformed. From tired, grimy and barely holding up, we emerged clean, relatively tidy and in a celebratory mood. We patted the bikes, relieved of their panniers and resting against the motel balcony, and headed straight out for dinner.

Whitehorse was wonderful. It had everything we needed – primarily a bike shop and a great deal of food. The next day whizzed by in a blur of eating and restocking. We bought eight inner tubes, multiple repair kits, a huge handful of extra patches, new tyres and a pannier rack. The shop offered to fit it. 'Great', I said, and headed for a second breakfast, followed soon after by lunch. Chris was busy establishing the basic logistics of a fantasy canoe trip on Wind River as I searched various gear shops for a pair of leggings to replace the pair I'd somehow managed to lose. They were probably still drying on a rock somewhere. Back in a café I scrabbled to bring the journal up to date and then retrieved Rocky and all too soon it was evening. I hadn't even begun to work on the blog, which had abruptly ended in July. 'Anyone reading it won't even know whether we're alive, let alone that we've made it to the Yukon,' I said.

'Too bad,' said Chris. 'You're not spending the evening blogging. You're coming out to dinner. With me. Same place as last night?'

I was partly exasperated and partly relieved. An evening with a computer or with Chris, eating fabulous food. Not really such a hard call. The restaurant was a tip-off from the motel and, disguised as a bland looking run-of-the-mill place attached to the Motor Inn, it was in fact an oasis. A lovely atmosphere and great music – a sort of mix of Spanish and North American with occasional songs in Arabic – as well as the fabulous food. 'Jesse Cook,' the waiter told us. 'He's Canadian. Very popular.' We ate cannelloni and Greek salad and cranberry cheesecake and drank a seriously delicious bottle of merlot, dry and velvety, the first wine for many weeks.

Next morning, we were slow getting away. It was a dry, cool day, with raw strands of sunshine scattering through the clouds. We climbed a long, steady hill out of Whitehorse, and into extraordinary scenery. Bare, rocky hills, patches of dark green conifer and then the aspen, already further into autumn after only one day and a few more northerly miles. Swathes of yellow and occasional splashes of orange, vivid against the conifers, like frozen fire. The distant hills were blue until they moved into the intermittent sunshine. Then whole hill-sides were revealed as yellow and green, so beautiful it made me call out loud. 'Wow! Oh, look!' Orange, yellow, dark green; the shapes changed and shifted and I had to keep stopping, captivated by the colours and bombarded by potential photographs that formed and then dissolved as we moved.

After forty miles, we pulled off the road to eat cold pizza and the most amazing cranberry bread pudding courtesy of a Whitehorse bakery. A cluster of information signs described a massive forest fire back in 1958. The conifers were, it said, taking unusually long to regenerate, hence all the aspen.

'Aspen are colonizers. One of the first trees back after a fire.' Chris had been boning up on his Suzuki tree book. [50] 'A single tree can cover several acres with suckers from its roots,' he said. 'Then the conifers return after the aspen are established.'

'But why aren't the conifers regenerating now?' I asked. 'Climate change?' The signs didn't say but, since conifers flourish in a lower temperature range and since the temperature was already edging warmer across the Canadian north-west, it seemed likely.

After lunch the sun went in. It was almost a relief to be free of the compelling photograph stops, though the relief was shortlived. We startled a black bear just below the road, his eyes following us as we swooped past. Then a massive shape in the verge, its head in shadows,

[50] David Suzuki & Wayne Grady (2004) *Tree; A Life Story* Greystone Books

brought us to a halt. 'If that's a bear, it's enormous!' Chris whispered.

'With antlers?' I giggled.

The shape moved and resolved into a moose. The moose, watching us, munched on some bush tops and then walked slowly across the road, his antlers huge and heavy, held high above incredibly long legs. In seconds, despite his size, the creature had melted soundlessly into the woods and disappeared. We stowed the cameras again and carried on, the mountains off to each side edging closer. They were big and rounded and looked old, like the Scottish Cairngorms. Indeed, one of the mountains was shaped extraordinarily like Lochnagar in Deeside, a former favourite of mine, its wide shoulder curving round to steep cliffs above a high coire. Ahead of us was a younger, spikier range; as if the Cairngorms and the Skye Cuillin had magically come together in the same vista. The spiky mountains were in fact the Saint Elias. Snow capped and dramatic, they included Mount Logan, the highest in Canada at a little under 6000 metres. Huge, permanent, high icefields lay behind those first peaks. And beyond them, the ocean.

At Haines Junction the next day, the Alaska Highway swung northwest, running alongside the Saint Elias Mountains and the Kluane National Park. Haines Junction had held a romantic attraction for me ever since a Canadian couple told us they'd stopped for gas there twenty-five years previously and never left. We soon began to wonder if we would ever get any distance from Haines Junction ourselves. Chris had a puncture. We fixed it. Then we hit a gravel section, with roadworks. Tracks through the loose stone made by trucks – almost every vehicle here was a truck – made cycling just about possible but it was hard, slow going. Another puncture left us sitting by the side of the road, with the leaking inner tube.

'What we need now is for a roadworks person in a big truck to tell us it's too dangerous to cycle any further,' I said.

A truck drew up. 'Too dangerous to cycle any further,' said the man inside. He had incredible brown eyes, and looked a little like George Clooney. 'I'll take you to the visitor's centre at Sheep Mountain,' he said, with a heart-stopping smile. Bikes loaded in the back, the truck sped effortlessly across the rough road. We sat in the warm cab, secretly hoping that Sheep Mountain was many miles away. Minutes later, he stopped. 'There,' he said, pointing high up on the mountain's flanks, 'sheep.' Tiny off-white blurs were barely discernible against the steep rock. The Clooney-man waved, and drove away, his truck wheels spitting small stones.

We finished fixing the puncture and cycled on, suddenly aware of our own, familiar, slow speed. Then, 'My back wheel feels wobbly!' said Chris. I fell back and cycled behind him. His back wheel was visibly swinging from side to side as it turned. 'Oh heck,' I said quietly, as the rain returned. Not longer after, we came to a campsite. Enough is enough, we both agreed, despite the day's relatively low miles. A sign said, 'No Tenting – Bears!' but the man in the office took pity on us and said that the bears had not been through for a couple of days and that we'd probably be okay. A photograph taped to a notice board showed a large grey grizzly who appeared to be grinning, at a beautiful spot right by the lake – the spot we were advised to camp on, in fact. But, as we curled into our warm bags not all that long afterwards it was back wheels, not bears, that weighed on my mind.

Next morning, as rain hammered on the tent, we scrunched up inside eating blueberry bagels and I dug out the back half of *Richard's Bicycle Book* from the bottom of a pannier. [51] I'd torn the book in half at the beginning of the maintenance section and retaped the spine with parcel tape, a weight-saving measure that the pile of David Suzuki classics could arguably be held to have rendered pointless. I looked up 'buckled wheels', ignoring the bit that read 'by far the best idea is to take the wheel to a bike shop,' and focusing instead on, 'but if you're determined to have a go, or have no choice...' The rain eased. I took the tyre off and put the back wheel back into the frame, and slowly span it, using a pencil held as a fixed point against the wheel as a marker. The buckle was not exactly hard to find. The rim of the wheel danced rhythmically from one side of the frame to the other as it turned. I worked away, tightening spokes on one side of the bulge and loosening those on the others. It was absorbing and, once I'd recalled what 'turn anti-clockwise' actually means in relation to spokes on an upside-down wheel, gratifyingly effective. Gradually the wheel span truer, its kink slowly unfolding until I was spinning an almost round specimen. I cleaned up in the wonderful warm toilets and waved cheerfully at the campsite owner as we cycled away. It was

[51] There are more recent versions but the original and still (extremely useful) classic is Richard Ballantine (1983) *Richard's Bicycle Book* Pan Books

still raining, but we had a tail wind, and our wheels were all turning. I felt a little smug.

Ten minutes later, Chris' wheel buckled again. This time, the result was a major wobble, worse than before. Unrideable. We pulled off the road onto a gravel shoulder and I started again, feeling pessimistic. If my straightening efforts hadn't worked before, why should the same procedure work now? But there wasn't much else we could do but try. I re-straightened the wheel and then gently tightened all the spokes a little, in turn. Two horrible splits in the rim lengthened a fraction as I did it. Any tighter and the spokes would pull the rim apart. Not tight enough and there wouldn't be enough tension to hold the buckle at bay. Basically, the wheel was trashed. My smugness had utterly evaporated. Why the hell hadn't I checked Chris' wheel properly in Whitehorse and taken it to the bike shop? Of the two of us, I was by far the more experienced cyclist and Chris, doing what he could, was nevertheless taking his lead from me in terms of maintaining the bikes. I'd known about his wheel wobble but had somehow simply forgotten about it, distracted by the sheered pannier rack and the split tyre and all the punctures.

I took as much weight as I could from Chris, stacking his share of the tent, books and stove on top of the pile of stuff already on top of Rocky's panniers. Chris had been carrying a bag of food and I was horrified at the weight. 'We're cycle touring, Chris, not on a gourmet trip. What's with the fresh pesto in a GLASS JAR?' We left via the bins and parted with the pesto. Destruction Bay was ahead of us and we decided to try to reach it rather than turn back immediately. We cycled gingerly away. The mountains had moved in alongside the road. Their bare tops were a mustard colour, strewn with green and gold flecks, like no colour I'd ever seen on a mountain before. But I could hardly take them in. I was trying to decide whether I should prioritise hitching back to Whitehorse with Chris, or finishing the trip.

The wheel made it to Destruction Bay – apparently named for the road-building equipment routinely blown away during the construction of the Alcan back in the 1940s. 'It was officially completed in '42,' said the owner of the café. We'd stopped to eat, and to consider our options. 'But it wasn't really passable until the next year. On this section, all the permafrost melted and the road buckled up. That was 1943. We still have road problems now.'

So did we. It seemed clear to me that going back to Whitehorse was our best bet. We were about a hundred and seventy miles away – a very short hitch by Canadian standards – and we could guarantee a good bike shop and a new wheel in Whitehorse. There were few towns ahead. They were further away and even Tok, the largest, was small. The chances of finding a new wheel before Anchorage were very slight indeed. For me, the only real question was what I should do. This was my fault. If I'd been more on the ball in Whitehorse this wouldn't have happened. I should help sort it out. That could involve waiting for Chris here, and looking after the bikes, or hiding Chris' bike and riding on to wait at the next town, which would shorten the remaining journey. Or we could hide both bikes and I could hitch back with him. Alternatively, I could just keep going and leave Chris to catch up whenever he could. That would give us the best chance of getting to Anchorage, but it felt unfair.

Chris, though, saw it all differently. 'If I go back and you wait, we'll lose at least two days,' he said. 'We don't have a spare two days.' This was true. 'And if I go back and you carry on and the snow comes in, we could end up stuck on different sides of the Alaskan border. I think we should just carry on until the wheel actually collapses and then I'll hitch forward rather than backwards.'

'But then you might not get a wheel in time to finish the trip. You might not ride into Anchorage,' I said.

'I know. But the priority is for you to finish the trip, not me. Whatever happens I'll only have done some of it. And it's been fantastic, wherever I finish. I'm not that bothered about Anchorage.' Chris was being generous, and I knew it.

'Chris, this is my fault. I'm sorry.'

'No it isn't,' he said. 'And anyway, that's not the point. You need to finish the trip and I don't want to go back to Whitehorse,' he said. 'So let's carry on.'

Not for the first time I thought of various girlfriends' assessment of Chris. 'This guy's a keeper,' they'd said. 'Do NOT dump him.' I hugged him. We carried on.

Rather bizarrely, the rest of the day was one of the best day's riding for weeks. The wind swung around and we picked up speed as it gathered strength behind us. This was particularly helpful for me as, even with the tail wind, I could feel the extra weight as a constant

251

strain in my knees. The road rang alongside Kluane Lake for most of its seventy-kilometre length. At the end of the lake, we ripped through the tiny town of Burwash Landing, passed a sign reading 'Bed, Grub, Booze - Long Live the USA!' and cycled on into the evening sunshine. Now the Kluane River, huge and ribboned, ran beside us. The river is a major spawning ground for chum salmon who, gorged full of seafood, swim upstream for fifteen hundred miles to the place they were born. At the end of this astonishing journey they lay their eggs, and die. Decaying salmon in the rivers provide so many extra nutrients that they support the forest growth, and eagle and bear depend on the live salmon for extra-fattening food before the onset of winter. In the days when people travelled regularly by dog-sledge, chum or 'dog' salmon had been used as high-energy husky food. I wondered whether this was the origin of a certain well-known dog-food brand, but no-one seemed to know. I also wondered what happened to salmon, and the rest of the ecosystem that depended on them, when their rivers were dammed to feed our ever growing need for water and power. I was pretty sure I could guess the answer.

That night we decided we could, given the wheel situation, stop with honour after only sixty-eight miles. It was well after eight and we were both more than ready to rest. Never in my life had I experienced as many techi-hitches - punctures, wheels, pannier racks - in one trip before. Perhaps every cyclist has a designated number of punctures and collapsed wheels for their life, like heartbeats, and Chris was getting his quota all at once. We followed a track leading off the road and camped on a disused Landrover track, now thick with grass, leaning the bikes against a stowed yellow steamroller. We used its roof as a bear hang, climbing up over the cab with our bags of food. Then I sat in the tent doorway, trying to work out tunes on the Canmore flute. One for the god of the tailwind, to invite him to stay with us. And the other a bear tune, to invite them to leave us be.

~

A huge wind came through in the night, and no bears - or none that we knew of. We woke to grey skies that turned to rain. I felt mightily uninspired to get up, retreating into the depths of the down bag to the sound of rain on canvas and sinking back into delicious warm sleep after breakfast in bed. An hour or so later I crawled out into temporary dryness and worked on Chris' wheel. By the time we'd finished packing it was raining again and we rode wet and cold until our bodies heated up – a slow process. Miles and miles of spectacular mountain ridge line ran alongside us, fresh snow on the tops and yellow aspen at the base. I kept thinking of the massive icefields stretching away on the other side of the ridge, invisible to us beyond the line of peaks that flanked our road. A whole different world lay up there, and I fantasised about coming back and spending time on those wild, remote, high plains of ice beyond the first range.

At a chilly lunch stop we brewed tea on the Trangia, carefully watched by a small gaggle of polite but definitely hopeful ducks. Not long after, I hit a large pothole. My back derailleur instantly stopped working. A café-cum-rock shop appeared. I stopped to try to coax the derailleur back to life. Then I massaged Chris' wheel back into relative straightness, too. By now, we were stopping to do this several times a day and it had become almost routine. Then, hands frozen, we went in for coffee.

An elderly couple sat inside. She was large, with short, blonde, curly hair and a deeply lined face. Her husband sat silent. 'The café is closed,' she said. 'No proper toilets. We've been shut down.' There was a pause. 'I could *give* you a coffee though.' We told her how many closed cafés we'd encountered and she told us that many places were closing permanently. 'We're not on the mains up here. Everyone runs on generators. But diesel is getting more and more expensive.' Another pause. 'I expect you're cold. I could give you a cinnamon roll ...'

We sat with our coffee at the table in the middle of their store, surrounded by an extraordinary muddle of rock chunks, polished stones, fossils, bizarre ornaments and a glass-fronted cooler cabinet with WD40, chocolate, packets of nails and dog food on display inside. Animal furs and jewellery were stacked in piles on the floor. They had been there thirty-eight years, she said, spending the winters – from about now until the end of April – in Mexico. They were leaving in the next couple of days, in fact, if they could manage to pack. They weren't sure if they'd ever come back. It had been a particularly hard year. Cold all summer, neither of them feeling well, and she was losing her eyesight.

A television in the background gave news of a Canadian private killed in Afghanistan. The man, who hadn't acknowledged us at all, suddenly started to speak. 'They should take no prisoners when it comes to the Taliban,' he said. 'And destroy the opium poppies.' Then a deluge about immigration, and how outrageous it was that asylum seekers should get money and access to health care that people like him had worked sixty years for. They'd worked and worked to build this place back when there was no electricity and no phones and no TV and they'd had it collapse when the permafrost thawed and then they'd built it again. Despite his anger at the world I felt at ease sitting in the muddle of their stuff, in the warmth of their wood burner, listening to their stories and enjoying Buddy, a lovely-natured amber coloured labrador cross they'd rescued from a man in Arizona.

'I might have a wheel,' the man said, to our surprise, as Chris' predicament came into the conversation. 'In the Bike Department.' The bike department was in a shed outside. He opened the door to a huge pile of rusting wrecks in a tangle. We looked politely at the chaos and claimed regret at not having tools to remove a back wheel. 'How about the bus?' he said, clearly determined to help. 'Three times a week to Anchorage. Next one is tomorrow.'

'Now that is good to know,' said Chris, with evident feeling. We thanked them both and wished them luck. There was a part of me that would have liked to stay, and simply help them pack. It was help I think they would have accepted, in a matter-of-fact way, just as they had accepted the permafrost melt buckling their hard-built store. Melting permafrost could buckle us all, I thought, recalling Annie and her chilling explanation of positive feedback. We didn't stay. Cycling off into weather that was now glorious, I wondered if they would make it to Mexico and, if so, whether they would ever return. The sun shone. Vast swathes of golden yellow aspen glowed at the feet of the mountains and scattered dots of yellow were picked out all the way across the higher mountain rock faces. Best of all there was a tailwind.

The next day, at the diminutive town of Beaver Creek, I worked on both bikes while Chris tracked down a bus timetable. Rocky's gears were disgruntled and had not functioned properly since the pot-hole incident. I tightened the gear cable and readjusted the limit screws and tweaked the angle of the shifter over the chain, but no matter what I did I couldn't get it to shift into the top two gears. At least I had the lower ones. Then I fixed Chris' late-evening puncture and worked on his wheel, ending up with something that was beautifully round but, as I realised when I stood back and looked at it in relation to the rest of the bike, a good inch closer to one side of the frame than the other. Quietly cursing myself, I loosened the spokes and started again.

'Today's bus has already gone,' said Chris, over a late omelette breakfast in a café full of stuffed animals, photos of huskies, and old wooden skis. The chef made us sandwiches. It was noon before we got on the road. Two minutes later, the wheel crumpled into a major wobble. From behind it looked manic, lurching from side to side as it turned. We pulled off the road and I sat with the wheel on the dirt edge, easing it back into a more or less round shape, though it still kinked to one side as I span it. I took the brake blocks out so the wheel didn't rub at the buckled section and I retaped the split rims with duct tape. Minutes later, the wheel punctured. Chris fixed that while I worked on the wheel, already kinked so badly it was rubbing on the frame. Neither of us said a word, but we both knew it was nearly the end. The next puncture came only minutes after we'd set off. Several spokes had broken and stuck out at bizarre angles. The rim was buckling upwards at the split section under the duct tape.

'Chris, I'm beat,' I said. 'There's nothing more I can think of to do to keep this together. I'm so sorry.' We'd already agreed what should happen next. Chris would hitch and I would ride on alone.

Unfortunately, we were now in a stretch of no-man's land between Canada and the US, about five miles from the border. There was little traffic. 'I'll walk with you to the border,' I said.

'Thanks, but no. Get going,' said Chris. 'Get some miles done. It's late already.'

He was right. And, in truth, I was impatient to get back on the road, frustrated with all the delays and the constant stopping and starting. But I also felt awful. I'd made two big mistakes. First, I'd dissuaded Chris from getting front panniers. Never having liked or needed them myself, I'd completely failed to take into consideration that Chris, several stone heavier, already had considerably more weight over his back wheel than I ever would. And then there was my failure to get the wheel checked at Whitehorse.

'Go!' said Chris, helping me move all the stuff I'd been carrying for him, back onto his bike. I left the stove with him, too, so I could travel as light as possible, and then we hugged goodbye. I choked back tears of frustration and sadness on Chris' behalf. Turning back at the hillside I waved and took a photograph: Chris, pushing his bike steadily along the road, his red jacket bright against the aspen.

Sometime later I stopped at a wildlife information centre. It was closed. I ate one of the sandwiches and read about the fur trade on a series of information boards around the shuttered, silent building. Fur had brought waves of fortune hunters here since the arrival of the early European pioneers. Beaver hats were no longer *de rigeur* but, depending on current fashion, a single lynx pelt could be worth $600,000. $600,000! I felt a shock of fear for these animals, reading that. How could something as erratic and essentially meaningless as fashion have driven the near extermination of creatures as gentle and beguiling as beavers or make a lynx's pelt worth well over ten times more than the annual income of, say, a college lecturer? Why did we tolerate these horrible, random effects of our economic systems?

I dug out my music, wanting a change of mood. As the rhythm of 'Crazy' kicked in I stood on my pedals to pull away and felt an uprush of exuberance. I felt rotten about lynx pelts and rotten about Chris and his wheel. But it was a relief to be moving and I couldn't help but notice that part of me was glad to be on the road alone again. I could feel good humour breaking back in, despite everything. The landscape was flat, though the road somehow still contrived to be hilly. There was little traffic and I felt for Chris, pushing his bike in this no-man's land between Canada and Alaska. I cursed the few trucks that went by without him. The border was nondescript. I pulled up to one of the small glass-sided booths and was asked where I'd come from, and what was in my sandwich. 'Strictly speaking, ma'am, we should confiscate that,' said the guard in the booth, 'but given your circumstances...' I told them to look out for a British man on foot, pushing a bicycle and looking for a lift. And then I cycled into Alaska.

Low lakes glinted among acres and acres of tiny, dwarf conifer trees, many at strange angles. Hundreds of aspen were spotted across the dull green like a pointillist painting: a huge canvas of yellow and green dots stretched out for miles ahead. Behind me, the mountain ranges we'd cycled alongside were reduced to occasional glimpses of sheer white peaks, almost ghostlike, on the now distant horizon. I was heading north-west, towards Northway Junction. 'A few miles before

Northway there are two RV sites. Second one is your best bet,' the café chef had told us. 'Northway Junction is just a gas station. And after that, there's nothing till Tetlin.' Tetlin Junction was well out of my range but the campsites turned up sooner than expected. I'd only done fifty-four miles and it was only quarter to eight. I could carry on and wild camp. Or call it a day and give Rocky some attention. He'd developed a back wheel wobble I'd been studiously ignoring but that was definitely getting worse.

Lakeview campsite had a small toilet block and a row of lakeside sites currently occupied by a solitary RV and a distinctly hostile German couple. They sulkily confirmed there were no further campsites ahead, but their lack of friendliness did nothing to mar the view. It was beautiful. Sod it, I thought, I'll stop here. With a growing sense of peace I pottered about under some trees, putting up the tent and admiring the lake. Then I turned to the wheel, heaving Rocky upside down and watching the wheel from behind as I span it. A very distinct wobble. And, looking closer, a broken spoke. Bugger! It must have been that bloody pot-hole, I thought. Ironically, I'd joked with Chris that my own back wheel would probably fall apart as soon as I'd left him. Now it looked horribly as if that could indeed be on the cards. The broken spoke was on the same side as the block and, though I had spares, I was not going to be able to get it out to change it. The best I could do was to try to straighten the wheel around it. I worked away for ages, tightening and loosening spokes. Then I taped the broken spoke to a neighbour and pumped up the tyre. And then I sat by the lake eating the remaining sandwich and watching tiny, distant ducks glide on the far shore while the evening sun coloured the water gold around them.

I was only half appreciating it. My head was in a mental loop, reviewing the situation, and my mistakes, again and again. Now we might end up with both bikes off the road in different places, unable to communicate or join up, and hitching separately to Anchorage! I decided the only way to make sense of the whole situation was to make peace with it. It wouldn't do Chris and me any harm to be apart for a few days. Already I could see, and with sudden and unnerving clarity, how irritable I'd been getting and how consistently generous he'd been. I was ready to be alone again and it wouldn't do our relationship any damage either. As for my wheel, there was nothing I could do.

I'd just have to see what happened. It was the 6th of September. If the wheel held together and if I could do about ninety miles a day for the next few days, I – or we – should get to Anchorage on the 10th. If my wheel collapsed and if there was no bike shop in Tok, then that would be the end of the ride for me. I'd have to hitch or catch the bus to Anchorage. But I would still have cycled to Alaska. I would still have cycled through some of the most beautiful landscapes I'd ever seen, through deserts and over mountain passes. I would still have seen bears and moose and met many lovely people and been joined by a man who could turn out to be a true partner. I would still have had time really to think about climate change and, hopefully, to move my thinking – and feeling – forward. Not such a bad outcome.

Back at the tent I realised I'd left the bear hang rope with Chris. I packed my (rather pitiful) food – one muffin, some cheese, a muesli bar, some chocolate and a few dried cranberries – into a pannier and put it in the toilet block. Then I went down for a last look at the dark and shining lake. As I stood on the shore a muskrat emerged from some weeds and swam slowly across the still water in front of me. It felt like an affirmation. And a reminder. I was cycling through the habitats of a multitude of other creatures. A central part of the point of it all was to find a way to use the trip to speak on their behalf; to campaign against climate change and other ways in which our lifestyles threaten them; threaten them to the extent that conservation areas alone – even these vast northern refuges and even joined up as in the Y2Y – could not possibly provide protection. This lake was part of the Tetlin National Wildlife refuge, an area of over 600,000 thousand acres of mountains, glacier-fed rivers, forests, tundra and wetlands. It was probably home to thousands of muskrats. It was also home, I read in the tent, to forty-one other species of mammal, numerous birds – the reserve fell across part of a major migration corridor – and a single, extremely well-adapted amphibian; the largely terrestrial, water-averse wood frog, able to survive the winter by increasing the amount of glucose stored in its cell fluids. The glucose acts as antifreeze and prevents the frog's skin cells from freezing as it hibernates through the bitter winterssszzzzz ... I fell asleep reading about the reserve animals and woke in the night to the beautiful, haunting sound of coyotes calling across the water.

Next morning I was on the road relatively early and dreaming of a big omelette breakfast at Northway Junction a few miles ahead. Having left the stove with Chris, I no longer had the option of lingering over a mug of tea in the tent, and this greatly speeded up the camp-dismantling time. A grocery store, a launderette and a gift shop huddled at the junction behind a sign reading 'Town For Sale'. The store specialised in Twinky bars and toilet rolls. I rooted around and found some nuts, a highly processed berry pie, and a solitary muffin. The road beyond was hilly and hard work, rolling up and down like solid waves in a sea of yellow aspen. Telegraph poles leaned randomly towards or away from the road, as if a bit worse for wear after a long night out. I wondered where Chris was. My best bet was that he'd spent the night at the RV site just across the border and was still behind me. But he could have gone by after I'd pulled off the road or, more likely, before I'd got going. There was no way of knowing. Nor whether my wheel would hold up. For the first few miles it had creaked and pinged ominously as the adjusted spokes settled in but now it was quiet – and still turning. I passed a sign saying 'Tok 56 miles'. Next stop. Maybe the wheel would be okay. Maybe we could still make it. I began to relax.

CHAPTER FOURTEEN
What a Wonderful World

'For we have arrived at a turning point, perhaps the most significant in the history of humanity. It is now clear that there is no more urgent intellectual task facing the human species ... than thoroughly to re-imagine its relationship with nature. [N]ature is neither backdrop nor storehouse, neither product nor chattel, but a community of which we are inevitably a part.'

Robert MacFarlane [52]

'We abuse the land because we regard it as a commodity belonging to us. When we see land as a community to which we belong, we may begin to use it with love and respect.'

Aldo Leopold [53]

Several hours later a small RV with bikes on the back hooted and pulled over. Chris! I felt an up rush of emotion as he got out, red jacket and big smile, and walked back towards me. Two people and a dog piled out of the van behind him and joined us. They were going to Tok, now about sixteen miles ahead, and then Fairbanks. I arranged to meet Chris at Tok, at the Burnt Paw motel. Then we would make a plan. The RV drove off and I pedalled on, relieved that Chris was fine and in good spirits, even if not in Anchorage. The road levelled out and the surface improved. My back wheel was still intact and not too badly out of shape, though the residual buckle still rattled a pot of vitamins in my pannier like maracas.

Tok was small but long, spread out along the main road. Chris was sitting outside the Burnt Paw, reading, his bike leant against the wall beside him. Its back wheel was absolutely trashed. The rim had buckled upwards and Chris had wrapped the numerous broken

---

[52] Robert MacFarlane (2006) 'Turning Points' in David Buckland et al (eds) *Burning Ice: Art and Climate Change* Cape Farewell

[53] Leopold has justifiably been called the grandfather of environmental ethics. Aldo Leopold (1949) *A Sand County Almanac* Oxford University Press

spokes around the hub to facilitate pushing. They stuck out at weird angles like the spines of a dishevelled hedgehog. We headed for a café to eat and swap stories. Chris had had a frustrating time. Several folk had stopped but been unable to help – they were going the other way or they had no room – and a good many more had just driven by. He'd ended up walking the seven miles to the border, where the guards were sympathetic and expecting him, but also unable to help. He'd pushed on to the RV site. By this stage his wheel had pretty much disintegrated and it was almost impossible even to drag the bike. He'd spent the night in the RV motel as the only guest, eating with the helpful, friendly family who ran it. The motel was all lopsided. 'They said it's because of the permafrost melting,' said Chris. 'Did you see the telegraph poles? Like the drunken forests, they're standing in the melting permafrost and leaning all over the place.' And releasing massive amounts of methane, I thought, an extremely potent greenhouse gas. It rather took the edge off the humour.

Up early and on the roadside with the tipsy telegraph poles, it had taken Chris until noon to get a lift. I was surprised. Even with the bike, I hadn't imagined hitching would be that difficult, not here where a broken bicycle could mean a very long walk. The good news was that a bus ran the next day, from Tok straight to Anchorage. Chris was done with hitching. He planned to stay in Tok for the night, and catch it. Not entirely sure where I'd be, I stocked up at a downright luxurious grocery store, buying bagels, burritos and a peach while Chris checked into the Burnt Paw – complete with possibly the most beguiling form of canines on earth: husky puppies.

I left the puppies – and Chris – a touch reluctantly. A comfortable night at the Burnt Paw was definitely appealing but I'd only done fifty-six miles. I was now aiming at about ninety-five a day. With luck, Chris would be able to buy a wheel and come back to meet me for the final day's ride, leaving us three days in Anchorage before the ferry south. We'd hoped for a week to explore and follow up on contacts but three days would be better than nothing. And we needed a bit of leeway. We couldn't afford to miss the boat. It was the last ferry south from Anchorage until the following spring.

I turned off the Alaska Highway – heading north-west for Fairbanks – and onto the Glenn Highway. From here it was south-west all the way to Anchorage. There were road works for the first mile or so. My heart sank as I crunched onto gravel but a pilot car directed me to a bike path and for seven miles I had a ribbon of new, smooth asphalt all to myself. Bliss! Then out onto the road, a lovely new surface for miles. Quite suddenly, the mountains were back. Astonishing colours, deep pink and yellow, vivid against the dark conifers, like nothing I'd ever seen before. I was heading for a town called Mentasta Lake, having decided that ninety-five-mile days could reasonably also be motel and shower days. The bus stopped at Mentasta and so, I reasoned, it had to exist. It was a beautiful ride. I rode on and on and when I started to fade I put the music on and rode on again. At about eighty-five miles I began to wonder when Mentasta Lake was going to show up. At about ninety miles, I passed a small cluster of houses and a sign saying, 'No Access to Lake, Resort Closed'. It looked as if Mentasta Lake was nonexistent after all. The next town, Slana, was a good thirty miles ahead and I was losing the light. So much for my motel and shower fantasy. Time to look for somewhere to camp.

A few miles later a track turned off the road. I rode along it. The track split into three – one branch leading, I guessed, to a house, another back to the road, and the third to an open gravely space surrounded by woods. A defunct white plastic sun lounger sat in the middle of it, next to a bonfire site and a cluster of tiny aspen. Perfect! I put up my tent on the far side in the first fringe of trees, out of sight, I hoped, to any chance human visitor. I ate the peach and put the rest of the food in a pannier and hung it in a tree. The trees were small and I didn't think any self-respecting bear would take more than a minute to figure out how to reach this feeble attempt at a bear hang – but at least it was away from the tent. It was still and almost silent, save for the occasional and, from the perspective of a wood-bound gravel patch, rather bizarre sound of a duck. Curled up warm in the tent, I wrote my journal and then opened the mosquito net to watch the full moon come up behind a stand of conifers and light the lower edges of the clouds. Part of me was at peace, loving the landscape and the sounds and the beauty of the trees in the moonlight. And part of me was distinctly uneasy. It was irrational, and faintly irksome, but I felt edgier alone than I had done camping with Chris. 'For goodness sake! I said to myself. Why should a bear bother you? And if, for some strange reason, a bear did attack the tent, would it really make any difference whether there was one person in here or two?' My logic was sound but it didn't entirely help.

Later in the night, having a pee on the edge of the trees, the moon was small and high and hard silver in the dark sky. As I stood enjoying the sheer beauty of it, Bill's mountain lion story came, unhelpfully, back into my mind. I found myself wondering whether there were mountain lions in this part of Alaska. My back was against the woods and who knew what was watching me. I legged it back to the tent. Over the years, I'd camped hundreds of times in all sorts of places, and often alone. Mountains, deserts, beaches, forests. But I'd never been so aware of being in a habitat where I was, potentially, a prey species. No question about it, it gave a different perspective. It wasn't all bad. I felt alert and alive and the edginess was perhaps the beginning of some deeper kind of humility. Understanding intellectually that I was part of an ecosystem like any other animal was quite different from actually *feeling* it. I most certainly did not want to be a bear's breakfast. Yet this growing knowledge that being human didn't take me out of the food chain felt unexpectedly positive. In my tiny tent in the woods, any assumption of human superiority was hard to maintain. I was there on pretty much on the same terms as every other animal, plant or insect in the neighbourhood. It was an oddly liberating feeling.

~

I slept for ten hours and woke to a wonderful morning, cold but brilliant blue with the sun just reaching the far end of my clearing and lighting the aspen on the hillside beyond a brilliant yellow. Spinning Rocky's wheel with the bike upside down, I could see a distinct bulge. I decided to leave it alone. We headed off into the cold, glorious sunshine. Mentasta Lake materialised about ten miles later. I could have had a hot shower after all. But I was glad to have spent the night where I did, rather than indoors, comfortable but cut off. It would turn out to be the last night's wild camping of the trip.

I rode past Mentasta without even slowing down. I would go on to Slana before I stopped. And then, I thought, I would have earned a big egg breakfast. Layers and layers of hills stretched away from the road, furry with dark green conifers and brilliant yellow aspen. Occasional glimpses of mountains, pale tops beyond the hills, snowy and remote. The colours across the hillsides constantly changed shapes. Sometimes the hills were patchy, with yellow and green in equal measure; sometimes they were mostly green with yellow splashes. Occasional vivid streaks of red and orange across the whole canvas made the hillside glow.

Slana was about thirty miles down the road and, by the time I reached it, I was vague with low blood sugar and in that state where the easiest decisions are impossible to make, the simplest tasks almost overwhelming. Slana seemed to consist entirely of Midway Store, a big wooden building set back from the road with an array of cabins and sheds scattered around it. A huge bonfire of rubbish in front of it periodically gave a very loud bang and exploded into flames. Rocky's gears were playing up and needed attention and I needed to eat. But in which order? I gazed blankly at the gears for a while and then shambled inside. A large store, no café, not much food, free coffee. A woman with long grey-brown hair handed me a coffee with unspoken understanding and no comment and waited while I ate a muffin. As I came to, she began to chat, voice husky with cigarette smoke. She and her husband had been running the store for the last eleven years.

'We stay open all year,' she said. 'Many of the locals work away in the summer. But they come back in the winter. Lots of hunting.' The phone rang. 'Someone from the First Nations' village at Mentasta. For you,' she said, handing the phone to her husband. He was thin and smiling, and smoked as he talked.

'They want me to go and shoot a grizzly that's been hanging around and scaring the kids,' he said. 'For some reason, they don't want to shoot it themselves.'

'Are there many bears around here?' I asked, casually.

'Yes,' he said, inhaling deeply, 'more and more. They're killing the moose and the caribou. They know it's hunting season and that there's meat around so they hang around to see what they can get. They're in a funny mood this time of year. Aggressive.' The wisdom of wild camping was beginning to feel a little dubious. 'We had a couple of cyclists from Oxford stay here once,' he said. 'I never saw such skinny people eat so much! On their way to South America.' He told me they'd stayed long enough to learn how to shoot, and that they'd loved riding into the backcountry on four-wheelers, learning how to track bear and moose and how to kill an animal cleanly. 'We sent them off with tins of smoked salmon and still get emails from them,' he said. 'Do you eat fish?'

'Not really, to be honest,' I said.

'Well, I'd have given you some,' he said, unperturbed. We chatted on amongst the rows of guns and camouflage jackets. I was finding something deeply attractive about the hunting culture – when it was associated with people who lived in these places and who shot to eat or to be safe. The guns, the quad bikes, knowing the land and understanding the animals, and all a bit rough and ready round the edges – but with a strong ethics of respect and understanding and community. As I left, the man offered me some chain lube, wondering if it might help with my gears. It was touching and thoughtful. This is almost what I'm looking for, I thought, almost the place to stay awhile. Outside, a man was holding court by the bonfire. 'I had to fix the radiator myself,' he was saying, waving a roll of duct tape in the air, 'no-one else on the bus had a clue. Ended up putting duct tape on duct tape ...' I felt a certain affinity as I cycled away.

My response to these hunters took me a bit by surprise, given that I'd been vegetarian for a good twenty years. Eating higher up the food chain – feeding plants to animals and then eating the animals rather than the plants – is almost always less efficient, and very much more costly in terms of carbon. This is not so, of course, when animals are fed on grass in places where only grass could grow – though even in this case they may massively compromise local biodiversity. (Witness the biodiversity-impoverished Lake District fells and their over-liberal coating of sheep.) The vast majority of meat we eat in industrialised societies has, though, been fed on concentrates. As Colin Tudge puts it: 'Cattle, pigs and poultry now consume half the world's wheat (the principal staple), 80 per cent of the world's maize, virtually all the barley that is not used for brewing and distilling and well over 90 per cent of the world's soya, now grown more and more in Brazil at the expense of the rainforest and the Cerrado. Animals raised in traditional ways – on grazing, browse, surpluses and leftovers – add to our food supply... Animals fed on staples that could be feeding us are not supplementing our diet. They are competing with us.' [54]

---

[54] Colin Tudge (2010) 'How to Raise Livestock – And How Not To' in Joyce de Silva & John Webster (eds) *The Meat Crisis: Developing More Sustainable Production and Consumption* Earthscan. This book does an excellent job of setting out all the links between high levels of meat consumption, climate change and other environmental problems – and is up there with the scariest books I've ever read.

I would, in fact, be happy to eat meat occasionally, if it was raised 'traditionally', with a low environmental footprint and with very high animal welfare. Given the extreme scarcity of such meat anywhere in the industrialised world, it's much easier to be vegetarian. But Alaska was a different context. You could probably keep a few farm animals in 'traditional ways'; but in any numbers, farming livestock in Alaska would almost certainly have a higher environmental cost than hunting. And to be vegetarian in Alaska, with such a short growing season, you'd have to rely on food with very big air miles. Better to hunt, then? But, when I saw a moose grazing at the roadside the sheer amazing reality of that particular form of life left me feeling the last thing I would want to do was kill and eat it. On the other hand, these moose lived a free life and, shot cleanly, their death was almost certainly better than almost any in a slaughterhouse. It was not straightforward. If I lived here, I thought, I'd want to go hunting and let the experience – and my emotional response to it – help me think it through. It was an odd conclusion to reach.

This train of thought took me all the way to Christochina, where I planned to eat, as ethically as possible, in large quantities. A single Bed and Breakfast sported a 'No Vacancies' sign and that seemed to be it until Posty's materialised. Posty's was a small store with a coffee machine. A woman with short blonde hair, pink top, white jacket and jeans stood behind the counter, chatting with a very slim lady with a high-pitched voice and a gentle weirdness it was hard to put a finger on.

'Are you the cyclist whose partner is on the bus?' the blonde woman asked. I nodded. 'Bus stops here. But they're running a good hour or so late. Leaking radiator.' Ah ha, I thought. I bet I know how that was fixed. The slim woman took a coffee and sat outside on the wooden porch with a cigarette. I took a coffee and an apple – no muffins – and joined her. She was forty-five and had lived in the area since she was three. I nudged the conversation towards global warming.

'Seen many changes here?' I asked.

'Glaciers,' she replied. 'The big one further down the road. It used to reach the road. Now it's miles away.' She paused, drawing hard on the cigarette. Then, 'Fewer and fewer mountains have snow all year. And the winters are much less cold.' She said she remembered her school closing when the temperature reached minus fifty. 'I would sit by the thermometer, willing it to go down a couple more degrees. We used to get off school a lot in the winter. Hardly ever happens now.' Her sense was that global warming was definitely underway. 'The First Nations people say other things have changed, too, like the quality of the fish. I think the folk who live out here, who pick berries or hunt or hike, we're more in touch with these changes than folk in the cities. More connected. So many people just go to work, earn money, go home, watch TV...'

She suggested I go and talk to the woman who used to run the store. 'She still lives round the back,' she said, stubbing out the cigarette. 'I'm sure she'd love to talk to you.' I was torn. The woman at the counter had said there was nothing on the road between Posty's and Glenallan. Glenallan was fifty miles ahead and it was already four. If I stayed another hour or so I'd be well into darkness before I arrived and the aggressive bear story had left me with uneasy vibes about wild camping. I wanted to keep going, to get to Glenallan. Within ten minutes of leaving I was thinking I should have stayed. A woman who had set up her own business in Alaska, forty-odd years ago? A woman who had lived here all her life? She would have had so much to say, would have been a goldmine of stories and insights. And I had traded this opportune chance encounter for a fixation on getting fifty miles further.

This internal conflict was not helped by my imagination. By the time I was ten miles down the road, the woman-who-still-lived-behind-the-store had become the archetypal, interesting, sweet-but-feisty grandmother, who would have been delighted to have company, plied me with tea and food (unspecified but in large quantities), and turned out to be a wise white elder. We would have formed a lasting bond and emailed regularly for the rest of her life. Why oh why had I not stopped? It wasn't really to do with bears, I admitted, though it was to do with wanting to reach Anchorage with a few days in hand. I didn't want to get there only to have to jump on the ferry and leave. I wanted to meet people, to begin the job of making the trip work for the muskrats. But if I was honest, it wasn't just about that. I was trying to prove something. Trying to prove I could still do the long days. If I made it to Glenallan it would be something over a hundred miles. The rational part of me said, Big Deal! And who, it asked, was

I trying to prove this to anyway? Myself? Stupid! But the part of me still stuck in the story of this journey as some kind of epic challenge; the part of me that clearly did have something to prove; the part of me that just found it easier to crank out the miles than stop and engage; and the part of me that actually positively relished the chance to push the miles hard while Chris was on the bus – that part was still winning out. I didn't turn back.

A loud hooting thankfully disrupted my thoughts, and a blue and white 'Alaska Lines' bus pulled off the road just ahead of me. Chris jumped down the steps and gave me a hug, while the whole bus cheered and clapped. The driver leaned out of the window and asked if I wanted a lift too. She grinned and hooted for Chris to return as I declined, flashing the hazard lights as they drove away.

I broke the remaining miles down. When I reach seventy miles, I can have a piece of chocolate. At eighty, I'll put the music on. Occasional glimpses of large snow-covered mountains showed through off to the left. But mostly the weather closed in and it was just me and the sleek, dark, grey wet road. A thin band of aspen lined the asphalt with yellow. Dark conifers hunched behind the aspen and behind them, the huge grey sky. Grey, yellow, dark-green, grey. A simple world of three colours and close horizons and constant, endless pedalling. Intermittent rain and intermittent headwinds were the only variables. I thought about what the woman at Posty's had said about the cold winters changing and the glaciers shrinking and about people going to work, earning money, coming home, not in touch and not concerned. Disconnected.

Reconnection, that's the key, I thought. We need to find a way of reconnecting ourselves to what we unwittingly endorse, simply by taking our place in the system. We become part of it, not asking whether it merits our endorsement and not resisting if we think the answer is, at least partly, 'No'. Of course, there is much to celebrate about western lifestyles. Our material needs are met, we have health services, longer lives, regular education, fantastic art and music ... but so much else is wrong. The impact of our lives on desperate poverty elsewhere; the way our domesticated animals are treated; the immense environmental impact of our high-consumption lifestyles. And in all of this, are we, the privileged, really living our human potential to the full? Or are we trapped, working nine-to-five for the best years of our lives, earning money to buy stuff we largely don't need; convinced that we need this stuff to be happy, to be successful, to lead a good life?

'We need to wake up!' I found myself shouting to the trees. 'Wake Up! WAKE UP!' Refuse to be part of this unfolding environmental tragedy! Kick up a stink about the utterly unjust chasm between richest and poorest. About the fact that we are precipitating a change in our atmospheric system that is likely to profoundly threaten the lives of our own children. And once awake? Well, then we need to cut down our own impacts as far as we can, and hold our politicians to account for the structures that prevent us doing more. Above all, we need to find less materialistic, less damaging ways of being happy; ways of living more lightly that are not about living with less, but living better. Ways of living that have more space for creativity, music, adventure, exploration, friendship, community, connection with nature...

On this idealistic and probably slightly deranged high I reached the Anchorage/Fairbanks junction, and a huge gas station called The Hub of Alaska. There was a motel, I learned from a small gang of teenagers inside, about a mile and a half down the Anchorage road. Another mile and half suddenly seemed too far. I slouched back out into the dark, and nearly cried with relief when a tailwind picked me and Rocky up as we turned south, and took us all the way to the door of the rather posh-looking Caribou Hotel. Inside, a very large man was making coffee. Slowly. He carried on making coffee for some time before strolling reluctantly back to the check-in desk, where a book called 'Bible Preaching for Beginners' lay open, festooned with yellow post-it markers. 'Yes, we have a vacancy,' he said, with a distinct tone of regret. Biblical quotes covered the walls in the small, overpriced room. The bathroom was distinctly grubby and the water was brown – stirred up, apparently, by a minor earthquake earlier in the day. I did not care. The computer read one hundred and three miles and Rocky's wheel was holding up. I dared to think that getting to Anchorage under our own steam was back on the cards. I had a bath *and* a shower and slept for a very long time.

~

Chris phoned the next morning. He was in Anchorage, at a bike shop and his wheel would be replaced within the hour! The mechanic had said he'd never seen anything like it, and thought the wheel must have been faulty. The bus, with Chris and his fully functioning bike on it, would come back out of Anchorage the following day. 'There's not a huge choice of places to stay ahead of you,' he said, 'but we did pass a place called Sheep Mountain Lodge. About the right distance. How about I come and find you there for breakfast tomorrow?'

There was another large Christian male on duty at reception but this one was much friendlier. 'Sheep Mountain Lodge? About seventy miles from here.' Seventy miles! It would be an easy day. I used the hotel internet to track down some information about the Mayor of Anchorage, Mark Begich, who had just signed up as a Cool City Mayor. I sent emails and had a very large breakfast. And then I went to the store to stock up on bagels, bean burritos and fruit. Finally, Rocky and I sauntered away a little after eleven into sunshine almost warm enough for shorts.

For some reason, I stopped on the road a little while later. A range of snow-covered mountains, invisible in the rain the previous day, shimmered in the distance behind us. These were the Wrangell Mountains with Mount Sanford at the northern end of the range, a little over sixteen thousand feet. Off to the left I could just catch glimpses of a huge glacier, the Matanuska, stretching down towards the highway. As I stood at the edge of the tarmac, soaking it all in, something moved off to the right. To my astonishment, a lynx walked out onto the tarmac and stood, just in front of me, looking intently up the road ahead. For perhaps half a minute, we both stood motionless, the lynx with one paw lifted, stripped like a tabby cat but very much larger, distinctive sharp ear tufts dark in the sunshine. Then she turned, saw me, and was gone, vanishing in a flash of fur into the small trees by the side of the road. 'No way!' I said out loud to the woods. Lynx are incredibly hard creatures to see. The chance of encountering one in its own habitat, let alone sauntering onto a highway, is remote. *This* is what this journey is really about, I thought, for the second time in as many days. It's not about me and my mileage. It's about the lynx and the muskrat and all the other species threatened by what my species are up to. 'I'll do whatever I can,' I said to the trees where the lynx had vanished. And then I cycled on.

I was bursting to tell someone when I stopped at a lodge for a sandwich, but some intuition warned me to keep quiet. I had no way of knowing whether a lynx in the area would be considered an astonishing privilege, a fur-coat opportunity, or even a threat. The lodge was in an idyllic spot. I ate a huge cheese salad sandwich alone on a sunny, warm balcony above a bend in the creek. The river sang constantly below me and the river sands glowed a pale dun under the running water. There were 'recycle' stickers in the porch but the owner's view of global warming was emphatic. 'A pile of crock,' he said, as I paid the small bill. 'A bunch of scientists making money out of it. We shouldn't be polluting, though.'

The apparent contradiction was intriguing. 'So, why don't you think global warming is happening?' I asked.

'Evidence,' was the reply. 'If it were happening, sea levels would be rising. They're not rising. So it isn't happening.'

As I struggled to think of a response that wouldn't get us into, 'Oh yes they are. Oh no they're not,' the conversation moved on to aviation school, and what he'd learned there about how efficient engines could be.

'We should all be using this technology,' he said, 'no doubt about it. But the powers-that-be in the oil industry prevent really efficient engines coming onto the market. And look what happened to De-Laurean.' This last leap of logic rather defied me as, while I would confess to appreciating the shape of the iconic gull-winged sports car, I'd never understood it to be a model of environmental efficiency. But perhaps I was wrong.

'What's the road ahead like?' I asked, changing the subject.

'Oh you've got a couple of pretty steep, long climbs,' he said, with a grin.

'First time I drove this road from Anchorage,' said an RV driver sitting in the corner, 'I couldn't wait to get out of the mountains. All these passes. Awful.'

Given that I only had three gears and was counting on an easy day, this did not sound like good news. Rocky's back derailleur had gone on strike completely and I had only the front three gears for variety. Luckily, 'steep long climb' is a relative term and the RV driver had clearly never been to Colorado. The climb was a gentle, meandering, steady pull for a couple of miles. An 'awful mountain pass' it was not. The views, however, were something else. Huge sweeps of heathery purple fell away to one side and huge sweeps of yellow and green rose up to massive, folded, white-capped mountains on the other. I sat on the plateau for ages and even after I'd dragged myself away and cycled on, kept coming to a halt, besieged with views requiring to be photographed. I was filled with a wonderful sense of vast space, and, despite the lay-bys parked up with hundreds of trucks, a huge sense of peace. Finally, the sun sank below the craggy skyline and I was released to cycle on.

Despite the view gazing, I was at Sheep Mountain Lodge by about eight. An early finish! I planned to use the time to catch up with the journal, eating through my stash of bagels in my room. But Sheep Mountain Lodge was an unexpectedly alluring (and expensive!) place. The restaurant featured a range of irresistible vegetarian meals and, even more irresistible, it boasted a hot tub. I gave up resisting, ate Hungarian mushroom soup and a vast bean burrito smothered in sour cream and spent what I thought was to be my last night on the road with an entire cabin to myself, sprawled across a massive bed after an hour in a hot tub with power jets running up and down my spine. The contrast with the previous night was hard to ignore. I would probably have been just as happy in the tent, albeit in a very different way. But I wasn't in the tent; I was in a plush lodge. Clearly, my own resistance to consumer attractions still needed considerable work. Or perhaps the occasional night of downright luxury had its place.

~

Chris arrived in time for breakfast next morning. 'It's all downhill from here,' he said, transferring a ton of weight from Rocky onto his bike, its new back wheel shiny in the cool sun. I was unexpectedly tired. Perhaps because the end seemed to be in sight, I found myself suddenly struggling to cope with the lack of gears and the frustration of having to unload the bike to shift to a larger or smaller back cog. The 'thirty miles of nonstop downhill' might have appeared that way from the bus but, on a bike with few gears, it was distinctly up and down. I tried to focus on the still-glorious views, the swathes of yellow and green peppered trees and the glacier, whose massive, chunked-up, gnarly ice snout butted up almost to the road. But I definitely felt ratty.

At lunch we pulled off the road by the river and Chris dug out a surprise picnic of grapefruit juice, veggie wraps and praline chocolate. The road was getting busier. It was a Sunday, and herds of trucks and RVs, many towing small 'alternative terrain vehicles' – ATVs or quad

273

bikes – were heading back into town. The ATVs typically had guns strapped to their sides and six-packs of beer stowed on the back. These were the modern hunters, out for the weekend to drink and shoot and roar around off-road, a completely different hunting culture from the traditional one. The atmosphere was distinctly aggressive and it was one of the very few times either of us had felt unsafe on the road. In fact, I was feeling much more allergic to traffic than when I'd started, unsettled and edgy at being back on a busy highway. And to make it to Anchorage that evening as planned we'd have to cycle about a hundred and twenty miles on these roads.

'Can I suggest a Plan B?' said Chris, who'd used his time in Anchorage to great effect. 'Friends of Anchorage friends live near Palmer. We'll still have done a good distance and we can get to Anchorage in the morning.'

'But we don't have any friends in Anchorage, do we?' I asked.

'We do now!' said Chris with a grin. He'd tracked down a university lecturer who taught outdoor education, and we now had an Anchorage base camp. 'His name is Paul, and he has mates nearby. They're half-expecting us tonight.'

The friends lived and worked at Spring Creek Farm. We left the main road for a series of minor ones. As we turned onto the farm road, a small pack of welcoming dogs raced out to greet us. 'Over here!' shouted a group of people waving beside a table stacked with food and beer. The farm was attached to Alaska Pacific University [55] and we'd turned up on the night of their welcome bar-b-q for new students. It was a great evening. Food, beer and conversation. A range of outdoor and environmental courses were taught at the farm, which had been bequeathed to the University by an astonishing woman called Louise Kellogg. Kellogg had bought land, ten cows and a cabin here in 1948, a time when no farmer in Alaska would sell a farm to a woman. Described – in what was possibly the understatement of all time – as 'not a woman to sit home and knit', she'd been one of very few female pilots (known as the Powderpuffs) in the 1920s, had worked as a 'Miscellaneous Specialist' in the war and, as well as developing the farm into a highly successful dairy business – to the utter surprise of the all-male farming community nearby – had founded

---

[55] Their website is http://www.springcreekfarmak.org/

museums, volunteered for hospitals, helped rejuvenate the Iditarod husky race, and been active in Republican politics. She'd also joined the board of what was then the Alaska Methodist University. Still driving 'like a bat out of hell' in her nineties, she'd put 700 acres of farmland into trust for the University when she retired, wanting a place where students could spend time with nature. 'Let there be no doubt about it,' she'd written. 'My aim is to protect the land for use by private educational institutions, for without the serenity of fields and woods, animals and friendly birds in their natural setting, a private educational institution can offer only book learning, not real education.' Also described as 'a friend to all dogs', this was a woman I would dearly have loved to meet. It was hard to think of a more appropriate place to have ended up.

That evening, the conversation constantly returned to the question of quality of life. How could we sustain or even raise it – for all of us, not just a privileged few – at the same time as drastically lowering our carbon footprint? If technofix is not a complete answer then the only option has to be rethinking what 'quality of life' actually involves. The many cyclists we'd met over the miles often seemed well on the way to living out a travelling, nomadic version of low-impact, high-quality life. Spring Creek Farm offered a different, more static model. Amongst other things, it demonstrated the huge benefits that come from being lucky enough to do work that really means something. And those who worked there encountered, in a truly practical way, the value of reconnecting with particular natural ecosystems; the way in which experiencing our existence as part of ecological as well as human communities can be deeply fulfilling.

We spent the night in the farmhouse and, in the morning, opted for a last minute detour. Pete and Alys, regular guests at Spring Creek Farm, had written the cycling guide to Alaska. They were also, like us, keen sea kayakers – and had Icelandic ponies to boot. They lived a mere seven miles away. It would be daft not to. Pete and Alys had taken footprint reduction several leaps further. They lived off the grid, running their electrical appliances – including a freezer they'd rescued from a nearby dump – on solar. They earned very little money, and needed less. They spent a lot of time cycling, paddling and messing about with ponies. They had a lot of freedom, and a lot of fun.

Quality of time. Quality of experience. Strengthened connections to other species and natural systems. Strengthened human communities. Much less stuff. A multitude of ways of working this out in practice and not all of them would look anything like Pete and Alys' life, or Spring Creek Farm. None of these particular examples were the whole answer, and nor were they answers everyone could or would want to adopt. But they did all seem to offer some very strong clues. It was almost as if, knowing we were out of time, the universe had thrown a couple of really compelling case studies in our path, just to be sure we got the message. Got the message, and passed it on.

It was gone four in the afternoon before we were back on the road, with lots of waving and plans for reunions. It was September 11th, a beautiful sunny evening, two days now before the last ferry south. Dusk was falling as we rode into Anchorage, and it was dark before we rode up to Paul's house. Rocky's computer read 4553 miles as we stopped at Paul's gate. On the main road into town, a moose and two calves sauntered out in front of us. 'I love this place!' I said to Chris, as they ambled across the street. I wasn't sure if I meant Anchorage, Alaska or the world. I'd started in the desert and ended with glaciers running down to the ocean; and all within the temperate zone. Three months on the road had really brought home to me what an extraordinary, diverse, wonderful, wonderful place the earth is. It had left me feeling passionate about the need to protect it. How ironic that we needed to protect it against ourselves; yet how profoundly heartening that we could still choose to change direction.

EPILOGUE
New Normal

'It's easier to change your light-bulbs than your values.'

Charlie Kronick [56]

'THERE IS NO PLANET B!'

Climate change protest banner

It has taken me a long time to see where it is I reached, at the end of that lengthy and, as it turned out, not so leisurely bike ride. It's taken me even longer to see what it is I want now to write. It is about coming back to the beginning. To the ordinary world; to the bike as magician with the intermittent power to bring that world, taken for granted in the background of our lives, back into vivid focus.

The ordinary world – our modern 'western' world – can be taken for granted no longer. That, above all, is what my ride eventually allowed me to see. It gave me just enough perspective, enough distance, enough disorientation to ask questions and to glimpse again that utterly disturbing dark side of our everyday existence. The challenge is to hold that focus.

We all need to see the ordinary world, really *see* it. And then we need to transform it. Our ordinary Western lives – privileged, comfortable, in many ways wonderful – are also fantastically damaging. They are systematically degrading the ecological systems we, like all living beings, depend on. They are causing mass extinctions, rendering the climate dangerously unstable, changing the pH of the entire ocean, undermining our own life support systems. Our ordinary lives are marketed as the embodiment of progress and success and something to aspire to across the continents. Yet they are utterly unsustainable and totally inequitable. They are three-planet lives. They cannot be shared without ecological meltdown. This is the ultimate, underlying and extremely 'inconvenient' truth. Our ordinary lives are both threatening, and profoundly under threat. We, ordinary people,

---

[56] Charlie Kronick, Greenpeace UK Senior Climate Advisor. Personal interview just before the trip (2006)

aren't necessarily either stupid or evil; very few of us wake up intent on trashing nature. But we are heading for a very literal Wasteland unless we change direction.

~

Back in 2006, I set off with a question I took to be simple. How can we make ourselves and our ways of life climate-friendly? I found as many new questions as I did answers and I came back with a whole lot of complexity – a tangle of contradictory ideas, partial solutions, debates, inspired examples – shot through with strands of clarity.

I found a thousand reasons why any particular individual might not be taking action. Lack of information. Distorted information. No information. More urgent short-term concerns and problems. The belief that we are not smart enough to understand the issue or strong enough to tackle it. The belief that even if we do, it won't make any difference, and so really there is no point. Or that it's the government's job, not ours. That it can't be that bad because if it were, the government would sort it. That it *is* that bad and the government will sort it. That God will sort it. That the world is going to end anyway so it really doesn't matter.

I found that it's critical to break through all this, somehow to reach, explain, inspire. And yet also that it is not as simple as exhorting individuals to do their bit, crucial though that is. Individuals live in societies; and in most western societies it's not only normal to have a high impact, it's often genuinely difficult to do otherwise. Sometimes there just aren't low-carbon alternatives to the things we choose or need to do – we need our transport, finance, energy, food and other systems [57] to change around us, so that living with a low impact becomes easy and routine.

I found that it's not as simple as calling on individuals to do their bit for more sinister reasons, too: that we need to be wise to the vested interests, the vast accretions of wealth and power distorting democratic systems, supporting fossil fuel use, distorting science and media alike. I glimpsed the immense power and staggering wealth of some of those whose interests are deeply entangled with oil. I glimpsed a handful

---

[57] Forum for the Future is among those groups leading the way on system transformation. Their website is http://www.forumforthefuture.org/

of ways in which this power is used to *stop* us changing, controlling information though astonishingly influential media outlets like Fox, manipulating and misrepresenting the scientific evidence, dominating the political arena – doing, quite literally, whatever it takes to protect the fossil fuel and related industries.

I collided with my own naïvety yet again, and became more aware of my own multiple-planet activities, my arrogant assumptions and hypocrisies, myself as a microcosm of wider damage and denial. I returned more alert to my own complicity and less naïve about power.

I found the consistent kindness of strangers and the overwhelming beauty and strangeness of the world. I found inspiring examples of leadership from the middle, across a range of different sectors. I found them in politics, in business, in NGOs, in conservation, and in education. I found the Banff Centre, working in a hundred different ways to support joined-up leadership, running courses of a kind I hope my own university – which also has a beautiful mountain-town campus – will one day also offer. No doubt there are a thousand other examples whose paths I didn't happen to cross. None offer a single-bullet solution. Some might even be mistaken; perhaps none are radical enough. But they are all doing *something*. And they all provide springboards to bounce off, critique, take forward, transform.

I found all too many examples of climate change-related impacts which are already being felt on the ground. The devastating fires and the dying cactus. The National Park named for the glaciers it will surely lose and the withdrawn, diminished and dirty ice of the Athabasca Glacier, miles from its former reach. The cheat grass and the early-waking bears and the complex, collapsing relationships between beetles, trees, people and fire. The unravelling Rocky Mountain ecosystems.

I found immense swathes of dying forest, hundreds of miles of dead yellow pines swathed like an all-season autumn across entire mountainsides. I learned that the ongoing devastation of millions of trees and the ecosystems they are part of is by no means confined to distant rainforests, and that arresting this devastation is as critical as tackling our addiction to fossil fuels.

And of course, I found no shortage of oil-hungry, high-energy, high-consumption lifestyles. I still see them characterised in a series of images: the glittering Aspen shopping malls, the Hummer, the heli-skiing, the acres of golfing grass in the high mountains, the Montana family with their four or five trucks. I realised how unexceptional these are. In industrialised societies, even those of us without Hummers, who don't rate heli-skiing amongst our top forms of recreation, and who only shop when pressed into it – even we have grossly oversized carbon footprints as a matter of course.

~

A great deal, of course, has happened since 2006. A great deal that is positive and yet also terrifyingly little. Climate summits and presidents have been and gone. But the vested interests in the status quo, in maintaining our voracious appetite for fossil fuels, remain; and they remain immensely powerful. And our multiple-planet lifestyles continue, largely unchanged. Meanwhile, the bottom line is this: *across the world, greenhouse gas emissions are still rising.* In response to the shocking 2010 figures, the chief economist of the International Energy Agency said that, while we could still avert the disaster of runaway climate change with 'bold, decisive and urgent action', it was 'becoming extremely challenging.'[58]

As individuals, we need to walk a difficult tightrope. We are simply deluding ourselves if we think we are doing our bit – and doing enough – because we do the weekly recycling or because we've changed the lightbulbs. 'Every little helps' is as dangerous a concept as it is potentially constructive. We need to be honest and we need to get real – both about the scale of the challenge and the consequences of not rising to it. Runaway climate change is not just a bit of bad weather. It will bring drastic, sudden, major discontinuities in our weather systems and cause catastrophic social and ecological disruption and collapse. To have a hope of preventing it, we need very big reductions indeed. Working backwards from the maximum amount of CO_2 and other greenhouse gases there can be in the atmosphere if average global temperatures are to be kept the right side of the likely 'runaway' tipping point, most analysts conclude we must reduce greenhouse

---

[58] A record 30.6 gigatonnes of CO_2 was added to the atmosphere in 2010, a 6% rise on the previous year and the highest output in history. The unexpected rise – mainly from burning fossil fuels – occurred despite major economic recessions across the world. Source: International Energy Agency, reported in *The Guardian* 29th May 2011

gas emissions by eighty percent across the industrialised world. *Eighty percent!* By no later than 2050. With a *very* substantial chunk of that in the next decade or so.

The figures tell us loud and clear that we need greatly to ratchet up our own personal contributions to carbon-light living, in any and every way we can. Everything from energy saving in our houses (yes, including the lightbulbs! It sounds like a contradiction. But read on ...) to cutting back on flights, to looking at what's on our dinner plates with an informed and carbon-critical eye.[59] We need to do it in the full knowledge that it's not enough, but that it still needs doing. Every little *does* help, so long as we don't then give climate change a mental tick and assume it will all be okay. We need to know the truth about what we are facing – and to tell everyone around us. We need to be catalysts for change where we live, where we work, where we socialise. As much as *can* be done by individuals does need to be done.

But we're also mistaken if we think it's all up to us. Being satisfied with nowhere near enough is the fall that lies on one side of the tightrope; the belief that as individuals we bear total responsibility for turning this around is what lies on the other. Berating ourselves for not changing things we can't change is a pointless waste of energy. We can't personally and individually change the systems and structures our lives are embedded in.[60] Transport structures, economic structures, legal structures. But we *can* be an awful lot more demanding of the governments and businesses and organisations that do have this power; that could profoundly alter the structures that in turn shape our everyday lives. We can lobby, vote, boycott, campaign, write, demonstrate, organise, gather. We need not to tolerate it, but to DEMAND that they get on and make the changes that *will* make it possible to eat, drink, heat our houses and move ourselves with a vastly reduced footprint – or not do them at all. We need to demand these changes, no matter what this 'costs' us in the short term, no

---

[59] Mike Berners-Lee (2010) *How Bad are Bananas? The carbon footprint of everything* is really helpful on how to prioritise personal actions – and an engaging read.

[60] With the possible exception of Polly Higgins! Information about her campaign to change international law can be found at http://www.thisisecocide.com/ Her book *Eradicating Ecocide* won 'The People's Book Prize' in 2011.

matter that it might make diesel more expensive or cheap flights a thing of the past. Are we really going to exchange cheap flights for our own future? Do we really value cheap fuel and consumer freedom more than we want to protect our children's lives?

But wait – what about the hope that advances in technology will allow us to tackle climate change while keeping our lifestyles essentially intact? It turned out that someone *was* crunching the numbers. Tim Jackson, in his book *Prosperity without Growth* (initially a report for the UK Sustainable Development Commission) shows that every dollar of growth in the year 2006 generated an average of 770g of CO_2 or equivalent greenhouse gases. To hit our climate targets, the figure needs to fall to 7g by 2050.[61] Seven hundred and seventy to seven! That's an off-the-scale improvement of efficiency. Not factor ten or even factor twenty – but factor *one hundred and thirty*. No-one, not Amory Lovins, not his colleagues at RMI, not *anyone* comes close to showing how this could be done. We can't do it now, and pinning everything on the ungrounded hope that advances of this magnitude are just around the corner is simply delusional. It's magical thinking. Technology may be a critical part of the solution, but it's nowhere near enough.

In the end, though, it's not just about the numbers. Technological changes alone, even the most brilliant, the most welcome and the most to be celebrated,[62] can't and won't turn our ordinary lives into one-planet lives, because this kind of approach leaves a host of deeper problems completely untouched. Climate change, for all its seriousness, is only a symptom. It is a symptom – one of many – of an entire system heading in the wrong direction. The whole trajectory of the industrialised and industrialising world is badly off-kilter. Putting it back on track requires shifts that are deep as well as hefty. Changing our worldview will be every bit as important as improving our technology.

Seen from the future or from another planet, the dominant worldview of modern industrialised societies – our worldview, for

---

[61] Tim Jackson (2009) *Prosperity Without Growth: Economics for a Finite Planet* Routledge.

[62] For a shot of sheer technological brilliance try Jeremy Rifkin (2011) *The Third Industrial Revolution* Palgrave Macmillan

the most part – would surely seem just as bizarre as that of the rapture believers, and as profoundly disturbing in its impacts as that of the Europeans arriving in the 'new world'. Those early settlers had a worldview, a set of beliefs, values and assumptions, that made it seem normal and acceptable to hunt down and persecute the people who already lived there. To outlaw their religions, throw them off their lands, massacre them in great numbers. Our set of beliefs, values and assumptions makes it seem normal and acceptable to lead three-planet lives. Normal, acceptable, desirable and feasible.

In fact, it is none of those things. Our worldview tells us we can expand forever on a planet with limits; that progress means more and more and more material wealth, way beyond the point of meeting our needs or even making us happy; that we can pursue this progress forever. Our worldview tells us that quality of life is about quantity of stuff. It tells us we are not part of nature, that we are disconnected from other forms of life and vastly superior to them. It tells us that the whole of nature, the whole wonderful world from lynx and bear to swallows and starfish, ravens and aspen trees, is merely a set of resources that we can exploit indefinitely, for any purpose, and that it really doesn't matter if we damage or even destroy. And it tells us that appalling abuses of power and economic systems utterly dependent on impossible destructive growth is just what it takes to carry on. It is this worldview, the deepest, most powerful shaper of our ordinary lives, that we most need to bring into focus. To see, to question and most definitely, to change.

~

These, then, are the strands of clarity I uncovered on those long, high roads. To cross the great divide from where we are to where we need to be, changing our worldviews will be key.

What sort of changes?

First, we need some new stories. We need, as Thomas Berry said some time ago, a new story about who we are and how we relate to nature. [63] The Wild West version is dangerously misaligned. No longer searching for gold or for beaver pelts we still, nevertheless, have a frontiers mentality, a mad commitment to indefinite expansion. But we can't carry on endlessly pushing into new lands, conquering

[63] Thomas Berry (1999) *The Great Work* Bell Tower.

and taming the limitless wild. The wild is not endless and we've pushed it back far too far. We're not just cowboys galloping across it, we *live* there; and the wild we inhabit has limits that we're crashing full-speed into.

Second, as many others have argued, we desperately need reconnection. Our ordinary lives, by and large, reinforce our feeling of disconnection rather than confront it. We don't witness the impacts of our lifestyles on natural systems and other species, and we don't feel part of the ecosystems we're damaging. We spend more and more time with computers and televisions and less and less time 'in' nature, around other species, aware of the 'vividness and vibrancy' of life. Our political leaders and powerful elites are often even more disconnected than we are, isolated from the feedback we badly need to receive and from the kinds of relationships with nature that might inspire its protection.

Third, we need some new values – or to revitalise old ones that are currently smothered in a morass of glitz. We need to question these most basic of assumptions – that growth is always good, and that our happiness is, above all else, tied up with money and *stuff*. We need to change the excessive value we put on our freedom as consumers to buy and do whatever we like and can afford; the way we prioritise this freedom over a liveable planet. We need to be clear that protecting our own habitat – and that of a zillion other species – is not just a personal pet passion. It is, or should be, the core value of any civilisation.

It's also a profoundly practical value that we must have in place if we are, quite simply, to carry on. We like to think we are the most intelligent species on earth, and yet we are systematically undermining our own habitats. What better use for our big brains than figuring out equitable ways of living really well, within the ecological limits of our own planet? Is out-of-control consumerism really the best version of the good life, the best version of progress and success for human beings that we can come up with? We need to throw our intelligence and our creative energy into re-imagining quality of life in better, richer, different ways.

We need, in sum, a new normal. Normal to live low-impact lives. Normal, acceptable, easy, attractive, trendy. Normal to have a rather different take on quality of life; to have more time, less work or better work, strengthened communities, more contact with nature. The glimpsed insights about quality of life shared by the cyclists and the Spring Creek farmers and the off-grid neighbours need to become mainstream. It's not just about giving things up; it's about finding the win/wins and living better than we do now. And this, maybe bizarrely, is perhaps the most effective thing any one of us can do about climate change: to step back from our ordinary lives and ask what really makes us happy. And then to throw all our ingenuity, creativity, intelligence and passion into coming up with single planet answers. [64]

We know where we are trying to reach. Low impact, high quality lives that could be enjoyed by all. Ordinary lives that are single-planet lives. Crossing this particular divide is a huge challenge. We all need to take it on, in whatever way we can. It's urgent and not always easy. There will be many hot headwinds and seemingly endless climbs on the way. But there will also be amazing encounters, heart-stopping vistas, an undeniable sense of purpose. There will be increased sense of connection, ordinary adventures, a different kind of dream. And what a destination.

For more information about climate change, including links to useful sites and suggestions for action please visit the website:
www.outdoorphilosophy.co.uk/thecarboncycle

---

[64] Acknowledgements due, again, to WWF for the idea of single- (and multiple!) -planet living.

About the Author

Kate Rawles studied philosophy at Aberdeen University, and environmental philosophy at Glasgow and Colorado State University. She was an indoor philosophy lecturer for nearly a decade before escaping to work freelance in 2000. Kate now works half-time as a lecturer in Outdoor Studies at the University of Cumbria – teaching environmental issues – and half-time as a freelance outdoor philosopher, writer, lecturer and campaigner. She is passionate about the need to find urgent, effective and suitably radical responses to our multiple environmental challenges (including giving our values and worldviews a thorough overhaul) – and firmly believes our quality of life can go up rather than down in the process. Kate is a keen hill-walker and sea-kayaker (with a particular love of remote islands with lots of wildlife) as well as a long-distance cyclist. She is a Fellow of the Royal Geographical Society and sits on the Food Ethics Council. She lives in Cumbria with her partner, Chris.

More information about Kate, the Carbon Cycle and Outdoor Philosophy can be found at *www.outdoorphilosophy.co.uk*

Changing the Climate